Bawaajimo

Bawaajimo

A DIALECT OF DREAMS

IN ANISHINAABE

LANGUAGE AND LITERATURE

MARGARET NOODIN

Michigan State University Press | *East Lansing*

♾ The paper used in this publication meets the minimum requirements of
ANSI/NISO Z39.48-1992 (R 1997) (Permanence of Paper).

Michigan State University Press
East Lansing, Michigan 48823-5245

Printed and bound in the United States of America.

20 19 18 17 16 15 14   1 2 3 4 5 6 7 8 9 10

LIBRARY OF CONGRESS CATALOGING-IN-PUBLICATION DATA
Noodin, Margaret.
Bawaajimo : a dialect of dreams in Anishinaabe language and literature /
Margaret Noodin.
pages cm.—(American Indian Studies Series)
Includes bibliographical references and index.
ISBN 978-1-61186-105-1 (pbk. : alk. paper)—ISBN 978-1-60917-396-8 (ebook)
1. Ojibwa language—Dialects—North America. 2. Ojibwa language—Folklore.
3. Ojibwa literature—History and criticism. I. Title.
PM854.Z8N66 2014
497'.333—dc23
2013012250

Book design and typesetting by Charlie Sharp, Sharp Designs
Cover design by Erin Kirk New
Cover art is "Spirit Tree 0254: 'May Moonrise at the Spirit Tree'" © Travis Novitsky
and is used courtesy of the photographer (www.travisnovitsky.com). All rights reserved.

Michigan State University Press is a member of the Green Press Initiative and is committed to developing
and encouraging ecologically responsible publishing practices. For more information about the Green
Press Initiative and the use of recycled paper in book publishing, please visit www.greenpressinitiative.org.

Visit Michigan State University Press at www.msupress.org

N'gii ozhibii'amawaag ingitizimag, nishime miinwaa ndaanisag.
N'miigwechwinim Zhibaasige miinwaa Chibinesi zaam nisidotawiyeg.

In saying the word, *nindinawemaag*, or my relatives, we speak of everything that has existed in time, the known and the unknown, the unseen, the obvious, all that lived before and is living now in the worlds above and below.

—Nanapush's afterword to Louise Erdrich's *Last Report on the Miracles at Little No Horse*

Nimbwaawinanigoomin.
We are still here.

—Chapter title from Jim Northrup's book, *The Rez Road Follies*

K'gah baugwaushkaugameetchigaemim beenish mukwaenimikohing.
We will stir the waters until one remembers.

—Call of the *maemaegwishuk*, included in Basil Johnston's *Ojibway Ceremonies*

Wanaki anishimo wanaki. To live in a place of peace, to dance away in a place of peace.

—Round Dance Chant from Gerald Vizenor's *Chancers*

Contents

N'digo: Preface

With the simplest act of translating this starting point I am reminded of the distance between two languages. *N'digo* is the phrase used to share identity; it signals an act of self–translation; it stands as the personal preface to a narrative.

N'digo Giiwedinoodin, waabzheshiinh debendagoziyaanh, Minnesota onjibaayaanh. Chizhaazhagwa n'okomisag miinwaa n'mishomisag gii ni dagooshinowaad iwedi giiwedinong ChiOnigaming. Noongwa nd'kinoomaage Kchikinomaagegamigong Wisconsin-Milwaukee zaam geyabi Niswi-Shkode-bimaadizijig minobimaadiziwaad miinwaa kchinokiiwaad ji-zhaabwitoowaad Anishinaabemowin, ezhi-Anishinaabemaadiziwaad. The audience for an introduction in Anishinaabemowin is small in print right now, but vast across time. If a *manidoo* or Nanabozho or my great-great-great-great grandmother stood before me, this is what I would say.

In English, on paper, online, and in classrooms I say I am from the north, from among the pine martens, from a place where Ojibwe and Lakota cultures mix with Irish, German, and Scottish settler traditions now mixing again with Afghan and Mexican influences. I teach at an institution that is heir to the history of cosmopolitan commerce that preceded both the United States and Canada, steward of a language that is wandering wounded into a new century. I listen to lessons offered by degrees and seasons. I write curriculum that traces paths others can follow. I use the old words to release the past, and I make new words to explode the present in a way that will splash indelibly on the future. And every day I give thanks to those around me, elders, students, rocks and trees, the ones who balance and inspire me. These are the things that should be said before beginning, the bits of spirit that should be shared before asking others to listen.

N'miigwechwiwaag:
Acknowledgments

Baatiinag bimaadizijig gii naadamawigoog. N'gii zhawenimigoog kina gikinaamaw-iwaad, zaagiwaad. Gaagige n'gii minotanan zaaga'iganan, mitigoog, nengawan miinwaa asiniig miidash gii gashkitooyaanh nakinigeyaanh ezhi-enendamoyaanh. I have been blessed with many lessons. In addition to the lakes and the trees and the sand and the stones who served as inspiration, there are many people to thank for these ideas becoming a book. Those who first shaped the contents as part of my doctoral thesis were Maria Damon, Genevieve Escure, Ed Griffin, Carol Miller, and Larry Gross. Those who shaped it most recently at Michigan State University Press were Julie Loehr and Elise Jajuga.

As the ideas moved from one form to another, many colleagues in Native studies supported my poetic-socio-linguistic theorizing including Gordon Henry, P. Jane Hafen, Ginny Carney, Gwen Westerman, Patrice Hollarah, LeAnne Howe, Jill Doerfler, Nigaanwewidam Sinclair, Kim Blaeser, Chad Allen, Lisa Tatonetti, Beth Piatote, Stephanie Fitzgerald, Simon Ortiz, Daniel Heath Justice, Jodi Byrd, Robert Parker, Robert Warrior, Fred White, Pete Beidler, Sandy Momper, Petra Kuppers, K. David Harrison, John Nichols, and Rand Valentine.

Thanks as wide as the sky to the many elders and fluent speakers who took time to teach me Anishinaabemowin: Collins Oakgrove, Helen Roy Fhust, Howard

Kimewon, Alphonse Pitawanakwat, Bev Naokwegijig, Martina Osawamick, Pat Osawamick, Dan Jones, Roger Roulette, Patricia Ningewance, Kenny Pheasant, Shirley Williams, Jenny Blackbird, Barb Nolan, and Francis Fox, along with Hap McCue-ba, Orien Corbiere-ba, and Porky White-ba. And although we all see each other far too infrequently I owe a debt of thanks to my generation of second language speakers who know what it feels like to move from constant correction to confidence in the classroom. May we all live long enough to see the generations behind us teach and talk and sing for many more years.

I also owe a debt of thanks to the strong women, my sisters in song, of Miskwaasining Nagamojig (the Swamp Singers): Stacie Sheldon, Marsha Reeves, Linda Purchase, Christie Bieber, Michelle Saboo, Jasmine Pawlicki, and Karen Schaumann. Many nights your voices were the medicine I needed to carry on with the great and small of getting things done. Ari Weinzweig served as a formidable editorial intellect outside the small circle of scholars who share a love of Anishinaabe linguistics. The beloved and magical Heid Erdrich made me realize the importance of taking time to make books and poems real, and she always had an extra ounce of encouragement when it was needed. Jim and Pat Northrup gave me pure syrup for my coffee and gallons of good advice as I navigated the many changes of my life. My parents Terry and Alice O'Donnell have always believed in me and gave me an early love of words and stories. My sister Shannon O'Donnell never forgets to say ISYLB, which is so very important for every writer to hear. Shannon and Fionna Noori have been listening to Anishinaabemowin since before they were born, and I am forever grateful for their appreciation of something so important to me. With their dad, Asmat Noori, they gave me the gift of many hours driving to one more language class, one more family camp, one more ceremony under the moon. Michael Zimmerman has reminded me to laugh in winter and stay strong through the longest summers.

Ziibaaskobiige: To Set a Written Net

Aanii ezhikidoying . . . ? How do we say . . . ? Two words or four words, it is the same incessant question that haunts the students and teachers of language. Many, many times on the journey of learning Anishinaabemowin I have repeated that question, first in English, then in Anishinaabemowin without knowing exactly what each part meant. Eventually I learned the "say" in the center was *kido*, and I began to understand the *ying* means all of us with you included, instead of *yaang*, which would mean just us without you. And finally when I said it again in Anishinaabemowin I knew that the *ezhi* softened and expanded the phrase, beyond the answer of the moment, to "This is the way this always happens." The path into a language is clear when the sounds come together as shared meaning to exchange.

Aanii ezhikidoying "dream"? I asked, and was told *bawaajige*. Much later, maybe years later, I told Howard Kimewon, *Mindimoye n'gii bawaanaa* ("I dreamed of an old woman"). *G'gii waabaamaa* ("You saw her") he offered, telling me that depending on how you are speaking of the dream you should sometimes simply use the word "to see" because, as he pointed out, "That's what happens in a dream." *Bawaajige* and *wabaamaa* ("to dream" and "to see") stuck in my poet's mind with *bawa'am*, the word I learned from Jim Northrup for ricing;

and *bawaagonan,* a word I once heard for brushing snow off the low roof of an ice-house. The brush of rice falling off the stalk was clearly echoed in the sweep of snow, which made me wonder if in dreams we sweep reality away, cast time aside, and see the other side for a while. There is no way I can know for certain if these words grew from the same stalk, but I can see patterns as a linguist and hear the stories as a poet. More importantly, these questions led me to rethink the way I "see" Anishinaabe literature. Native American literature has a place in the American literary canon, and many authors have included specific tribal details that merit consideration in the context of tribal nations and confederacies. What I try to do here is take a walk with four authors through Anishinaabe literature using language as my eyes. Thinking differently about possibility, moving beyond the basic truths of nature, spirit, and old stories, I try to connect the meaning of words in a way that brushes the world away to show what is underneath. And the underneath of Anishinaabe language and literature, at least in this dream, is a central tension, an energy fueled by opposition, that frames the way both language and story are woven together. By connecting the words and their patterns of use to the stories and their meaning, we can hear the *ishkwa* (after) in the *ishkode* (fire) and question the relation of burning to being. Some traditions explore the truth of the phrase "I think, therefore I am." The Anishinaabe eschew a single word for think and instead attach *endamo* to every way they can dream of being . . . *gichinendamo* (delighted), *giiwinaadendamo* (crazy), and *bekaadendamo* (at peace) are only a few of the many options, and this is only one of several endings to consider, and endings are only one category of comparison. Verification of existence is not tied to thought as much as to connection and direction. The project at hand is to explore ideas of connection and direction in Anishinaabe language and literature.

In Anishinaabemowin, words fall together according to particular patterns, with sounds and meaning constructed around an Anishinaabe worldview. A prominent non-Native scholar of indigenous linguistics during the early 1900s, Edward Sapir, said in his book *American Indian Languages*: "No two languages are ever sufficiently similar to be considered as representing the same social reality. The worlds in which different societies live are distinct worlds, not merely the same world with different labels attached" (209). His theory follows on centuries of cultural comparison in North America. When Gabriel Sagard wrote in 1632 "Les mots de Gloire, Trinité, sainct Esprit, Anges, Resurrection,

Paradis, Enfer, Eglise, Foy, Esperance & Charité, & autres infinis, ne sont pas en usage chez-eux (The words Glory, Trinity, Holy Spirit, Angels, Resurrection, Paradise, Hell, Church, Faith, Hope, and Charity and a multitude of others, are not used by them)" he was noting the difference between Anishinaabe and French culture (35). Today these are common words in Anishinaabemowin, but the literal interpretation of them reveals differences in cultural perspective. For instance "hell" is simply *maji-ishkodeng*, a bad fire without the implications of religion and darkness carried by the English word, which reaches back to Old Norse definitions of a cavern or concealment. Words can represent worldview and identity. Language can shape narrative and leave traces of that shape long after it has been translated. The readings of literature offered here are based on structural analysis of Anishinaabemowin combined with patterns of composition and meaning in Anishinaabe literature. Basil Johnston has said:

> Language is a precious heritage; literature is no less precious. . . . As rich and full of meaning as may be individual words and expressions, they embody only a small portion of the entire stock and potential of tribal knowledge, wisdom and intellectual attainment; the greater part is deposited in myths, legends, stories and in the lyrics of changes that make up the tribe's literature. (*Think Indian* 90)

It is important to reverse-engineer the Native critical landscape, to create paradigms and methodologies that stem from indigenous systems of thinking. By thinking of the stories in an Anishinaabe context first, we set a differently woven net. This is not the only way to read tribal stories, but it is one that can move careful readers toward less colonial interpretations that acknowledge the connections of A language is shaped by centuries of use and communal exchange. Some facets are merely a reflection of human cognition and pronunciation; some are markers of specific histories. As language becomes literature, theories of meaning and interpretation are possible. A close analysis of language and narrative patterns is one way to read indigenous literature within and around both national and pantribal identities, bringing the stories of the past into the current language of contemporary writers by connecting the present writing with the thought patterns of the ancestors. Readers are invited to unravel the web of knowledge contained in Anishinaabe words. Poets can learn how to carry the language and images forward.

Pii Anishinaabebiigeyaanh	When I write in Anishinaabemowin
Nd'shkitoon	I am able to
nagamobiiyaanh	sing idea strings
nambiing, nibiishensing,	of underwater leaves
wiigwaamigong, chigamigong.	of birch places and deep spaces.

The sound *bii* could relate to the *bii* of water, the *bii* of tree veins, the *bii* of a flowing *ziibii* (river), or the black on white *bii* of *zhibiige* (to write). Language can teach what it means to meander, bringing life through water, through lines of meaning. Contemporary Anishinaabe authors exhibit, to varying degrees, and with varying levels of intent, familiar patterns of language and narrative construction that can be connected not merely to the identity of the author, but to the history of storytelling in the community.

This book begins with a short description of the language itself, its place of origin, its sound and structure, and an update on its current state. I've also included an overview of Anishinaabe literature and storytelling culture to serve as further backdrop for the theories of later chapters. The core of the book is what Margaret Kovach calls a "round dance of indigenous inquiry" in her book *Indigenous Methodologies* (23). Four authors who represent the range of contemporary Anishinaabe literature are introduced, and through an examination of their use of Anishinaabemowin and traditional Anishinaabe stories we find that they each connect in different ways to a shared worldview.

The four Anishinaabe authors included in this survey were not chosen solely because they lived through the same turbulent times or because they share ethnic heritage defined by blood quantums. They are people held together by a culture of tales, songs, and beliefs. These authors define themselves as Anishinaabe and are accepted as such by others who do the same. Each of them has heard, or studied, or written extensively in Anishinaabemowin, making their heritage language both a part of the backdrop and sometimes the medium of their work. These particular authors are known for their works in English. However, Anishinaabe words often "color" the text and add dimension to the narrative. In some cases translations are provided; in other instances definitions are only implied. In a few cases, readers who do not speak Anishinaabemowin become outsiders and are never invited to move beyond a point of observation. Each writer has been immersed in the language differently, some by inheritance as children, others by choice as adults. In each case, to varying degrees Ojibwe has become a part of their work. For all of these authors, the Anishinaabe language is a way to ensure cultural continuity.

Louise Erdrich is part of an Anishinaabe community in a diverse urban neighborhood. Jim Northrup lives on Northrup Road near where he grew up on Fond du Lac Reservation. Basil Johnston lives near Cape Croker Reserve. Only Gerald Vizenor lives far from the land of the Anishinaabe in an academic community. Although they have lived very different lives, the choices they make in textual production demonstrate a common cultural, linguistic, and literary heritage. Erdrich creates stories that illustrate the ways Anishinaabe people view themselves as others. She traces the complex lives of people who live in many directions at once and relies on narrative ambiguity that is possibly rooted in pronoun structures. Jim Northrup demonstrates the art of careful observation, *weweniganawaabi*, and through this he shows how contextualizing a life can support survival, even against the *wiindigoog*, the evils of human existence. His laughter is a legacy intended to spook the *gichimookomaanag* and awaken the next generation. Basil Johnston is a true *daebaudjimoot*, one who tells the truth through stories. He explains the creation of Anishinaabe communities and reflects the distinctly Anishinaabe system of classification in his stories. He has worked hard to continue the remembering that is the responsibility of every generation. Neither his visions of young Nanabozho long ago, nor the experiences of his uncle "Crazy Dave" can be discounted if the Anishinaabe are going to survive. The fourth author, Gerald Vizenor, is often considered the least like any of his cultural counterparts, but reading his work in an Anishinaabe context, it is not hard to see he is familiar with the long shadows cast by Anishinaabe language and culture. He finds in contemporary Anishinaabe communities the supernatural ways of the past that often go unnoticed. He twists time and tradition to make sense of tricksters and dream songs.

Each of these authors connects with the central ideas of observed truth and the importance of maintaining a crossroad of possibilities. Erdrich explores the way personal and community identity can be mapped onto familiar spectrums that allow for many ways to be Anishinaabe. Northrup shows how careful observation of the options in life related to tradition and change can keep a language and storytelling culture alive. Northrup also demonstrates the way traditional forms of linguistic play connect to narrative patterns of satire and survival. He shows there is more than one way to say almost anything. Johnston explores the importance of central myths as archives of cultural truth. His stories also lead to taxonomies of knowledge that align with Anishinaabe noun classification and the dominance of verbs in the language. Vizenor shows how old stories can offer new ways to observe history and map the future. He also ensures that Anishinaabe literature is one piece of the international literary conversation. He also shows how Anishinaabe names and dream songs are a part of the way the Anishinaabe define themselves and offer infinite options for the creation of Anishinaabe literature.

As Basil Johnston has said, "Much work and study remains to be done in order to understand Anishinaubae [*sic*] ideas and institutions. Until that study is done, the Anishinaubae peoples and their teachers cannot fully understand the philosophy or the philosophic basis for their institutions, cannot transmit them to their children" (Johnston, *K'd'Inawaewininaun* 51). He continues:

> In the course of learning language, much more than speech is received. In the study of language much more than the ability to utter words or to express simple wants and sentiments is expected. The end of language is to glean some understanding of the transcendental, the abstract, the world, life, being, human nature, and laws both physical and human-inspired—as embodied in literature. (Johnston, *K'd'Inawaewininaun* 51)

Study of the actual firmament of indigenous literature, the language itself, allows connections to be made even more clearly. The aim here is to invite readers to think in an Anishinaabe way, not just think about the Anishinaabeg because when that is possible, readers will find in Anishinaabe literature unceded identities and a way of looking at the world that resists stasis, defines existence and energy in motion, and requires constant observation for survival. A particular problem in postcolonial communities is the duality of existing always either as an untranslated identity or as an assimilated translation of oneself. The aim of this book is to work beyond the oppression of that dichotomy by inviting readers of all nations to read Anishinaabe literature through the reality of the Anishinaabe language and storytelling culture. Certainly many other cultural and political readings are possible, but it is important to confirm the validity of constructing literary theories based on the structure of an indigenous language without reference to hierarchies of difference . . . or to at least offer a new way to turn over a new leaf and see the stories in the trees, the kind I can write about in Anishinaabemowin to honor the old ways while creating the new.

WAAGAAMITIGOOG

Anishinaabeg gii owaangawi'aawaan
weweni owaagibizhaawaan
waawiyebii'igankewaad
aadisookaanag biskinaawaan
wiikwiiwin waamdaanaawaa
wiikonogewaad ji-wiiwaji'owaad
enji-waatebagaa tenon.

CROOKED TREES

The Anishinaabe tamed them
bending them carefully
making compasses
of stories folded
of energy visible
an invitation to freedom
in each bright leaf.

CHAPTER ONE

Anishinaabemowin:
The Anishinaabe Language

*Kchigaming, miskwaasini'ing, maashkodeng miinwa mitigwaakiing mii sa Anishi-
naabewakiing.*

The Great Inland sea, the swamp, the grasslands and the forest are all Anishinaabe
country.

Although the Anishinaabe people are often called a "woodland" culture, there
is much more to Anishinaabe identity. The center of *Anishinaabewakiing,* or
Anishinaabe country, is the life-giving *gaming,* the "vast water." The roll of "g"
against "m" is still heard when people speak of Lake Superior as *Gichi Gumee,* the
biggest, most *kchi,* of all seas. The sound is also echoed in the word *Michigami,*
which appeared on Vincenzo Coronelli's map *Partie Occidentale du Canada ou
de la Nouvelle France* in 1688 and became the name Henry Schoolcraft gave to
the territory that became a state in 1837. Anishinaabe elders still say that all the
lakes, now named separately, once shared a single name and identity, *Chigaming.*

Beyond the water are *miskwaasini'ing,* the swamp, and *mashkodeng,* the
grassland. In these words are echoes of *miskwa* (blood), *mashkiki* (medicine),

and *mashkawizi* (strength). This middle ground between the bays and rivers is important and an indelible part of Anishinaabe culture. One does not move from the mutable seas to the stationary pines without traveling the land between. On the other side of the circle is *mitigwaakiing*, the woodlands, which blends several descriptive concepts including *mitg* (tree), *aagawaakwaa* (to shade someone), and *aki*, commonly translated as "land" but closely related to *akina*, the term for "everything" or "unity."

Anishinaabeg / The Anishinaabe People

Anishinaabe language and culture is more than the woodlands, more than the lakes, more than artifacts and ceremonies. It is also the sound of a language that continues to evolve in this place among these people. A billion years ago continents fused, 500 million years ago a shift occurred, and over 5,000 years ago ice formed then melted. These distant events are chronicled in Anishinaabe stories of cataclysmic change and flooding (Grady). Traditional tales describe these vast seas without ever mentioning migration from the area of the Bering Strait, which, Vine Deloria Jr. points out, is an omission "to be taken seriously" (*Spirit and Reason* 92). Careful readers will see connections between Western science and indigenous narratives, between maps of land and the etymology of language and culture. Language and culture overlap, and sites of inquiry are more complex and diverse than at first imagined.

Many indigenous languages are now endangered, and at the core of most language revitalization is the belief that the language reflects the culture, and cultural practices are connected to identity, and place exerts some level of influence over both language and culture. These are complex claims that have been debated for years. What I aim to do here is explore the truth of these ideas while taking into account both community wisdom and academic scholarship. In the examples that began this chapter, it is clear the words to describe Anishinaabe habitat are connected to concepts of what is required to thrive. Mary Isabelle Young beautifully summarizes the community perception of language and worldview. In her book *Pimatisiwin: Walking in a Good Way,* she shares her own belief that "as aboriginal people we look at things our own way [and] a lot of that is rooted in the language" (115). Like many Anishinaabe people striving to keep the language alive, she finds this idea echoed across genders and generations and in venues of all kinds. Participants in her study repeatedly connect concepts of grammar and morphology to worldview and well-being. Nouns are not simply classified in two categories; they are "infused with spirit" that one informant, Aanung, explained as a connection between language and worldview. "We see all living things as having spirit and I don't believe we worship these things. It's just that we have a relationship with them as living beings and we respect them" (Young 139). Leroy Littlebear puts it another way when he talks about his language: "What I carry around is a combination of words. We become skillful at combinations. . . . The language encompasses all of the following: a constant flux, moving, recombining, energy waves, spirit, animate, relations, renewal and land. . . . I believe that if I do not speak the Anishinaabe language the way my Father taught me, I am underestimating the life force and the spiritual significance of the language" (Young 29). Furthermore, teacher Shirley Williams maintains that we need to move the language into the future so that life as it is lived now can be encompassed by the Anishinaabe language. "Language is a living thing that evolves with the times. Some things are hard to describe, but . . . we are in the new Millennium and although this has never been done before, it is urgent that speakers coin new words to describe such things as Plexiglass or a time clock" (Burnaby and Reyhner 223).

These explanations at first seem emotional or spiritual, but time and again they relate to specific points of grammar, morphology, syntax, and semiotics. Studies in the philosophy of language explore the way worlds are described and truth is communicated through language. I would suggest that indigenous linguistics might advance studies in this area, as metaphors and meaning are mapped differently in societies with alternate values and perspectives. Language is a social practice, co-created and constantly re-created by users who build circuits of understanding. These patterns of language should be as fully explored as possible when reading indigenous literature. Story, sound, and meaning cannot be separated from one another, or from the people who communicate with them. As Roger Spielmann concludes in his book on Anishinaabe discourse analysis: "If a person loses his or her language, lost also are the ideas and culture-specific ways of relating to each other" (239). These culture-specific ways of using language are reflected in the stories of the Anishinaabe people.

The word *Anishinaabe* can be translated as "original one" or the "first good human being lowered here" and is the term understood by Native speakers to be the most accurate description of the people who share a language and culture in the Great Lakes region (Vollum and Vollum 274; T. Smith 6). *Nishin* is still used both formally and informally as a term for one who is "doing well" or something that happens in a good way. *Naabe* is the term for one half of the creation equation. It is used to denote male versus female, but will also sound to speakers like the small term added when something is put "right here." Of course there is no way to say what the first speaker meant by the term, and Anishinaabe names and words are infamously mercurial, but fluent speakers revel in the intellectual paradigms and possibilities. To pretend there is one supreme interpretation is contrary to the spirit of the language itself.

As an ethnic and political term, *Anishinaabe* has a long history, considerably predating such commonly used terms as *Ojibwe* or *Chippewa*, which seem to be of eighteenth-century origin. The 1795 Treaty of Greenville refers to "the Chippewas," and William Warren noted in 1852, "'Chippewa' does not date far back. As a race or distinct people they denominate themselves Anishinabe [*sic*]" (14). In the 1960s, through the efforts of Gerald Vizenor and others, the word *Anishinaabe* made its return to popular discourse. In Vizenor's words, "Today the people named odjibwa, otchipwe, ojibway, chippewa, chippeway and 'indian' still speak of themselves in the language of their religion as the Anishinabe [*sic*]" (*Everlasting Sky* 11). Vizenor's effort to make the term *Anishinaabe* more prevalent in both Native and non-Native circles has met with success and was echoed by counterparts in Canadian communities.

According to traditional stories, *Gichi Manidoo*, the Great Spirit, took four parts of Mother Earth (perhaps the soil of the lakebed, the swamp, the prairie, and the woods) and blew into them using a sacred shell. "From the union of his breath with the elements, man was created" and then lowered to earth (Benton-Banai 3). Tradition holds that *Gichi Manidoo* placed the first people slightly east of the land they now inhabit. Much later they migrated to the land surrounding Lake Superior (Vecsey, "The Ojibwa Creation Myth" 12). Anishinaabe communities are now estimated to number over 500,000 people living in an area extending east to west from Lake Ontario to Lake Winnipeg and north to south from the Severn River basin in Canada to the Wabash River basin in America. Many more Anishinaabe people have migrated with family, toward work, to urban communities and are reflected as a growing population in the U.S. census.

The earliest written records of the Anishinaabe were compiled by French and English missionaries and explorers who came to North America in the 1600s. The immigrants imagined they were discovering a "new" world, when in truth they became "cocreators of a world in the making" (R. White 518). By the seventeenth century, warfare, disease, the economy of fur trading, and the rising number of immigrant settlements had changed the Anishinaabe landscape irrevocably. The cultural collision of this period is preserved in the oral stories of the Anishinaabe and in the writings of the foreign men who walked among them, including Nicolas Perrot, Alexander Henry, Frederic Baraga, and Henry Rowe Schoolcraft.

Anishinaabe communities are part of what is now North Dakota, Minnesota, Wisconsin, Michigan, Ontario, Manitoba, and Saskatchewan. As people living in a shared place, migrating from the east to the west of the lakes, the Anishinaabeg were known as a confederacy of several ethnicities and many small communities. Theirs was the Three Fires Confederacy, and they are considered indigenous to the Great Lakes because theirs is the oldest living memory that has survived in this place. Early in the 1600s Champlain began to use the name *Algonquian*, which has been traced to either the Micmac phrase *algoomeaking* ("place of eel spearing") or the Maliseet term *elaegomogwik* ("they are our relatives"). In the early 1800s Henry Schoolcraft further complicated matters by combining the terms *Allegheny* and *Atlantic* to create "Algic." Embedded in these tangled linguistic roots is at least a kernel of undeniable truth: there were multiple large groups of people, whose languages and practices were distinct enough to be sometimes unintelligible, yet recognizably connected in practice and community. Today, linguists classify Anishinaabemowin as one of 27 Algonquian languages and acknowledge it as the ancestral language of over 200 communities in the United States and Canada. This broad group is sometimes divided into three parts indicating the languages used in the plains and in the central and eastern parts of North America. Anishinaabemowin is part of the central group that also includes Cree, Miami, Menominee, Naskapi, Shawnee, Fox, and Sauk, among others, and speakers of these central languages can often easily understand one another and share storytelling traditions.

The Anishinaabe have always insisted on their distinctiveness as a people. In 1885, when his book *History of the Ojibway Nation* was published, mixed-blood Anishinaabe interpreter and legislator William Warren noted:

> During my long residence among the Ojibways, after numberless inquiries of their old men, I have never been able to learn, by tradition or otherwise, that they entertain the belief that all the tribes of the red race inhabiting America have ever been, at any time since the occupancy of this continent, one and the same

people, speaking the same language, and practicing the same beliefs and customs. … There are differences amongst its inhabitants and contrarieties as marked and fully developed as are to be found between European and Asiatic nations—wide differences in language, beliefs and customs. (60)

Early maps indicate the edges of linguistic groups, paths of trade and shifting political alliances. Today many smaller sovereign nations exist where once a more connected confederacy controlled the region. Despite modern quantums and linear descriptions of descendancy, families are still defined in broad strokes, and clan affiliations remain in place as networks that defy time and modern templates. Anishinaabe people see themselves as connected in many ways to one another.

Anishinaabemowin / The Anishinaabe Language

Anishinaabemowin is the language of the Three Fires Confederacy, a political construct that has shifted in use over time. Most speakers today understand Odawa, Potawatomi, and Ojibwe to be ethnic communities present in many combinations on various reservations, while the term *Anishinaabe* connects the broader linguistic and cultural community. Each of the ethnic groups has its own dialectal and cultural identity. Odawa stems from the word *adaawe*, meaning to trade. The term "Potawatomi" references the word *boodwedi*, the act of working to build a fire together. Some say the term "Ojibwe" stems from the word *jibakwe* (to cook or roast) because the people wore moccasins that were puckered at the toe. However, it is possibly more productive to connect the initial sound *jib* to such other words as *jibwa*, meaning "before," and *jiibay*, meaning ghost, which carry implications of the past. In fact *jibakwe* itself connects back to the concept of putting a plate out for the *jiibayag* (the ancestors who came before us), which makes sense because the role of remembering or retelling stories is the role most often associated with the Ojibwe. In her travel memoir, *Books and Islands in Ojibwe Country*, Erdrich herself extends this analogy, connecting the term *ojibwe* to the word *ozhibii'ige*, which is the verb for "he or she writes" (11). Some of the stories other Anishinaabe authors write might continue this exploration of sound and meaning to consider the echoes of the crane clan centered at the place of the rapids, the *jijaakwag onjibaaweting*.

The term *Anishinaabe* is a verb in the language and becomes a sentence when conjugated: *Nd'Anishinaabe*/I am Anishinaabe. Adding *mo* to the end of the verb means "to speak as an Anishinaabe": *Nd'anishinaabemomin*/We speak Anishinaabe. Adding *taw* changes the form of the verb and implies a speaker and listener: *Gd'anishinaabemtawigo*/We all speak Anishinaabe to you. Adding *win* to the word makes it a noun. This transformation may seem tangled to an English speaker, but it is a window into a world of meaning shaped by action and addition rather than presence and pronouns. The slip of definition between seeing language as a noun and having a way to peel it back to a common verb is the difference between cultures. To say, "I speak English" or "Je parle français" requires use of a pronoun that stands alone and a verb, "speak" or *parle*, to say what is happening with that thing, the language, "English" or *français*. To convey a similar message regarding Anishinaabemowin, I say *nd'anishinaabem* as one word with the pronoun *nd* (I) added to the front and the *win* noun indicator removed. Other speakers in the region might say *nd'ojibwem* or *n'boodewaadmiimomin* to indicate they are speaking the language of their Ojibwe or Potawatomi community. This shifting of verbs depends on understanding the changes that occur at the center of the message, rather than positioning of subjects and objects. Of course there are times when an object is desired, as in "I love you," *Je t'aime, G'zaagin*. Watching that phrase move from three separate words in English to two words and an enclitic pronoun in French to a single transitive animate verb in Anishinaabemowin is like watching clouds come together. In this and several other ways, including noun classes and negation, French is closer to Anishinaabemowin than English. It is not the subject of this book, but one does wonder if that had any subtle influence on the course of history. Regardless of that particular debate, it is clear that the way meaning is constructed differs from one culture to another, and ideas of possession, classification, positioning, and accuracy can differ greatly.

To build theories and identify aesthetic trends based on language, it is important to know the sound and rhythm of Anishinaabemowin. Many Anishinaabe authors find in the language an echo of the place. Ignatia Broker wrote in her memoir of an Ojibwe childhood, *Night Flying Woman*: "When the forest weeps, the Anishinaabe who listen will look back at the years. In each generation of Ojibway there will be a person who will hear the *si-si-gwa-d* who will listen and remember and pass it on to the children" (1). In Anishinaabe culture trees have long been considered markers of meeting places and messengers to other dimensions. Desperate women and young warriors sometimes become trees in Anishinaabe stories. Little people known as *apa'iinsag* capture children and teach them lessons under trees. When Broker urges young people to "listen to the trees" she is not only asking that they hear the pattern of syllables and dance of vowels between the consonants, she is also asking them to listen for meaning not always on the surface. In the words chosen for the tree names, or words used for the actions associated with certain trees, there are networks of meaning in the sounds that should not be ignored. If we listen, the trees tell us who they are: *zesegawandag, zhingwaak, mitigomizh, ninatig, azaadi, wiigwaas, giizhik* (white spruce, white pine, oak, maple, aspen, birch, cedar). The numerous vowels, absence of "l" and "r" and presence of consonant pairs "zh," "gw," and "nd" mark the words as Anishinaabemowin. Helen Fuhst and her brother Stanley Peltier, who have been teaching the language for many years, say there are meanings in the sounds that cannot be forgotten. Fuhst has written a book about a sound-based method of language instruction with the subtitle *Nisosataagaadeg Akina Initaagawaziwinan E-Noondaagaadegin E-Akidoong Akiodoowining* ("understand all the sounds that are heard, that are said in words"). Knowledge of sounds can help explain definitions. For example, *ozhaawashkwaande* is hard to define in English. It has come to stand for "green" most often, but elders will say it once was used for both blue and green and represents all the blue and green of fir needles, sage leaves, the place where lakes merge, or that spot on the horizon where water becomes sky. Others may hear different images in these sounds, but the Anishinaabeg have built connections between words, an audible etymology, that causes the mind to leap in a certain way from one image to another. Only the most fluent speakers can understand all of these implications and connections, but it is something students can aspire to and readers should recognize.

For centuries these sounds were transferred from one generation to the next reinforced only by the environment and community. If you forgot the word for pine you could ask a *zhingibis* (grebe) or a *zhingos* (weasel) or just *zhingishin* (lie down) on a layer of dry soft needles and think about it while ice fishing . . . or you could ask a friend or elder who might say you are *zhiingizi* for forgetting. Today you can check with Jim Northrup on Facebook, look it up in Basil Johnston's thesaurus, or go to class at any one of several universities and tribal colleges to find out. But until colonization, Anishinaabemowin was an oral language, which is partly why there is still no standard orthography. There was a brief period of literacy and cultural exchange as writing came to the continent, but it was followed by swift and effective linguistic genocide in many communities. The current era is one that supports recovery of indigenous languages, but spelling is still evolving and can be considered a matter of preference. While students and teachers tend toward standardization, no variation attempting to represent the sound of a Native speaker accurately should be denied legitimacy. Although many explorers included word lists in their travelogues, the first Anishinaabe dictionary was compiled by Bishop Baraga, who interpreted Ojibwe according to Latin linguistic structures. *A Dictionary of the Otchipwe Language Explained in English* was first published in 1853 by Jos. A. Hemann in Cincinnati and remains in print today. In the late 1990s, dictionaries by Richard Rhodes and John Nichols and a comprehensive grammar by Rand Valentine became common. In this century, technology has made online dictionaries and archives more common, but students and speakers should always know that any representation of sound and meaning is never absolute if the language is living. In fact, it is likely that the cultural tenet of looking in all directions and making change possible has impacted the desire to ever render the language fixed in black and white. It is quite possible that several forms of writing, syllabics, and a few variations of type will evolve together and be learned by future students as regional branches of understanding.

Most teachers in the United States use the system based on the roman alphabet that was devised by Charles Fiero in the 1950s and adapted by John Nichols in the 1970s. The Fiero system uses the roman alphabet and a series of "double vowels" to represent each sound. This system has the advantage of being highly predictable. The long "e" sound is always represented by "ii," while one "i" is always short. Thanks to technology, interested students and scholars can hear many examples of speech and song online now. At *Noongwa e-Anishinaabemjig* (www.ojibwe. net) we have posted lessons on pronunciation and examples of stories and song. Many of the teachers in Canada prefer the syllabics system, developed by James Evans in the early 1840s, which more accurately manages vowel and consonant differences, but is difficult to publish. In this book, the double-vowel system is used most often, but in direct quotes, the author's spelling is preserved as it was originally published. In some instances, variant spellings reflect a change in an author's knowledge over time.

To understand how the language and literature relate and in turn can be connected to cultural theories, it is important to have some sense of how Anishinaabemowin works, how the bones of grammar work with the muscle of verbs. When teaching Anishinaabemowin, I often find myself saying, "There is no word for —— in Anishinaabemowin" when in fact what I should be doing is taking time to explain which words there *are* in Anishinaabemowin. Often, it is the case that an English noun is an Anishinaabe verb. Each language has its qualities, and one is not better than the other, but in some cases they are differently accurate. A lake might be named for the man who built a town around it or it might be named for the color of its leeches. Think of the explanation of Anishinaabemowin I provide here not as an algebraic equation with English on one side and Anishinaabemowin on the other, but perhaps as a tour of the parts of town the tourists rarely visit. Think of the language as the back settlement of literature, the network of dirt roads and deer paths that can take you into the woods and lead you out the other side.

Anishinaabemowin is an agglutinative language. This means words are long strings of meaning that can be shifted by speakers to clarify what is happening. There is a tendency to prefer variety over standardization, and there is sometimes great fun to be had by speakers who build the longest word possible that can be easily comprehended by others. Paula Giese, a Lakota student who dedicated many years to learning Anishinaabemowin, described learning the agglutinative quality of the language from an elder who taught her the word for computer, *mazinaabikiwebinigan*, which is a combination of the words *mazini* (to design), *aabiki* (metal keys), and *webinigaazo* (to throw it away). Her long explanation of how the computer came to be known as "the thing that uses keys to make designs that you throw away" not only shows how the language is agglutinative but also shows how the perceptions of young women working with metal type keys in the 1930s and plastic keyboards in the 1980s shaped one of the words used for computer. As an interesting side note, Giese and her instructor then came up with a new word to use for computers, *mazinibiiangwaazakone*, which means "designs made of glowing light." The Nichols dictionary still cites the older word, *mazinaabikiwebinigan*, but who knows what the next edition will contain?

A second defining feature of Anishinaabemowin is the use of verbs. There are four categories of verbs. While this may sound like the making of a linguistic riddle, it is actually the source of much of the complexity of the language. It is the progression of complexity that creates incredible variety. For instance, consider the difference between *wiisini* (eats), *miijin manoomin* (eats rice), and *mwaa mishiimin* (eats an apple). Eating without mentioning what is being eaten is *wiisini*. Once the food enters the conversation, a speaker has to choose either *mwaa* or *miijin* based on the type of food. None of the root verbs are the same, but each of them has related words; for instance, *miijin* is close to *miijim*, which is the generic term for food; and *wiisini* is close to *wiinin*, the word for fat and *wiishko-* and *wiisaga-*, the prefixes for sweet and sour. Sometimes the verb forms are related to one another instead of other concepts. For instance, *gii waabaanjigaade* (it was seen), *waabam* (to see), *waabmdaan psagak* (to see the board), and *waabamaad mitig* (to see the tree) all share the root verb *waab*, which connects with *waaban* and *waabang*, the words for "east" and "tomorrow." In this case, the variation of the verb conveys ideas of light, diurnal cycles, and the science of sight. Learning how these verbs move from one form to another and remembering that action must be specifically connected to the object of that action are important markers of fluency. This complexity is based on accuracy. Anishinaabemowin complicates meaning in a way that reflects the origin stories. Words stem from the center, the way stories say life began with a spark of light and earth was made from a speck of dirt. Meaning radiates from a central spoke of action, and diversity of interpretation is important. There are rules of morphology to help create words, and grammar that guides the construction of phrases, but a high value is placed on creating meaning that can be specific to the context and yet open to interpretation.

A third important feature of Anishinaabemowin is the classification of nouns. Nouns are secondary in importance to verbs, and they are always marked as one of two classes. That they are secondary to verbs is evident by the fact that in many cases a noun is created by adding *win* or *jigan* to a verb. Verb stems tend to have relatively fixed meanings across dialects. Nouns are more transitory and capricious. Their names vary from region to region, sometimes also by household, gender, or generation. The most important thing about the name of a thing is that it says clearly what one can do with it. A personal favorite noun is the western version of coffee, *maakademaashkikiwabo*, literally "black medicine water." Early curriculum often refers to noun classes as "animate" and "inanimate," which can be as confusing as the more scholarly linguistic term, "gender." Anishinaabe noun classification has nothing to do with animacy or gender, merely the level of complexity a speaker wants to indicate. For instance, when speaking about a person or animal, it is obvious that the speaker would need to indicate some level of complexity in the relationship. For this reason, people and animals always fall into the class of nouns that can be used with the most complicated verb form. It is not particularly easy to teach these forms because they need to be memorized through listening to and speaking Anishinaabemowin. A student cannot use English terms or perspectives to predict the noun classes. The fundamental lesson is that a speaker must know which class any noun falls into or be willing to choose one based on the dialect of the region or the direction a story may be taking. As with other aspects of Anishinaabemowin, everyone can be right and everyone can be wrong all at once. If I speak of a cross as a place where two roads meet, I might say one thing; if I speak of the object atop someone's gravehouse, I might say something else entirely. Some might agree with my usage, others might not; what is important is the ability to know the difference, not the need for universal consistency. I have often been corrected on classification when using the word "bread" by itself. Some say *bakwezhiganan*, some say *bakwezhiganag*. I have never been corrected when the word is part of a sentence. As long as I match the form of the verb "to eat" and say either *n'mwaag bakwezhiganag* or *n'miijinan bakwezhiganan*, I am left to believe what I want about the class of that noun. Variation within certain boundaries of understanding seems to be the key.

The fourth related concept is the system of pronoun indication. Verbs, as markers of action, are central to the language; therefore the system of indicating the actors is equally sophisticated and designed for precision. The universal sorting of self and other in the form of first, second, and third person occurs with more specificity of number and a complete lack of gender indication. One can say *niin* (I), *giin* (you), or *wiin* (the one that is neither of us) but not "he," "she," "him," or "her." This lack of specification of gender has often been suggested as an indication of the relative equality of men and women in traditional communities (Brizinski; Medicine; Ezzo; Ross). However, there are times when gender is indicated by speech. Some nouns, particles, and exclamations are used only by one gender. For instance, only women say *enya* to mean yes, and *n'iiji* is used only to indicate a male friend. In my opinion, this leads us to a conclusion that Anishinaabe language and culture acknowledge gender difference, but in a way that relies on choice and context rather than fixed and predictable rules.

Another way Anishinaabe pronouns can reflect the context is the way a speaker can include or exclude members of the listening community. For instance, *giin* indicates a singular second person (you), while *giinwaa* indicates a group (plural "you" or "you all"). This means it is important to know who is speaking, who is listening, and who is being spoken to. The "listening" and "being spoken to" categories are not always the same. For instance, kids standing in a group who hear *Aanii dash gii ezhichigeyeg ina*?! know they all stand on trial. That version of "Why did you (plural) do it?" is able to clarify that all the listeners are being questioned. If instead two sisters heard *Aanii gii ezhichigeyin ina*?! they would both know that the *yin* at the end of the verb instead of a *yeg* means that only one of them needs to reply. This ability to clarify the audience is also evident in the first-person plurals *niinwi* and *giinwi*. Both translate into English as "we," but the difference between them is whether the speaker is including or excluding the listener. There are times when a story is told to someone not involved in the event, and there are times when a speaker wants to indicate that the audience is part of the story. This always comes up when the drum group I sing with needs to sing what is now known as "The AIM Song." The song was first used by the pantribal group of Native American activists during protests in 1972 that followed the brutal murder of a Lakota man, Raymond Yellow Thunder, by four non-Native Nebraskans. The round of verses with its pattern of leads and vocables became a song known throughout Indian Country. From Alcatraz Island to Pine Ridge and the streets of Milwaukee, Minneapolis, Detroit, and Toronto, the song became recognized as a representation of Native American political unity. It calls listeners to stand as if at attention, as if gathered in prayer. With permission from a few of the original leaders of the organization, we've given it Anishinaabe lyrics that combine Jim Northrup's favorite word, *boochigo*, with new lyrics, *Anishinaabe-moying, ji-minobimaadziying* ("We have to all speak Anishinaabemowin to live well"). Before each performance we have to pause, size up the audience, and think about whether or not we expect them to speak Anishinaabemowin. If not, we tweak the ending and sing the song in a way that says we speak it with each other, but not with everyone there. The capacity to make these relationships audible is another feature of Anishinaabemowin that can be found in the writing of contemporary authors.

All four of these main features of the language indicate a level of flexibility that is uniquely suited to oral presentation and knowledge preservation. As Roger Spielmann explains, "legends, stories, and traditional teachings transmitted in Ojibwe are intricate and artful discourses . . . elaborately designed to do several things at once" (92). By adding to words, shifting verbs, indicating noun classes, and selecting pronouns, speakers control and direct their stories. Students can spend years becoming fluent, and elders often say they are still learning every day. There are many words and ways to use them that are important to master. But for understanding the way contemporary authors use the language and represent Anishinaabe identity, at least some language should be introduced. Beyond the structural differences in grammar, there are patterns of sound Anishinaabe speakers use to enhance their message. For example, repetition is one way to emphasize a verb. There are some prefixes that can be repeated and extended. In telling the story of a time when I waited, I might say, *n'gii baabinchige* (I waited). To add emphasis I might duplicate the first syllable to say, *n'gii baabaabinchige*. This would still translate literally as "I waited," but it sounds more like "I wawawaited" and allows the speaker to convey the extended duration of the action. Speakers might also change the order of individual words to give priority to one part of the sentence over another, or simply to vary the tempo of the narrative. Word order is not fixed in Anishinaabemowin. There are common habits, but it is also up to the speaker to say some words first and other words last. Additionally there are a range of particles a speaker can add to pause, connect, restart, or mark time in any story. Brendan Fairbanks has written an entire thesis on these discourse markers and the ways they function in speech. It is important to define *mii, mii'iw, miidash, miinawaa, mii sa,* and the many more *mii*'s and a few *igo*'s, *gwa*'s, and *gii'enh*'s, but it is also essential to know how they stop and start thought, creating a shared space in conversation for both the speaker and the listener.

Connections to Culture

The importance of language to the preservation of indigenous culture extends beyond one tribe or one continent. Tribal governments and scholars can trace the history of blood, quantum, and enrollment, but as nations exercise increasing control over their identities, culturally identifiable activities have become part of the equation, which is why attention must be paid to the use and maintenance of indigenous languages. According to the U.S. Census Bureau, the term "American Indian and Alaska Native" refers to "people having origins in any of the original peoples of North and South America (including Central America), and who maintain tribal affiliation or community attachment." In 2011 the U.S. National Congress of American Indians listed 581 federally recognized tribes, with an additional 24 tribes recognized by state governments. In Canada, where there are over 630 First Nations, the term "Aboriginal Peoples" is used separately from "Inuit" and "Métis" as an ethnic designation. The language of each nation offers yet another form of history that stretches beyond current national memory. In *First Nations Family Justice,* George Muswagon writes:

> Language is the medium through which history, culture and worldview are transmitted; therefore the best connection to historical roots [is] First Nations

languages. . . . It is their particular way of viewing the world, and their place in it, that sets First Nations people apart from non–First Nations people. This worldview remains intact in the language. (40)

For the Anishinaabe, the language is a source of history and a means of survival. Old words, newer words, patterns of speech, and changes in usage all document the history of Anishinaabe speakers.

In Canada, the relationship between politics and language was clarified in 1993 by the Declaration on Aboriginal Languages written by the Assembly of First Nations, which states: "Our languages were given to us by the Creator as an integral part of life. Embodied in our languages is our unique relationship to the Creator, our attitudes, beliefs, values and the fundamental notion of what is truth" (Champagne 2). In the United States, the passing of the 1991 Native Languages Act confirmed the connection between indigenous language and identity. In both Canada and the United States, the relationship between the government and Native Americans is one of denial and restriction of identity through numerous tactics intended to result in cultural erasure and assimilation. Blood, land, and language can be viewed as mediums of continued warfare. As early as 1819, the Civilization Fund Act provided money to societies who would "educate" Indian students. The goal was to "civilize" Indians by getting rid of their traditions and customs, including the very words they used to communicate. In 1879 Captain Richard Pratt, notable for his success during the Indian Wars, was given responsibility for Indian education in the United States. Considered a forward-thinking educator willing to give Native students a chance (if they abandoned all traces of their Native roots), he opened the doors of the Carlisle boarding school to continue the work begun by early French, German, and Spanish missionaries. Eventually, boarding schools and the myth of the "vanishing American" took hold, and increasingly fewer people used indigenous languages. At the 1988 Aboriginal Languages Policy Conference, Grand Chief Mike Mitchell related the following

What would happen to the Creator's law if the robin couldn't sing its song anymore? We would feel very bad: We would understand that something snapped in nature's law. What would happen if you saw a robin and you heard a different song, if it was singing the song of the seagull? You would say, "Robin, that's not your language; that's not your song. (Burnaby and Reyhner 18)

Chizhaazhagwa (in the long ago) there were of course Anishinaabe linguists who were the creators of the language, the namers and truth tellers who taught communities which words to use. In another direction at a different time, we find translators and orators, some of them Anishinaabe, who wrote about their language, including Andrew Blackbird and Simon Pokagon. Then there came along the road ethnographers who collected dates, dialects, and details. After all this, let's say around noon, American indigenous languages were studied in a serious way, not just as a matter of warfare, trade, and curiosity, but with a desire to truly understand how they work. For Anishinaabemowin this began in the 1930s with the work of Leonard Bloomfield and has continued through to the present with increasing participation from Anishinaabemowin speakers themselves, including work by Patricia Ningewance, Roger Roulette, Maryanne Corbiere, Basil Johnston, Howard Kimewon, Alphonse Pitawanakwat, Howard Webkamigad, Kenny Pheasant, Anton Treuer, Brendan Fairbanks, Michael Sullivan, and others.

Despite continued efforts to teach and document the language, use is sharply declining. Leanne Hinton, K. David Harrison, and Jon Reyhner have written useful books about the importance and process of preserving linguistic diversity. In the wake of the American Indian Movement, language programs began to appear in schools at all levels. On reservations and in urban communities, Anishinaabe people are relearning a language that suffered a loss of continuity across generations. Its chances for survival have increased with immersion schools in Wisconsin, Minnesota, Michigan, and Ontario, and more programs are being started for young children in communities throughout the Great Lakes. Both print and audio resources are limited, but the efforts of many teachers, the efficient power of technology, and the increasing number of Anishinaabe people earning degrees in language and education offer hope for a future that will allow for more creation and critique of Anishinaabemowin.

As you read how four authors bring the language and its patterns into their writing, keep in mind the structure and history of Anishinaabemowin. Whenever possible, try to hear the long frequent vowels and soft "zh" and "gw." Consider the fact that action is always central and speakers constantly think about how to communicate what is happening. Consider too that Anishinaabemowin is a language of options so diverse and extreme that the act of seeking a center is the focus. In a world of snowflakes, agates, and leaves there are patterns premised on individuality, and the view from a distance shows unity, while a look up close reveals infinite variety. These are some of the truths of a world where there are words for dreaming (*bwaajige*) and words for storytelling (*dibaajimo*) and nothing to prevent the creation of a new word that implies they might sometimes happen at the very same time . . . *bawaajimo* . . . for a very long time . . . *babawaajimoyaanh.*

CHAPTER TWO

Anishinaabebiige:
Anishinaabe Literature

Anishinaabe literary history is both ancient and imminent, traceable to the sound of stones and adaptive as white winter fur, evolving in order to survive. Today Anishinaabe authors move from one language to another by choice and necessity. The language of the original stories is now endangered, but translations and contemporary creations still reflect indigenous Anishinaabe patterns. A brief review of these narrative signs and the Anishinaabe literary canon provides some of the background necessary for identifying indigenous literary theories. To advance the study of Native American literature as a broad field, I offer here what Kim Blaeser would call "tribal-centered" criticism (Blaeser, "Native Literature"). In my view she calls us to focus on one nation but also to reach, when needed, beyond national and disciplinary boundaries to provide a "tribal" view of narrative. The point is less about revealing the details of one tribe that fit the current framework than about understanding how to view literature and language from a tribal perspective that involves creating new frames of reference based on indigenous ways of knowing.

Geteaansoke / Story Origin

Long, long ago, during winter, a boy set out to hunt for his hungry family. He captured only a few birds and then, exhausted by the cold, decided to rest beneath the shelter of a great stone, a dreamer's rock. There, in the curve of the earth, he heard the first story. He left a gift for the stone and brought back to his people the transformative power of memory, entertainment, escape, and understanding. According to the version in Anne Dunn's *Winter Thunder*, the boy returned throughout the winter, learning all he could until the stone declared, "You are the storyteller now. Where there are storytellers there will be stories and where there are stories there will be storytellers" (18). This is a narrative equation of offerings, gifts, apprenticeship, creativity, and continuity. Anishinaabe storytelling is recognition of human intelligence and ingenuity despite the limitations of the human condition. Dunn's tale of the first storyteller comes to her through her mother, Wasaygahbahwequay, or Maefred Arey, who was a curriculum developer for the Indian Education Program in Cass Lake. She explained the importance of storytelling to the Anishinaabe people:

> The telling and hearing of legends was important in the life of every Indian. Each tribe had their own cultural hero, teacher or mentor. Although all Indians were natural storytellers, it was usually the elder men and women who were the historians of the village. At that time they knew more about their tribal traditions. While family and friends were gathered around the lodge fires on long winter evenings, the elders held them spellbound with the mystery, humor and excitement of ancient talks. Story was a part of training for all children. (Dunn, *Winter Thunder* 11)

Arey described stories as education, entertainment, and archives.

Today knowledge is classified broadly as sciences, art, or literature, and within those categories are such branches as biology, physics, and astronomy; music, painting, and dance; and romance, mystery, and horror, to name only a few. In Anishinaabemowin, stories are either *dibaajimowinan* or *aadizokaanag. Dibaajimowinan* are usually thought of in the noun class sometimes called inanimate. *Aadizokaanag* are usually of the other noun class sometimes referred to as animate. The cast of *aadizokaanag* are familiar characters whose inclusion in any story adds layers of meaning. The English translation of these words and categories is inadequate. The closest literal translation is one that connects *dibaajimowinan* to the act of collecting and redistributing the truth that you've heard. This is a simpler, more direct narrative style. *Aadizokaanag*, by contrast, in poetry, would be the bones of self-knowing, the core means of communicating the complexity of life. Both are often translated as "story" in English. Sometimes *aadizokaan* is translated as "myth," but that term is laden with implications of fiction that are not necessarily part of the Anishinaabe classification. Together, the *dibaajimowinan* and *aadizokaanag* comprise Anishinaabe literature.

Although authorship was communal (and in many ways, still is), each story was told by one person, one story to one audience in one place at a time. Constructing a narrative that neither pretends to be too original nor comes across as too didactic and unadapted is still the mark of a good Anishinaabe storyteller. A good narrator needs to know the story's origins and have the ability to weave the content into the contemporary context. Anishinaabe elders often sit around and make up words by breaking old words apart and putting them back together, or by borrowing bits of sound and meaning from disparate corners of conversation. This is also the way stories are conveyed. Some have described Anishinaabe stories as "complex," "polyvocal," and "multimodal." It is true, the stories are layered, use multiple voices and communicate more than one message at a time. This can be related in part back to the primary features of the language, which emphasize flexibility and change. In the stories, as in the language, speakers place high value on the variation of familiar themes. To view Anishinaabe literature only on a stage built by other nations is to misunderstand the malleability and communal qualities of original Anishinaabe works.

If a stone was the first storyteller, perhaps a useful metaphor would be to think about the way stones themselves are changed. A review of Anishinaabe literature across time shows how stories change in sedimentary, igneous, and metamorphic ways. Sedimentary rocks are layers of time and earth shaped slowly by water and wind. These are the stories told by fluent speakers of the language, sometimes published by the storytellers themselves, more often published as part of ethnographic or literary collections. Examples of these stories can be found across the past two hundred years. Igneous rocks are formed suddenly in fire. Igneous Anishinaabe literature was formed in the 1800s as a result of cultural conflict and political pressure during times when reports of legal and military entanglement became a part of new histories and attempts were made to speak across cultures. The authors of these stories operate somewhere between assimilation and acculturation, arguably moving along that scale as needed. They speak of rebirth and conversion, yet like all children, their features and gestures reflect those who came before them. Sometimes these stories are burdened by the ghosts of future generations absent in America, as the authors of these stories believe they might be "the last" storyteller in their community. Eventually, Anishinaabe stories become like metamorphic rocks, changing shape without being completely melted, as they move entirely into English, creating an indigenous modernity still centered in the space of the Great Lakes. Pages are perhaps not sediment, digital mediums are not molten elements, but Anishinaabe storytelling still has weight and is continually being reshaped, recast, and reinvented by the storytellers of the community.

Oshkiaanjimo / New Ways of Telling Stories

The first written records of Anishinaabe stories surface in the writing of missionaries and explorers settled in the Hudson Bay and Great Lakes region to teach and trade. These French- and English-speaking immigrants initially relied on indigenous teachers and translators to help them survive. Eventually, commercial connections and missions of conversion became well established, and both the immigrant and indigenous communities became culturally curious. Native authors wrote in their own and the colonizer's language to continue their own stories and test new formats for storytelling. The shape of narration shifted. American and Canadian settlers began saving the stories they heard from indigenous people. These literary explorers often claimed authority and published their "discoveries" as part of the colonial process of exoticism and possession. While these early ethnographers, linguists, and writers began to retell Anishinaabe stories in print, the oral origin and original names were often not included. However, despite these attempts to capture the stories for the American market, a thread of linguistic and cultural continuity can still be recognized. Like *wiigob,* the basswood thread that has been used for centuries to hold together baskets, canoes, and dwellings, the language and identity of the Anishinaabe has given shape to a body of literature.

Bamewawagezhikoquay, known in English as Jane Johnston, was born in 1800 to an Ojibwe mother and Irish father. Her writing is the first work by an Anishinaabe author to be published in America. She continued the tradition of retelling by recording the stories of her mother, Ozhaguscodaywayquay, but she also she wrote flowing, fluent English verse perfectly suited to the times. Robert Dale Parker's book about her life, *The Sound the Stars Make Rushing Through the Sky*, is an eloquent tribute to this early author. She survived the War of 1812 and later married the Indian agent Henry Rowe Schoolcraft, who, for many decades, cast a long shadow over the history of her life.

Jane Schoolcraft wrote poems to pine trees and the Doric Rock, but she also wrote elegies and acrostics. She was biliterary, moving from one language to another. She was definitely able to compose her thoughts in different cultural contexts. "To the Pine Tree" is an early poem that celebrates the life of the tree. In it she refers to the tree as "*zhauwushcozid*," which means green, but uses an ending that implies animacy. This connection to the trees is echoed in the legend "Mishosha," which begins, "In an early age of the world, when there were fewer inhabitants on the earth than there are now . . ." These markers of place and perspective cross the boundaries of language and carry a culture from one time into another.

An important part of the Jane Schoolcraft story is her contribution to Anishinaabe literature through the collections of her husband. Henry Schoolcraft is often lauded as the "father of ethnography," but the long-ago, first-storyteller rock would say he was just another listener who found a few tales while out hunting. Not only did Henry have access to the resources needed to publish and build archives, he predicted that the pace of change would render stories in print more permanent than those told only orally at ceremonies or in winter. This must have been a contrary thought to Jane and her mother, and to many of the other "literary informants" whose voices have been collected. The permanence of speech and winter would never cause one to question the potential eternity of storytelling. Imagine a means of collection and preservation that was successful for centuries being so quickly and severely crippled. Like language loss, literary loss was swift and unforgiving as elders took their words and stories with them to the next world. Who could have imagined editors who would collect stories without giving credit to the original tellers? This is exactly what Cornelius Mathews did when he published his *Indian Fairy Book* of 1856 without crediting *Algic Researches*, which was published by Henry Schoolcraft . . . who did not credit translations of his wife, Jane Schoolcraft . . . who heard the stories from her mother, Ozhaguscodaywayquay. Jane was aware of the literary piracy going on and once told a traveler, Chandler Gilman, who wished to include one of her mother's stories in his own travelogue, "many of the oldest and most intelligent of the tribe (say) that the story of the 'Origin of the Robin-red-breast' has been current in the tribe from their earliest recollections" (Gilman, vol. 1, 159). In the word-melding tradition of Anishinaabemowin there is a perfect description for this activity, and it would be "copywrong." Returning to the voice of the times, it was Mathews who said in his introduction:

> To Mr. Schoolcraft, the large-hearted and able pioneer of the literature of the Indian race, the world is indebted for the discovery of such tales and legends and for their first publication in the primitive form as derived from the Aborigines, and interpreted by various competent persons. From this novel source the following volume is derived . . . the editor has bestowed on them, according to his ability, such changes as similar legends most in vogue in other countries have received to adapt them to the comprehension and sympathy of general readers. He has at times smoothed out or lengthened, or abridged the thread of the narrative to make it more obvious and more easily followed.

This cavalier appropriation began the erasure of communal authorship and a separation of language and literature. Much could be said about the powerful language of statements like this, the "discovery" by the white man of "primitive" forms that required smoothing, lengthening, or abridging to render them comprehensible to "sympathetic" readers. When reading across cultures, everything must be questioned—in all languages. The early Anishinaabe stories were also blended into "The Song of Hiawatha" by Henry Longfellow. They are circuitously credited in the verse itself to "the Ojibways" and "the Dacotahs," but the need to name a single source also drove him to claim he heard the stories "from the lips of Nawadaha," a singer from "Tawasentha." Interestingly, Tawasentha is precisely where Henry Schoolcraft was born, and it was his *Algic Researches* that served as the primary source for Longfellow's long poem. This literary erasure and reduction must be consciously ignored. Whenever possible, the oldest Anishinaabe stories should be recorded by someone both fluent in Anishinaabemowin and acknowledged by the community as capable of telling stories. The rocks and thunders must have said much about the garbled attempts of these newcomers. Only in the complex, unaltered, indigenous narratives are the richest deposits of knowledge found.

By contrast to Henry Schoolcraft, and similar to Jane Schoolcraft, Peter Jones was another bicultural and bilingual storyteller of the time. Kahkewaquonaby, whose name is often translated as Sacred Feather but more literally means "forever with a feather sitting," was born in 1802 to an Ojibwe mother and Welsh father. His translation of the Gospel of Matthew was published in 1832. He is mentioned not because he retold traditional tales or wrote original stories but because he continually spoke of the ways Anishinaabe culture could blend with the religions newer to the continent. Speaking of his own Methodist conversion he wrote: "The love of God being now shed abroad in my heart, I loved Him intensely, and praised him in the midst of the people. Everything now appeared in a new light. . . . The people, the trees of the woods, the gentle winds, the warbling notes of the birds, and the approaching sun, all declared the power and goodness of the Great Spirit" (McNally 52). His listing of various categories and directions and use of verbs as adjectives points to a fluent speaker of two languages.

Like Jones, Kahgegagahbowh, George Copway, used his language and story-telling ability to convert Native people to Christianity. Copway was born in 1818, and his autobiography is nonfiction, but in *Recollections of a Forest Life, or The Life and Travels of Kah-Ge-Ga-Gah-Bowh*, he included comments on the Anishinaabe language. He also offers interpretations of various origin stories about the earth and the cosmos that not only reflect traditional Anishinaabe worldviews but serve in some cases as cultural comparison. For example, he wrote: "The fruit of the earth teemed wherever I looked. Every thing I saw smilingly said *Ke-sha-mon-e-doo nin-ge-oo-she-ig*—the Benevolent spirit made me. Where is he? My father pointed to the sun" (9). His statement *Ke-sha-mon-e-doo nin-ge-oo-she-ig* would likely be spelled *Gizhemanido niin gii ozhi'ig* and means "God created me." Certainly he probably meant it as translation of biblical ideas, but it is interesting to consider that by saying it in Anishinaabemowin he could have been asserting that God as the Creator created the Anishinaabe right where he was, in the Great Lakes region. The very words themselves offer a repetitive emphasis of the action of creation. One wonders how the early Anishinaabe converts reconciled stories of Eden and the Holy Land. Copway may have been referencing *Midewiwin* teachings familiar to members of the traditional Anishinaabe religious community, reminding readers we are all made of the same spirit that is the Great Spirit and in that way we are equally imbued with life and potential. The point is that we may never know, but if we pay attention, we can at least ask these questions. Serious studies of the translations made during his time might teach far more than religion.

Copway also wrote several poems in English, which he refers to as "the language of the poet":

Once on the raging seas I rode
The storm was loud, the night was dark
The ocean yawned, and rudely blowed
The wind that tossed my foundered bark. (10)

He artfully translated his thoughts into the language of the times, but his style and subject remains Anishinaabe with Anishinaabemowin mixed into his prose like bark lingering afloat on *Chigaming*. Both Jones and Copway represented Anishinaabe voices making the transition to new subjects and languages.

Later in the same century, William Jones, who was born in 1871, gathered the stories of four Anishinaabe storytellers. In 1903 he visited Marie Syrette and Penesi in Fort William, and Wasagunackank and Midasugaj in Bois Forte. These stories, preserved in Anishinaabemowin and translated by the Fox linguist, demonstrate the Anishinaabe focus on verbs, the shifting use of tense and location to present supernatural scenes, and the use of vocabulary to preserve cultural ideas. For instance, in the first story, "The Youth Who Died and Came Back to Life," a boy becomes ill and leaves one dimension to learn about another. In the story he literally walks on a road in the other world, which is a concept reinforced by the verbs used to explain this in Anishinaabemowin. His mother pleads with him not to leave, saying, "You are only starting your life" by using the word *kiwimadcipimatis* (spelled *g'wii maajibimaadiz* now), meaning literally, "You are starting on your walk." Other stories of foolish maids, winter-makers, evil *wiindigoog*, cranberries, and belligerent crawfish are part of his collection. The use of particles (*mii sa, nindina*, etc.) and the word choices in these stories preserve authentic Anishinaabe literature.

William Whipple Warren was born on the island of La Pointe in 1825. His *History of the Ojibway People* is often referenced today for explanations of the western clan system and stories of settlement throughout the Great Lakes. His *dibaajimowinan* speak of tradition, politics, and survival. Although his writing is entirely in English, his focus on the specifics of the Anishinaabe culture, and comparison to surrounding tribal cultures, is extremely useful. He points out that the Dakota people do not have stories of sea-people, but the Anishinaabe do. He speaks of a time when life emerged from the Great Water and talks about the way a soul travels after life on a *che-ba-kun-ah* (soul road), which is also a term used by the Anishinaabe for the Milky Way (73). He describes a far distant, perhaps paleolithic, era when land, water, and people were positioned differently, and he contemplates how that ancient history may have led to change, conflict, and migration, even the possibility that such conflict, in combination with the position of sunset, may have contributed to the Anishinaabe belief that the west was the place of the afterlife. His sophisticated cultural theories are based on his knowledge of Anishinaabe stories.

> With their mode of transmitting traditions from father to son orally, it is natural to suppose that their present belief in the westward destination of the soul has originated from the above-surmised era in their ancient history. And the tradition of a once happy home and country, being imperfectly transmitted to our times through long lines of generations, has at last merged into the simple and natural belief of a future state, which thoroughly pervades the Indian mind, and guides, in a measure, his actions in life, and enables him to smile at the approach of death. (74)

Warren wrote, in 1840, before his own early death at the age of 28, about the way literature relates to the history and culture of a people. He included and explained the Anishinaabe terms for important concepts and pointed toward theories of literary hermeneutics and phenomenology, but unlike Sartre, Ricoeur, and others, Warren likely believed he was gesturing backward toward thoughts from the past instead of forward into modernity. The Anishinaabe tradition of studying ideas across time and dimension, creating cycles of ideas instead of chronologies, is evident in Warren's analysis of his people's stories.

When the Indian Removal Act was signed into law in the spring of 1830, Native culture became further dislocated, disguised, and in some communities, both. The Removal Act, devised by Thomas Jefferson and implemented by Andrew Jackson, allowed the government to relocate thousands of "Indians" who were actually members of many different tribes to a single area deemed "Indian Territory." The literary parallel of this is stories moving into English, without proper acknowledgment of the "Indian" authors. Not yet citizens of the United States, Native people came to be viewed as a single minority. The Creek War (1813), the Peoria War (1813), the Winnebago War (1827), the Black Hawk War (1832), and the Dakota Wars (1854–1891) all impacted the Anishinaabe people. Many more wars across the nation altered the cultures of other communities. These battles over life, land, and liberty were the reason indigenous people were not considered citizens, and as the wars ended, those who survived remade themselves into people of two worlds, one of the past and one of the future.

The General Allotment (Dawes) Act of 1887 allowed Native nations to be eroded through taxation and land tenure. After a lifetime of political and cultural turmoil and repression, Simon Pokagon published *Queen of the Woods* in 1899. His novel marks a literary move into the future for the Anishinaabe. He acknowledges the past in his preface, which describes the Anishinaabe language, but he speaks of his language as a dying art, a figment of linguistic memory. Like other Anishinaabe authors, he incorporates Anishinaabe words and narrative patterns in his work, but he is clearly writing for a non-Indian majority. Unlike those who either recorded the old stories or created imitations of the religious and romantic writing of the time, Pokagon's work is cunning and syncretic. Like the leaders of his nation, he sees the world changing and writes of his culture's decline by committing the very acts that forestall such an event. Pokagon is one of the first Anishinaabe authors to create an extended book-length plot of his own, blending autobiography and fiction. In his story, the lines of authorship and intent blur. He does not credit any portion of the story to other storytellers, and his text is laden with traditional metaphors, yet it offers a message of temperance and civility contemporary to the time. Although it poses as a trendy work of American fiction, his is still a story written from an Anishinaabe perspective.

In 1893 and 1895, Charles Kawbawgam, Charlotte Kawbawgam, and Jacques LePique told stories of the Marquette, Michigan, area. The stories collected by Homer Huntington Kidder elaborate and corroborate many other Anishinaabe stories about Nanabozho, the Anishinaabe people, and the way problems arose and were solved. They are detailed examples of unaltered Anishinaabe storytelling where old characters like Nanabozho turn into pine stumps and Frog Woman guards an underwater cave. They also mark the influence of other cultures in instances when spirits "act queerly" because the Great Turtle went "under the earth and got some of the whiskey that Black Cloud left there" (Kidder 49).

Finally in 1924, as part of an attempt to absorb the remaining Indians into America, and unprepared for their ability to live with duality and mixed identities, Congress passed the Indian Citizenship Act. It was probably helpful that America had survived its own Civil War and one world war with the help of many Native solders from many nations who fought alongside the settlers and industrial workers intent on continuing to build the nation now surrounding their communities. During the first half of the twentieth century a number of Anishinaabe authors began publishing their work for mainstream audiences. Joseph Anthony Northrup wrote under the pen name of Nodin in the 1920s and 1930s. *Wawina* was initially published in serial form in the *Carlton County Vidette* newspaper in Minnesota and later released as a book. According to his grandson, Jim Northrup, "It was the love story of an Anishinaabe daughter of a chief and a Dakota man. They tried to make peace between their peoples but when it didn't work they killed themselves at Knife Falls in what became Cloquet" (Northrup, personal email).

In the 1940s Angeline Williams from Sugar Island remembered stories of the dog people, while Andrew Medler shared the narratives of Walpole Island, with the special plea that they be preserved so that one day the children would hear them. William Berens shared his knowledge of traditional history, botany, medicine, psychology, and religion from the Berens River area. John Mink, Prosper Guibord, Delia Oshogay, Tom Badger, and Julia Badger of Lac Courte Oreilles shared stories of *Wenebojo* and the origins of the Anishinaabe people. All of these storytellers used Anishinaabemowin to preserve the distinctly Anishinaabe style and content well into the first half of the century.

With the founding of the United Nations in 1945, colonized nations across the globe sought permanent democratic freedom (U.N. Charter, Articles 1, 55, 73, and 76). But the United States interpreted this dictate differently. The Termination Act of 1953 effectively dissolved over 109 sovereign Native nations. The attempt by the United States to "decolonize" indigenous people in North America amounted to nothing more than assimilation and dissolution of Native cultures. The Relocation Act of 1956 was designed to lure members of Native nations away from their land to urban centers where they were guaranteed education and job opportunities. The result was a collection of intertribal urban communities scattered throughout the United States, dislocating language and literature from home communities.

In the 1960s and 1970s, as other groups stood up for equal civil rights, pantribal urban communities rallied with the occupants of reservations across the United States to assert the rights of Native American Indians. In 1968 Anishinaabe and Lakota leaders founded the American Indian Movement. Together Dennis Banks, Leonard Peltier, and Russell Means began a group that has been a part of many significant events in North American Native history. In 1969 AIM members participated in the occupation of the abandoned prison on Alcatraz Island in the San Francisco Bay. It was the same year that President Richard Nixon signed into law the Indian Self-Determination Act, which declared the government policy of termination to be "morally and legally unacceptable" (Fortunate Eagle 149). In 1978 the Indian Child Welfare Act was passed to prevent the systematic placement of Native American Indian children in white homes. That was also the year in which the American Indian Religious Freedom Act was passed to reverse state and local regulations criminalizing Native American Indian spiritual practices (Jaimes 17).

Enji-Oshkidibaajimowaad Chigamigong / Three New Storytellers of the Great Lakes

The decades before the new millennium were the beginning of an Anishinaabe linguistic and literary renaissance. During the 1980s and 1990s, members of Native communities, empowered by pantribal unity, began to record their own stories, often working across generations. Maude Kegg of Mille Lacs recorded memories of her childhood. *Oshkaabewis Native Journal* published the stories of Dennis Jones, Dan Jones, Earl Nyholm Otchingwanigan, and others. Anton Treuer collected the tales and oral histories of Archie Mosay, Jim Clark, Melvin Eagle, Joe Auginaush, Collins Oakgrove, Emma Fisher, Scott Headbird, Susan Jackson, Hartley White, and Porky White.

Local cultural revival movements spread across the Great Lakes, and when Ignatia Broker wrote *Night Flying Woman*, she dedicated it "to those Indian people who organized, incorporated, and built the Indian social groups, drum and dance groups, help and care groups, and educational groups, to those of the activist and conservative groups." Her novel of a young Anishinaabe girl, Nibowisegwe, who experiences relocation, includes layers of narrative that blend old and new stories of national significance and local relevance. Nibowisegwe hears the *sisigwad*, the voice of the pines, but she also sees the need to survive in the city. Many novels followed Broker's in the Anishinaabe community.

Those who still knew Anishinaabemowin, and those who wished they did, began speaking of the importance of preserving the sound and structure of the language. In *Wiigwaaskingaa: Land of the Birch Trees*, Arthur McGregor calls for the community to keep both the language and literature alive. For example, in the story "*Sinmedwe'ek*: Bell Rock" his use of *sinmedwe'ek* literally communicates the idea of a rock who speaks with an animate voice, while the English word "bell" denotes the source of a sound that might warn or gather people. MacGregor's story is told to remind the Anishinaabe people to listen to the stories and the stones and to see them as connected on the landscape. As Philomene George concludes in "*Nesendaawaa*: Breath of Life": *N'goding gegwa giizhigak, megesjig kabi waab-migwak, kaawiin kansastawaasiiyak ekidwaad, pkaan dazhigiizhwewok, pkaan gego debwewendaamoowin dabiidoonaa'aa.* A literal translation would be, "One time some day, strangers will be seen here; you won't understand what they say; they will greet the day differently, and they will bring different beliefs." Howard Kimewon includes the same message in *Anishinaabemowin Maajamigad*, his story about an ice-rink built to honor veterans. In his story about the importance of honor and respect in both cultures he says:

> *Gaawiin wiika Anishinaabeg gii nendsiiwag Anishinaabemwoin wii maajaamigag ... Zhaazhaagwa binoojiiyag gaa pa daminowaad kina igo gii Anishinaabemowaad miinwaa igo Anishinaabe bwaakenmaawaad boochigo gii zhoobiingwenid zaam wii Anishinaabemtawaad.* (The Anishinaabe never thought the language would leave ... Long ago all the children spoke Anishinaabemowin when they played and if another Anishinaabe person recognized them he or she would smile because they spoke Anishinaabemowin.) (Kimewon and Noori 21)

Thanks to these and other Anishinaabe storytellers, there is a chance that both the idea and the language will be preserved.

At the same time, elders and young writers were also recognizing that the stories should also be told in English if there was to be any hope that a collective memory of place and history would be transmitted to another generation. One example is Anne Dunn, whose 1995 collection of tales, *When Beaver Was Very Great*, is addressed to a vibrant and extended Anishinaabe audience. It begins with "my grandmother who presented me with wings, my mother who gifted me with strength, my father who provided the wind, and my children who loaned me the sky."

Another storyteller who once believed in English as a means of transmission is Eddie Benton-Banai. His *Mishomis Book* is written primarily in English with main concepts in Anishinaabemowin. The book serves as an all-ages introduction to *Midewiwin* teaching, mentioning at the very beginning that the best way to preserve the most important teachings is by memorization with some drawings on *wiigwas* (birchbark) scrolls. His stories of Nanabozho and the great migration connect with those of previous generations, while his lessons of seven grandfathers, four directions, and *minobimaadiziwin* connect with contemporary Anishinaabe teachings. Although he has preserved the stories in English, Benton-Banai advises all students today to learn songs and stories in Anishinaabemowin, warning that important teachings will be lost without the language.

Despite valiant efforts to preserve the language and encourage its use, by the end of the twentieth century, English was the primary language of many Native storytellers, and the Anishinaabe community was no exception. Powerful, inventive, contemporary stories about Anishinaabe life were being written, but the traces of Anishinaabe language were less visible. If there is any theme to modern Anishinaabe novels, it might be one of naming evil—the robbery of artifacts, the eruption of murderous *wiindigoog*, the commodification of stories. By recognizing the fissures in Anishinaabe life, authors illustrate the ways in which the truth has been buried and cultural messages are muted. The authors discussed later in the book, Erdrich, Northrup, Johnston, and Vizenor, are some of the most prolific, but they are not the only contemporary Anishinaabe authors. In Canada Ruby Slipperjack, Barry Milliken, Jordan Wheeler, Richard Wagamese, Janice Acoose, and Drew Hayden Taylor write about Anishinaabe life. In the United States, Winona LaDuke and Carole LaFavor represent other voices in the community.

Gordon Henry's 1994 novel, *The Light People*, explores old magic, new politics, and tricks of narrative. In it, he connects clearly to Anishinaabe trope and style without using many actual Anishinaabe words. His modern self-scrutiny of story clearly connects not just to nature in a vaguely Native American way, but to the tale of the first story in a specifically Anishinaabe way, especially when one considers that rocks are "grandfathers" in Anishinaabe metaphor. Oshawa is told by his uncle:

> Your grandfather claims the stone has gifts. Some stones carry earth histories, stories, songs, prayers, so their stone faces hold memories of the existences of other eras; other beings of the earth, air, fire, and water live on, embedded in shapes, in esoteric formations of strata and substrata, in scopic design and microscopic elementals we can only imagine in our limited view of the exterior. (Henry 41)

Stones are animate in Henry's book, and although we do not read these passages in Anishinaabemowin, the loss of that language is palpably mourned. Linguistic genocide is marked when young boys remember the way a friend's voice was stolen. Unlike many of them, who lose only the Anishinaabemowin, he becomes unable to speak at all, "though they walked away from the boy with the frozen words, they felt the breath-held syllables melt in their heads later in Native translations of circumstances and relationships that they never would have thought of without remembering the cold in their ears" (62). As readers are asked to relive these painful points of mourning and loss, Henry asks if truth can "recognize us from afar and run to catch up to us on a well-traveled road" (127). In many modern Anishinaabe novels, it does.

Another example of naming evil is the work of Joseph Boyden, whose book *Three Day Road* is a journey of travel in and out of identity. Early in the novel a soldier in World War I realizes, "This is where my life has led me. It's as clear as if I've been walking a well-marked trail that leads from the rivers of my north home across the country they call Canada, the ocean parting before me like that old Bible story nuns forced upon me as a child, ending right here in this strange place where all the world's trouble explodes" (Boyden 21). In a novel with only chapter headings in Cree and a few nouns exploding in the text, the metaphors and style are clearly connected to the Oji-Cree and Anishinaabe cultures. The notion of the *wiindigoo*, a psychotic killer with cannibalistic tendencies, and the reference to life as a walk (not a journey or any other general term) are very specific references to Anishinaabe experience. Certainly these ideas are found in the work of Silko, Alexie, and others, but the perfect word-for-word translation of Anishinaabe metaphors marks them as of the northern communities, connected to a particular language.

These modern authors explore the patterns of Anishinaabe narrative, use multiple languages as deftly as the authors are able, and define through well-wrought English prose the perspectives of a range of Anishinaabe characters, demonstrating the diversity of a single community. In David Treuer's novel *The Translation of Dr. Apelles*, the protagonist, a linguist and translator, finds a spark of interest in the world. "His life is different now. He has become interested in other people. He is now part of that half of the human race who takes an interest in the other half. With his new interests had come problems. All the formerly discrete parts of his life—his past, his work, his passions and the versions of himself he told himself and the versions of his life treasured and not told by others—were mixed up together" (195). Like the Anishinaabe people, like Anishinaabe fiction, Dr. Apelles is not just mixed-blood, he is mixed-story, mixed-language.

Modern Anishinaabe authors move across narrative forms to unite what we say in English are the separate genres of poetry, fiction, autobiography, drama, and song. Many American authors publish in more than one area, and many Native storytellers combine performance and song with narrative. However, the Anishinaabe version of genres might be something grounded in the structure of the language. Like the verbs, one could classify Anishinaabe stories by the depth and dimension of relationship between verbs. Imagine a theory of literature with a core and layers. Poem-like writings, the musings of one mind, might be the basic form, as simple as the weather, as complicated as the cosmos. If characters are added, as prefixes and suffixes can be added to a root word, then we might have something closer to fiction and nonfiction, narrative with greater detail expanding across a wider period of time. When characters become dimensional through the addition of color, movement, sound, and shape, then we have a presentation, a narrative ceremony that aligns with drama. Other permutations include self-reflexive works of memory, possibly called autobiography in English. This Anishinaabe way of describing genre could be represented by an author on an island surrounded by water, recognizing the story as form and nonform, sound and silence, line and line breaks, acts and intermission. Island utterances could be set in the sky, scratched in the earth, or set beneath the waves. Then in every direction, above or below, the layers of relations that increase in complexity align with the way words shift, like the difference between *debwemigad* (it is true), *n'debwe* (I am correct), *dibaadaan* (to tell about it), *dibajimo* (to tell of social events), and *debwetaaw* (to believe).

This might make it easier to locate Heid Erdrich's poems, allowing them to be read as history, play, and intimacy. Elvis, Kennewick Man, and the tracing of her own walks would break beyond the definition of poetry. And although they are edited beautifully and serve to recognize real talent in known arenas, Kim Blaeser would not need to collect thoughts and images in two volumes divided by style—one of poems, one of stories. Armand Garnet Ruffo, Mark Turcotte, and Pat LeBeau would be simply referred to as narrators, and each poem would have to be placed in a space of interpretation not so easily counted by rhyme, meter, and scansion.

This approach would also allow us to "read" songs as messages, perhaps muted or amplified, placed in the water of our paradigm. Anishinaabe songs recorded by Maingans, Bezhigwiwizens, Kitchimakwa, Debwawendang, Manidogiizhigokwe, and Nawajibigokwe at Red Lake, White Earth, and Leech Lake reflect ideas of life, love, healing, cosmology, and play. Their lyrics rely on the recombination of verbs and celebrate compound words that can express paragraphs of thought in a few bars. For example, *wiiondekwebiwag*, "they will put their headaches together," offers an interpretation of healing that implies empathy and requires use of one long, transitive, animate, carefully conjugated verb.

In the sky and on the shoreline would be the work of Alanis King and Tomson Highway. King is Anishinaabe from Manitoulin Island, and Highway is Cree from Manitoba. Both are celebrated writers who bring stories to life on stage. Highway's two short plays, *Rez Sisters* and *Ernestine Shuswap Gets Her Trout*, teach as much history as an epic poem or a long novel. Like Heid Erdrich, Gordon Henry, Jim Northrup, Kim Blaeser, and other Anishinaabe poets and novelists who move from page to stage, they transform narrative. When Ngashi tells her son Osawanimki he cannot forget his own power, she says, "You fail your spirit. If you ignore it now when you need it most it will go forever and you will be a body with an unbalanced mind" (A. King 52). This is a cross-cultural lesson for all times, but the echo of Anishinaabemowin is clear when she calls for balance. In Anishinaabemowin the word used to indicate illness is *akozi*, a relative of the word *agoozo*, which is the act of balancing. Health and happiness, living well, requires a balanced spirit.

Nawanj Moshkine-Aapkizid / More Than the Moon

On one hand, Robert Dale Parker's book *The Invention of Native American Literature* offers an excellent scholarly introduction to the academic and publishing landscape that defined Native American literature in the early years of its recognition. On the other hand, David Treuer provocatively declared the "non-existence" of Native American literature. In his book, *Native American Fiction*, he writes: "we should be free to construct narratives unchained form the projects of historicizing and pointing away, always away, from our cultural centers, and instead, claim the rights that other writers have enjoyed for centuries: to make larger the worlds of our prose through significant linguistic and cultural detail" (202). I think he means the moon is not enough . . . noticing the ring around the moon is not enough . . . knowing that a red ring foretells storms is close . . . *pii dibikigiizis miiskwaazhe wii nimkiikaa* is best, because then we preserve the idea of a night sun that shines a red light that reminds us of the *nimkiig*, the thunderbirds, and then a story begins.

In this still-evolving history of Anishinaabe literature there are patterns that define a narrative identity. *Nd'anishinaabebiigedibaajimowinkemi* would be one long word saying "We have a way to write as Anishinaabe and make stories." There is a way to use the language and build a story that is recognizably a part of the Anishinaabe community, a way that understands Anishinaabe commonality but celebrates difference as well. According to Anishinaabe literary genealogy, all storytelling has, in stones, a common point of origin, a common lineage. The patterns begun in the first tales have been preserved and are visible now in many Anishinaabe stories. Patterns of speech, signs of place and time, familiar characters, and common subjects all become embedded in the narrative.

The patterns of speech that mark Anishinaabe stories relate to the main features of the language. Some authors are proficient in the language and can insert phrases and paragraphs with long specialized words and verbs that reflect the context. Some of them are able to make those phrases indicate who is listening and who is being spoken to. In other instances, the authors and their characters gesture to these facts of language. Knowing that nouns have two classes, they can choose which to use and when. Knowing that none of the pronouns indicate gender, they can create conversations that evade that detail. Certainly the best way to write an Anishinaabe story is to *Anishinaabebiige* (write in Anishinaabe), but when that isn't possible it is important to bring the language into the work in any way possible. It is my opinion that every carefully considered use of the language has meaning and cultural significance; it may not be the same meaning and significance as long ago, but it lends an element to contemporary literature that is intentionally Anishinaabe. My children may not use the language as I teach it to them, but the fact that they use it has been my primary concern. If we wish to hear the language in the future, we can teach and continue to learn; we can set standards and high expectations; we can debate among ourselves, but we cannot dictate the future any more than we can control our own dreams.

Signs of place in Anishinaabe literature also echo the old stories while creating a new canon. Authors often begin, as the first storytellers did, in "the long ago." Stories frequently reflect the Great Lakes environment because, as the stories themselves tell us, the people and the place have a symbiotic relationship that is part of the way life is lived. It is not possible to understand Anishinaabe identity without knowing at least something of the way the sky looks from their perspective on earth, the way the land and water are part of time and the way presence includes all life—human, plant, animal, and a few things like rocks and the weather that are not commonly considered characters. All of this is part of place and the Anishinaabe literary identity. Certainly Anishinaabe writers have gone elsewhere and written stories, but the question is not whether the writer is Anishinaabe; the concern is with the provenance of the story. Where do its setting and imagery come from? With what eyes does it see the rest of the world? Many of North America's indigenous people have been called "nomadic." This is a term that doesn't sit well with many Anishinaabe, including Roger Roulette, who corrected the statement during a conversation in April of 2010, saying:

> *Mewenzha Anishnaabeg megwa babamiiaayaawaad gii babanametwaawag e-wii enji daapinamaagozig gii babamiiayaawag niswaak ge kwa naanwaak ge minik mi-inwaa neyap ji ge gii azhegiiwewaad gaa ge pii aayaawaad ji nagadanendamowaad da giimiiwaad.* (Long ago the Anishinaabeg moved around and left a presence while transporting things; they traveled for three to five years at a time and always kept in mind the places they had been.) (Interview)

This practice is *nametwaawaa*, which is a verb that can describe a relationship with a place, not random wandering, but enlightened stewardship that allowed people to circle a vast homeland, learning when to be where. This could also be applied to ideas of places beyond where we are. Many stories speak of places visited in dreams or visions, places like the sky or a cave at the bottom of the lake, or the kitchen table of *nokomisba*, who is no longer living. This ability to visit elsewhere, perhaps stepping out of time, is part of many Anishinaabe stories and can be found in the writing of contemporary Anishinaabe authors as frequently as the lakes and forests.

Classic Anishinaabe characters are both familiar and surprising: some can shift shape or operate in multiple times and places. *Manitous* impregnate humans, mermaids capture men who live with them for months, cats live below water, asses have speaking faces, and any number of other variations on reality are bound only by the storyteller's imagination and the Anishinaabe landscape. Humans are not always the primary players. In fact, the most accurate description of Anishinaabe stories would be that the action is the main character. Certainly, this bends literary definitions, but in a culture where most words are verbs, including the nouns, it is easiest to understand the characters through what they do. Many stories feature members of the community described by their role in the community, and events unfold relative to their impact on the whole community. Often the woman who dies, the girl who marries an old man, the child who is captured, or the man who turns into excrement, and so on, are only archetypes who exit the narrative before the narrative concludes. Stories focus on outcomes and sometimes have the air of *odaminokwedwinan* (riddles) *or nibwakawin* (wisdom). If individuals are to be named, the most commonly mentioned character might be Nanabozho, also known as Wenabozho and closely related to the Cree *Wiisajak* and Abenaki

Gluskabi. Another possibility would be *Kchi Manido*, or *Gizhemanido*, the Creator. Never seen or personified, the Creator often has an active role in the initiation or resolution of a story. The clan animals, including bears, sturgeon, otters, lynx, marten, deer, loons, cranes, and others are also commonly part of Anishinaabe literature.

There is no single theme that dominates Anishinaabe literature. Balls of light, trails of palm-to-paw prints, and leaps from earth to atmosphere are all common in Anishinaabe stories. Stories range from fascinating to frightening to educational. Cultural relevance, however, is required. Stories connect in some way to the culture and often serve to illustrate or elaborate on shared beliefs and values. Anishinaabe stories are intractably connected to four changing seasons and a need to predict and survive the extremes. The cycle of seasons is both symbol and metaphor, and the number four is a common point of reference, echoed in the four primary verb forms and the often-mentioned cardinal directions. Occasionally, a story will be used as a lesson or part of a ceremony. More than simply a series of events set in familiar landscapes, Anishinaabe literature traces and affirms the presence of a community. Anishinaabe authors may choose to write scripts for Americana action films, curriculum for American history, or ethnographies of strange academics to unravel the mysteries of their behavior, but that is not Anishinaabe literature.

Anishinaabe literature is an inheritance, a duty, an explanation and series of questions. It has been jolted by colonialism and remains lit by the energy of storytellers still living as Anishinaabe. *Ezhi-anishinaabebimaadiziyaang, mii sa ezhi-anishinaabeaadisokaankeyaang* ("The way in which we live, that is the way we write stories"). No single author, level of fluency, point of origin, blood quantum, or personal history can be defined as Anishinaabe. That would be nouning the stories. Louise Erdrich, Jim Northrup, Basil Johnston, and Gerry Vizenor offer some examples of maintaining and carrying forward Anishinaabe literature. They remember and write and rewrite and revise the past, present, and future. They know: *Aabdeg weweni aankenotaamwidizoyaang epiichi bababimaadiziyaang* ("We must carefully translate ourselves while liv-liv-living").

CHAPTER THREE

Gikenmaadizo miinwaa Gikenmaa'aan: Patterns of Identity in the Writing of Louise Erdrich

If we were to call ourselves and all we saw around us by our original names, would we not again be *Anishinaabeg*? Instead of reconstituted white men, instead of Indian ghosts? Do the rocks here know us, do the trees, do the waters of the lakes? Not unless they are addressed by the names they themselves told us to call them in our dreams. Every feature of the land around us spoke its name to an ancestor. Perhaps, in the end, that is all that we are. We *Anishinaabeg* are the keepers of the names of the earth. And unless the earth is called by the names it gave us humans, won't it cease to love us? And isn't it true that if the earth stops loving us, everyone will cease to exist? That is why we all must speak our language, *nindinawemegonidok*, and call everything we see by the name of its spirit. Even the *chimookomanag*, who are trying to destroy us, are depending upon us to remember and to use these words. *Mii'sago'iw*.

—Erdrich, *Last Report*

Giishpin Anishinaabemoying ("If we all spoke Anishinaabemowin")...Nanapush imagines this possibility and by doing so in Anishinaabemowin forces a speaker to choose an ending because *Anishinaabemo* is not a noun like "English"; it is a verb that requires one to say who speaks. Even the choices are unlike those in English. One can add *waad* to indicate a plural group of others excluding oneself, or one can speak too and then choose between *yaang* and *ying* to clarify whether or not the listener will also be speaking Anishinaabemowin. These choices indicate other ways of framing relationships, other ways to shift words differently, other views of translating reality through speech and story. *Aanikanootaage* means to translate, to speak for others, to explain something to or about a community, and *Aanikanootaagekwe* (a woman who translates) is a name that would suit Louise Erdrich. She speaks in circles about Anishinaabe language and identity the way a crow flies searching, the way a sunflower's seeds spiral, the way seasons cycle—with subtle, undeniable purpose. She knows the power of family ties, the importance of language, the need to listen to voices both real and imagined, and the mimetic power of words to awaken the senses and center a soul. Like someone choosing a name, she chooses each word carefully and then creates literature that reflects Anishinaabe identity. Many of her stories also reflect other cultures and sometimes a broader American Indianness that is also worth recognizing, but it is important to also take time to examine the ways her work is specifically Anishinaabe. Her stories are related, the way she is, the way we all are, to a certain space and time that offers many avenues of exploration. She uses language the way a hoop dancer relies on thin spinning branches of willow to bend the familiar into a visionary tool. She relies on tested and familiar patterns of language and storytelling. She inserts a language that is foreign to the majority of her readers into her books to shut them out, to invite them in, to teach them about the "self" and "other" in an Anishinaabe way. She is a modern Anishinaabe author whose work reflects, among other things, the specific language and narrative traditions of the tribe in which she participates.

Gaa Ezhi-bimaadizid / Life So Far

Born on June 7, 1954, in Little Falls, Minnesota, Karen Louise Erdrich was the first of seven children. Her parents, Ralph and Rita Erdrich, were teachers in a school run by the Bureau of Indian Affairs (Stookey 1). Her father's German parents ran a butcher shop in Little Falls. Poems about a similar butcher shop in her book *Jacklight* are dedicated to her Polish step-grandmother, Mary Korll. Her grandparents on her mother's side lived on the Turtle Mountain Reservation in North Dakota, where her grandfather, Patrick Gorneau, was tribal chair and a traditional dancer (Stookey 2). Like a network of veins and arteries, Erdrich's family is an interdependent maze of German, Anishinaabe, and French ancestry that she continues to trace in poetry and prose. Erdrich has explained how her cultural heritage is a source of chaos and inspiration.

> I think that if you believe in any sort of race memory, I am getting a triple whammy from my background—in regard to place and home and space. The connection that is Chippewa is a connection to a place and to a background, and to the comfort of knowing, somehow, that you are connected here and before the first settler. Add to that the overblown German Romanticism about place inherited from my father's family, and add to that the German part of my family is most probably converted Jews with the Jewish sense of searching for place, and you have this awful mix. A person can only end up writing—in order to resolve it. You throw in the French part of the background—the wanderers, the voyagers, which my people also come from. There is just no way to get away from all of this. (Chavkin 152)

Although many critics and readers have focused on her Anishinaabe heritage, Erdrich's experience is that of a mixed-blood who acknowledges all of her ancestral inheritances. This sense of being Anishinaabe along with a mixture of European nationalities is a common and important theme of many Anishinaabe writers.

Erdrich left what she has called "the flattest, most open, exposed part of the U. S." to attend college (Chavkin 152). She was among the first group of women admitted to Dartmouth, a college founded in 1769 with a mission originally defined as serving to educate "Indian youths and others," yet in 1972, the year Erdrich was accepted, only 12 Native American students had ever graduated (Chavkin 117). This was also the year that Dartmouth introduced a new program in Native American studies headed by a young anthropologist from Yale, Michael Dorris, whom she later married (Stookey 3). In 1976, Erdrich earned a BA in English from Dartmouth, and in 1979 she received an MA in creative writing from Johns Hopkins. Erdrich has said it was the combination of Native American courses at Dartmouth and work as communication director for *The Circle*, a Native American newspaper in Boston, that led her to pursue both her writing and her Anishinaabe background. "I didn't choose the material," she has said, "it chose me" (Chavkin 175).

Erdrich guards her family's privacy carefully as she continues to live her admittedly complicated life and create art from the circumstances she has been offered. In Anishinaabe tradition *Gichi Manidoo* asks each infant a question before birth, and life is shaped by the desire to remember and answer that question. In the spring of 2001 Erdrich told me: "Life is defined by learning what the question is, and by learning that the answer isn't everything. I believe in that" (Interview).

Gaa Ezhibii'iged / Writing So Far

Erdrich's still growing number of books, the *mazina'iganan* she has written, includes poetry, autobiography, and fiction for adults and for children. She is a best-selling author by any standard and a leader in Anishinaabe writing. Not only has she created an impressive and diverse body of work, she has inspired others to examine her stories. Students of her work now have *A Reader's Guide to the Novels of Louise Erdrich* by Peter Beidler and Gay Barton; *A Critical Companion* by Lorena Stookey; *The Chippewa Landscape of Louise Erdrich* edited by Allan Chavkin; and Hertha Sweet Wong's study, *Louise Erdrich's "Love Medicine."* All these authors connect her work to the Anishinaabe community, but to my knowledge none of them speaks Anishinaabemowin. When we relate her work to that of other Anishinaabe authors, we can throw into greater relief Anishinaabe literature as a whole and Erdrich's work in particular.

Erdrich's writing has earned many awards, including the Academy of American Poets Prize (1975), the Nelson Algren Fiction Award (1982), the Pushcart Prize (1983), the National Book Critics Circle Award (1984), a Guggenheim fellowship in 1985, and four Minnesota Book Awards . . . so far. Formal acknowledgment of her work has not been lacking throughout her career. She is an author who represents Anishinaabe life in her books, and she is also undeniably an author able to translate that specific experience into a universal dialogue. LaVonne Brown Ruoff sums up Erdrich's popularity in these words:

> Critics and scholars have praised her skillful weaving of Ojibwe ethnohistory into her narratives, masterful use of oral tradition, powerful portrayals of characters (particularly women), hilarious humor that ranges from mock heroic battles to survival jokes, unerring depictions of popular culture, and lyrical descriptions of

nature. Other Native American fiction writers have described their protagonists' quests for understanding their tribal and family heritages and have stressed the importance of achieving wholeness through integration of tradition, family, and community. Erdrich, however, charts a new path by describing in a series of novels the complex and shifting relationships of her characters within their communities. (Chavkin 183)

In spite of her success she once said, "I thought nobody would ever remember the books. The thought that someone reads them is always daunting. But not as daunting as knowing that my mother is going to read them. What I really care about is that it be real for the people who are my teachers and friends. I have this belief that if it's real for them it will be real for everybody" (Interview). Her insistence that she writes first for the people she knows, not an abstract idea of the craft of writing, is an important fact. She does not write about imaginary stereotypes or the ideal "Indian." She writes about the love medicine, the gambling, the losses and gains of real people. In her work we hear Anishinaabemowin and find traces of the language and literature of the Great Lakes.

Erdrich's publishing career began with poetry, and although she is best known for fiction, she has continued to publish verse. Her first book, *Jacklight,* was published in 1984. In four sections she uses poetry to tell the stories of runaways, hunters, and immigrant women. She introduces Old Man Potchikoo, who is a close fictional cousin of the Anishinaabe character Wenabozho, and in this first short collection of only 85 pages she sets the stage for her continued exploration of America from an Anishinaabe perspective.

In 1989 a second collection of poetry was published. *Baptism of Desire* focuses on "visionary and religious ecstasy and humankind's relations with the divine" (Chavkin 186). The poems of this volume are passionate, spiritual, and a mix of Anishinaabe and European traditions. In the poem "Sacraments," sundancers, sage smudges, and images of birth twist in words and images toward "the blackness of heaven." These are markers of contemporary tribal life in the prairies where Dakota, Lakota, and Ojibwe cultures often blend. She speaks of the landscape with its snow and ice and flooding spring waters. In the poem "Owls," she explains, "the Owl is '*gookooko'oo,*' and not even the smallest child loves the gentle sound of the word. Because the hairball of bones and vole teeth can be hidden under snow, to kill the man who walks over it" (75). In his book *Summer in the Spring,* Vizenor notes the same phenomenon of "Anishinaabe children [who] were warned by their parents in songs and stories that the owls would catch them like mice if they left the dwelling place at night" (149). While owls are respected by numerous North American tribes, use of that particular haunting word, which evokes the call of the owl "hidden under snow," is distinctly Anishinaabe (Sibley 278).

Original Fire: Selected and New Poems was published in 2003. Careful sequencing of the book gives shape to a body of poetry built from previously published and recent work. The work in this volume is mature in every sense. The added Potchikoo story is particularly delightful and reminiscent of the stories Anishinaabe elders tell. She also includes postcolonial prayers and views of life that become chants of modern motherhood. She speaks to stones in these poems as well as telling readers, "*Asiniig* (stones) are animate, the first storyteller was a stone. Some Anishinaabe still listen. Some stones still speak."

Many of Erdrich's novels explore the space between the fictional reservation Little No Horse and the rest of the world, especially Argus, North Dakota, and Minneapolis, Minnesota. The first to be published in this series, *Love Medicine*, was published in 1984 after chapters appeared as short stories in numerous publications. The love medicines of the title are "something of an old Chippewa specialty, no other tribe has got them down so well" (241). *Love Medicine* introduces contemporary Anishinaabe life on the reservation and remains one of the most widely read and studied of all her books. In 1993 she retold the tale with some changes for an audience with new expectations and perceptions.

In 1986 *The Beet Queen* explored events in Little No Horse and Argus between 1932 and 1972. Framed by a bazaar for homeless children at its beginning and a festival honoring the beet at the end, it is a novel of personal and economic depression and excess. Catharine Rainwater praises it for its ability to show how "many alternative kinds of ties, not biological, can link people" (Rainwater 418; Stookey 159). *The Beet Queen* is also known for stirring up debate in the field of Native American Indian literary criticism. The same year it was published, Leslie Silko wrote a review of it entitled "Here's an Odd One for the Fairy Tale Shelf." In her review she called the novel "a strange artifact, an eloquent example of the political climate in America in 1986 that belongs on the shelf next to the latest report from the United States Civil Rights Commission which says black men have made tremendous gains in employment and salary" (Chavkin 237). She described Erdrich's writing as the product of "academic, post-modern, so-called experimental influences" (237). Basically, Silko questioned Erdrich's desire and ability to speak for, and to accurately represent, Native American Indian stories.

Ironically, it is the external literary world that expects Silko to have an informed opinion of Erdrich's work. In fact, on many levels a Laguna Pueblo writer from New Mexico should not be expected to know anything about the authenticity of Anishinaabe life in North Dakota. Not only are the colonial histories of the area completely different (one French, one Spanish) the languages and story traditions are quite unalike—from creation stories to metaphors for survival.

Erdrich's next novel, and one of her most widely read, *Tracks*, was published in 1988. Although it is the third book to be published in her Little No Horse series, the story takes place before the first two and focuses more closely on changes in Anishinaabe culture between 1912 and 1924. Through various first-person accounts (sometimes purposely conflicting) she explores the changing relationship of the Anishinaabe to the land and to one another. *Tracks* is a highly emotional historical saga that relies on the cycle of seasons and traditional storytelling techniques to give a firsthand account of the past. In *Tracks*, history is shown to be subjective, and all versions of the story are influenced by the teller. As the elder Nanapush says in the novel, "there is no end to telling" because stories are "hooked from one side to the other, mouth to tail" (46).

Erdrich returns to Anishinaabe culture and the community of Little No Horse in many of her novels. *The Master Butcher's Singing Club* includes members of the Lazarre family familiar to Little No Horse readers, but primarily centers on the life and wives of German émigré Fidelis Waldvogel. *The Bingo Palace* reminds modern readers of the *missibizhiw*, the underwater lynx. *Tales of Burning Love* shows what happens when a man loses his "old time Ojibwa sense" of the land (153) and gets involved with the "place where skeletons gamble and evil spirits, *wiindigos*, roam" (384). *The Last Report on the Miracles at Little No Horse* invites readers to reconsider the spectrum of gender through Father Damien. And *Four Souls* allows Fleur Pillager to take justice and reparation into her own hands. Following John James Mauser to Minneapolis, Fleur avenges the trees lost at the end of *Tracks* by slowly devouring his life and soul. Perhaps the model for Mauser is one of the lumber barons of Stillwater, Minnesota, a town that rose in riches with the logging of the 1800s and became a ghost town in the early 1900s when supply had been drastically reduced. But another possible model is railroad owner James Jerome Hill, whose 36,000-square-foot home in St. Paul is now a historic site. His home was one of servants blended with family; it was a small business itself. Like other modern Anishinaabe authors, Erdrich exposes the *wiindigoo* capitalist spirit of the "empire builders" and the dangers of industrial greed. Other explorations of *wiindigoo* greed are woven through *The Painted Drum* and *Plague of Doves*. In both novels musical instruments, and those who encounter them, are possessed.

Although most of her novels are kaleidoscopic twists on a single imaginary location set amid real history, not every novel has connections to Little No Horse. *The Antelope Wife* and *Shadow Tag* paint harsh pictures of love and the pain it can endure. They carve out space in *Gakahbekong*, the Anishinaabe name for Minneapolis, Minnesota. *The Antelope Wife* is framed by a story of twins who bead light and darkness, joy and sorrow, into life. It is also a history of Anishinaabe relations with other tribes and cultures and a history of old stories and how they repeat themselves. *Shadow Tag* is the story of a postindustrial nuclear family disassembling despite attempts to give up alcohol and seek psychological advice. With characters named for continents, a quote from iconic American author F. Scott Fitzgerald, and a tie to Leadbelly blues, it is wrought in close connection to the literature of these United States, but has distinctly Anishinaabe connections.

Erdrich has also written a series of historical fiction for young readers that includes *The Birchbark House*, *The Game of Silence*, *The Porcupine Year*, and *Chickadee*. A map penned by Erdrich and placed inside the cover of *Birchbark House* shows the island in Lake Superior called *Monigwanaykanig*, or Island of the Golden-Breasted Woodpecker. The novel is the fictionalized history of Erdrich's own great-grandmother, who lived a seasonal Anishinaabe life alongside European traders, explorers, and the earliest settlers. The young protagonist, Omakayas, learns by listening to the stories of her elders. History, science, mythology, and philosophy are blended in these early Anishinaabe stories. As a toddler Omakayas lives through the winter of 1847, when many members of her extended family die of smallpox. The island is "the drum of the thunder beings," and of course Erdrich includes mention of the *wiindigoog*, the frightening, hungry winter creatures (13). As seasons pass, birchbark is harvested with the permission of the forest, and Omakayas has an encounter with a bear and her cubs. She apologizes in Anishinaabemowin to the mother bear for playing with her children: "I was only playing with your children. *Gaween onjidah.* (I am sorry.)" (31). By retracing the branches of her own family tree, Erdrich puts into print the oral conversations that keep both the language and the stories of the Anishinaabe alive in the community.

Occasionally Erdrich publishes nonfiction. In 1995 she published *The Blue Jay's Dance*, a memoir arranged around the seasons. It is an important gathering of personal thoughts and offers a way to understand how and why a contemporary storyteller becomes a writer as well as how a mixed-blood descendant of very different communities brings each to bear in the world of modern publishing. In it, she explains how her worlds have collided, sometimes gently, sometimes amid great pain and chaos, to compel her to commit stories to the page. In *Books and Islands in Ojibwe Country* she writes of a place where the United States and Canada recede in relevance, a place where the edges of Minnesota and Ontario let go and give way to the Anishinaabe traditions that extend as far back as collective memory can reach, and the record of her journey shares many of her thoughts about Anishinaabemowin and traditional culture. What both Erdrich's nonfiction works have in common is a woman's view of the world. Certainly one can read each for perspectives that are broadly indigenous, clearly postcolonial, and in many instances specifically Anishinaabe, but the dominant voice is that of a mother, a woman trying to manage the balance of caring for herself and her own sanity while also taking care of others.

Erdrich has given life to many stories. In *The Red Convertible* she explained the way the stories sometimes take on a life of their own: "They gather force and weight and complexity. Set whirling, they exert some centrifugal influence" (ix). This is the first lesson students learn about Anishinaabe word-making: the action is placed in the center, the "root verbs" begin to grow, bits of meaning clinging to every edge, telling stories within stories. Erdrich's perhaps unintentional echo of this basic structure is evident in all her work and has arguably become the one way to know her writing, its "centrifugal force." As with all authors and individuals, there are many valid ways to interpret efforts; however, one of the most productive ways to read Louise Erdrich is as an Anishinaabe storyteller whose works echo the patterns of Anishinaabe language and storytelling either explicitly or indirectly.

Gikenidizo / Knowing Oneself

In Erdrich's books, Anishinaabemowin is a way home, a source of comfort, a way to know yourself, other people, animals, spirits, and the universe. In the words she uses, and the way she places words in the mouths of her characters, Erdrich contributes to the definition of Anishinaabe literature and helps readers view the world from an Anishinaabe perspective. Language cannot be equated with identity, but it is an essential part of defining a distinct community. In her books the words protect and connect characters to a place, a place with others who share the same history, a place of origin, a place of evolution, a place to run back to and run away from, in circles of self-definition. Thinking about her years in boarding school, Lulu recalls the way Anishinaabemowin brought her home.

> I missed the old language in my mother's mouth. Sometimes, I heard her. *N'dawnis, n'dawnis.* My daughter, she consoled me. Her voice came from all directions, mysteriously keeping me from inner harm. Her voice was the struck match. Her voice was the steady flame. But it was my uncle Nanapush who wrote the letters that brought me home. (*Love Medicine* 69)

Although she has never claimed to be fully fluent and writes books in English, Erdrich's daughters might one day share Lulu's sentiments. They have certainly heard *n'daanis, nd'izhinikaaz, nd'anishinaabe*, words with the long vowels, different consonant pairs and bits added to the back and front. Erdrich has made Anishinaabemowin a part of her life, and even while writing predominantly in English, has taught herself and others the value of gathering the sounds and meanings of Anishinaabemowin.

Erdrich's knowledge of Anishinaabemowin has changed throughout her career. Early works include words in the way she knew them at the time—as distant relatives of another generation. Her later works show how she got to know that distant generation, how she herself became a source of words and ideas for others. Since her writing career began, Erdrich has spent considerable time learning vocabulary and grammar. The books in *The Birchbark House* series each include many words and a glossary at the end. By the time she wrote *The Last Report* in 2001, she had moved from knowing the few phrases that appear in the 1984 edition of *Jacklight* to teaching etymology through her characters. Father Damien, who learned Anishinaabemowin as a second language, explains the meaning of *manidoo*.

> Consider the word spirit, *manidoo*, and all of the forms in which it resides. That which we consider vermin, insects, the lowest form of life, are *manidooens*, and in their designation it is possible at once to see the penetration of the great philosophy that so unites the smallest to the largest, for the great, kind intelligence, the *Gichi Manidoo*, shares its name with the humblest creature. (*Last Report* 316)

Through Father Damien she shows how a non-Native language learner can appreciate the complex implications of Anishinaabemowin (also called Ojibwemowin). In 2000 Erdrich wrote:

> *Ojibwemowin* is one of the few surviving languages that evolved to the present here in North America. The intelligence of this language is adapted as no other to the philosophy bound up in northern land, lakes, rivers, forests and arid plains; to the animals and their particular habits; to the shades of meaning in the very placement of stones. As a North American writer it is essential to me that I try to understand our human relationship to place in the deepest way possible, using my favorite tool, language. ("Two Languages in Mind" 2)

She is committed to continuing what she calls her "love affair" with Anishinaabemowin because, as she puts it, "to engage in the language is to engage the spirit" (2).

Through use of Anishinaabemowin Erdrich shows how Anishinaabe people now and long ago have used the language to define both their own and others' communities. Her characters' ability to use their heritage language but also learn the sounds and perspectives of others is part of several books. In *The Birchbark House*, members of the community slowly begin to accept the fact that they need to learn to read *Zhaaganashimowin*, the white man's English. After a terrible smallpox epidemic both Fishtail and Angeline, two traditional Anishinaabeg, who previously had no use for English, begin to attend the mission school: "using a pointed stick to write in wet mud, Angeline showed Omakayas and Nokomis the meaningful signs, which looked like odd tracks" (190). Although this is fiction, this discussion about the way a new language enters a community is an important topic for Erdrich. She has inherited the tracks of the settlers and writes her own stories now in that language. In *Birchbark House* Nokomis (whose name is literally the word "Grandmother") looks at the letters written in sand and says, "*Howah*! Like our picture writing." Through her, Erdrich reminds readers that the Anishinaabe had been keeping records of their culture for many years. In the same book, she also mentions Fishtail's father, Day Thunder, who kept the records for the religious gatherings of the *Midewijig* and etched stories and songs on scrolls made of birchbark.

> Nokomis too, could etch pictures into bark. She also knew where certain marks had been placed upon lake rocks long ago. Some of the marks were made by the

spirits, some were made by humans; others were drawn by a giant race of people who had lived on earth in the old days and had disappeared. (191)

Erdrich places the story of stories within her work. She insists that readers understand that the book in their hands is only a part of the larger story of Anishinaabe language and literature.

Through her fiction Erdrich stresses that the Anishinaabe had their own systems and quickly learned others, creating an understanding of Anishinaabe linguistics and literature as strong enough to adapt without losing identity, able to be transnational and interdisciplinary without losing their original shape and significance. Readers also learn the Anishinaabe version of why another language would be learned and writing began to be used. The founders of the missionary schools insisted that learning English was a way to become civilized, but Omakayas sees the project differently. She does not see English replacing Anishinaabemowin, but only serving as yet another way to understand the newcomers. After the discussion of how English is written she sees Fishtail and asks herself, "Had he learned to make the white man's tracks? Had he learned to write his name? Had he learned to read the words of the treaties so that his people could not be cheated of land?" (*Birchbark House* 92). Of course, as the story unfolds, he does learn English, but that does not stop him from calling out in Anishinaabemowin, *Boozhoo, nindinaweymaganidok*, "Hello, my relatives" (92).

Later, the story of Native education became far more complex, as described by many writers, including Anishinaabe authors Jim Northrup, who discusses it in *Anishinaabe Syndicated*, Basil Johnston, who wrote *Indian School Days*, and Brenda Child, who wrote *Boarding School Seasons*. While the schools offered one means of survival, the impact on the language was erosion nearly to the point of extinction. Several of Erdrich's novels mention how these schools changed Anishinaabe identity. For example, in *Love Medicine*, Old Rushes Bear "let the government put Nector in school but hid Eli, the one she could not part with, in the root cellar dug beneath her floor. In that way she gained a son on either side of the line. Nector came home from boarding school knowing white reading and writing, while Eli knew the woods" (*Love Medicine* 19). Many years later the family would speculate on "why Great Uncle Eli was still sharp while Grandpa Nector's mind had left, gone wary and wild" (*Love Medicine* 19).

Lulu Lamartine also has memories of boarding school and how it impacted her sense of who she was. She recalls the "time of summer before school starts, before the leaves turn yellow and fall off overnight, before I would have to get on the government bus and go off to boarding school. Some children never did come home, I'd heard. It was just that time of summer when your life smarts and itches. When even your clothing hurts" (*Love Medicine* 280). Through Lulu, Erdrich gives us an Anishinaabe child's view of boarding school. More powerful than the adult debate about the politics behind the institution, or a sociologist's clinical opinion of its effects, she makes audible and emotionally tangible the heart-wrenching reality of a child being separated from family, language, and culture. Although the memories are written for the reader in English, there is allusion to the difference in sound that makes it clear that thoughts would still come first in Anishinaabemowin for the children; the language of fears and dreams could not be mandated by rules.

> I ran away from government school. Once, twice, too many times. I ran away so often that my dress was always the hot-orange shame dress and my furious scrubbing thinned sidewalks beneath my hands and knees to cracked slabs. Punished and alone, I slept in a room of echoing creaks. I made and tore down and remade all the dormitory beds. I lived by bells, orders, flat voices, rough English. (*Love Medicine* 68)

Erdrich's ability to use English to denigrate its very sound is an interesting twist of history. If she were to write in Anishinaabemowin, she would not reach her broad intended audience. So she uses English to speak reflexively about its more clipped, consonant-laden sound in comparison to Anishinaabemowin, which has fewer, longer words and far more vowels. Erdrich implies that the loss of a language is felt in your ears and mind and heart. The unfamiliar patterns of time and strange relationships with the earth that were imposed on the children are indecent. It is amazing that these children managed to adapt at all.

Erdrich continues to use English in other books to explain her belief in the importance of the language. Sometimes she explains with examples why an Anishinaabe word resonates more with her understanding of a concept, as with the etymology of the word for milk, *doodooshabo*, which translates to "breast water" (*Blue Jay's Dance* 213). At other times, her characters talk abstractly about the language. For instance, when Lulu and Moses come together on the island, she wakes "to find him speaking the old language, using words that few remember, forgotten, lost to people who live in town or dress in clothes. It was as though he had found his voice and it purred around me in a whisper" (*Love Medicine* 81). Perhaps he was saying *g'zaagin bazigem, aambe gizhaagame zaagaaganing*, which would be a purr unlike anything English could create. Moses represents a part of the Anishinaabe past that is kept separate from the present, but is proven to be very much alive and able to impact the modern world. Erdrich may not have inserted the actual words he used, but she felt it was important to make clear their power and difference and how they are connected to Anishinaabe identity.

The importance of old words also appears in *Love Medicine* when Marie Kashpaw explains her return to a language she once abandoned:

> Since she had lived among other old people at the Senior Citizens, Marie had started speaking the old language, falling back through time to the words that Lazarres had used among themselves, shucking off the Kashpaw pride, yet holding to the old strengths Rushes Bear had taught her, having seen the new, the Catholic, the Bureau, fail her children, having known how comfortless words of English sounded in her own ears. (*Love Medicine* 263)

Marie had reasons for abandoning Anishinaabemowin in her youth: pride; a desire to assimilate; perhaps to give the Bureau, the Catholics, and their language a chance to make her life better. But as she becomes an elder she also begins to demonstrate to the youth the power of cultural pride that includes knowing the original language.

Erdrich has used over 1,000 words of Anishinaabemowin in her books. Most of them she uses only once or twice, and many of them appear amid English. But they reflect the Anishinaabe system of creating words from verbs, classifying nouns, specifying the audience carefully, and allowing for multiple interpretations. One of the ways the language takes shape in Erdrich's work is as a means of identification. As she moves from English to Anishinaabemowin and back again, she highlights the way others are identified. One language is not better, or more civilized, than the other, but the Anishinaabe way of attaching information about relationships to the way one talks about what is happening could be viewed as a reflection of a verb-centered worldview.

Along with this positioning of self among others is the notion of spectrums of identity that shift easily from one extreme to another and allow for neutral positions. For example, the Anishinaabemowin third-person *wiin* is neither male nor female. As a story unfolds, it may become clear in which direction a character leans, but there is a way to speak, for a long time, in Anishinaabemowin without indicating gender. Other directions of identity manipulated by a speaker of Anishinaabemowin are "self" or "other" and "animate" or "inanimate." To say "I was laughed at," prefixes and suffixes must be chosen, and number but not gender must be made clear. One could say *n'baapig* (he/she laughed at me) or *n'baapaag* (they laughed at me). A speaker also has to choose between *waamdaan* (to see something that is inanimate) and *waabamaa* (to see something that is animate) any time the object of a gaze, a dream, or a vision is mentioned. It is not that other languages and cultures don't have these categories and ways to speak about them changing, but rather that Anishinaabe language requires attention be paid to them in a distinctive way and Anishinaabe storytelling tradition encourages stories and tellers who are adept at manipulating the extremes. Shifting, manipulated identity is a feature of the language and a characteristic of Erdrich's work. Her reflection of these concepts may have originally been unintentional. She didn't study the language and grammar and then work to reproduce the patterns in her fiction. More likely, the stories that she heard, the communities she encountered and then worked to re-create, had long lived with these patterns and choices in stories, and so this reading of her work is simply a reversal of that effect—a lesson in how to read Louise Erdrich from an Anishinaabe center, thinking around the many directions familiar to that particular community. The theory of literature that Erdrich's work illustrates is one of new ways to explore identity by using the distinctly Anishinaabe paradigm of self as a center with a myriad of connections. Furthermore, rather than striving to blend these selves or choose one to supersede the others, the most powerful self at the center is one that can move along the various axes as they are offered, become a bear when necessary, speak to the thunder, listen to plants . . .

To make space for this alternate view of the world, Erdrich defines what it is to be Anishinaabe, and it is not one thing at all. Her novels describe the Anishinaabe community as one that includes urban and rural life and is multinational with a history that reaches back thousands of years. In some cases, her repeated use of a word teaches others to recognize Anishinaabe culture; in other cases her language teaches ways the Anishinaabe recognize themselves.

Anishinaabemowin has made several lasting contributions to vernacular American English that date back to the first days of settlement. For example, *makazin* and *mooz*, now spelled "moccasin" and "moose" in English, are common English words and are used repeatedly in the *Birchbark House* series, indicating a few of the things with Anishinaabe names that seemed untranslatable to immigrant populations. Erdrich also uses both "Anishinaabe" and "Ojibwe" in her works to point out the difference between the diaspora of a large confederacy and the word for a specific ethnic subgroup within the Great Lakes landscape. Her use of *Gichimookomaan* also teaches readers an important part of Anishinaabe identity history. *Gichimookomaan*, which translates as "long-knives," describes, from an Anishinaabe perspective, the people who came to the Great Lakes. Her use of the words in *The Antelope Wife*, *The Birchbark House*, and *The Last Report* shows how the Anishinaabe viewed the immigrants. Two other words she uses, *Zhaaganaash* (British) and *Wemitigozhi* (French,) show how the Anishinaabe differentiated colonists prior to the American Revolution. Fluent speakers still recognize *zhaag* as a prefix meaning "weak" or "defeated" and *wemitig* as a pair of morphemes that sound together like "talking sticks," presumably because the Jesuits carried crosses.

Erdrich also uses Anishinaabemowin to show how the Anishinaabe recognize one another. For example, the particle *geget* appears in several novels. A simple word indicating agreement or certainty, *geget* can sometimes be a subtle sound-code used to determine the culture or fluency of a listener. An elder who answers a question *geget* and is understood may go on to say more in the language. If no signs of recognition can be found in the listener's eyes or response, then the speaker moves on in English. Erdrich's characters constantly check and recheck one another, sorting non-Native from Native, Dakota from Ojibwe, speakers from students, those who care and those who don't.

Gaawiin and *gego* are also used in a similar manner to clarify identity with a dimension of exclusivity. The two related particles, meaning "no" and "don't," can be code words in settings where negative comments or commands would not be polite or are best left disguised. Although they represent very small messages, they can serve as a way to create a language community where shared perspectives are not broadcast widely. *Miigwech* is another word that creates a circle of knowing. Although many use it like its closest English equivalent, "thanks," *miigwech* communicates an Anishinaabe perspective even when used by non-Native speakers who carefully learn Anishinaabe words in order to be included in Anishinaabe events and dialogue. In this way Anishinaabe language colonizes the conversation of others regardless of their ethnicity. *Miigwech* is a turn of the word *miigwe*, which means to give someone a gift. Like many Anishinaabe verbs, this one represents a core idea that can be made more complex. To receive and to give are equal in Anishinaabe; perhaps the word "exchange" would be a better translation if it did not signify trade and commodity in English. *Miigwe* is a gift given freely with nothing required in return. *Miigwech* is the acknowledgment of the gifting; used properly, it is conjugated as *g'miigwechin* or *miigwechwigo* to indicate "I thank you" or "we all thank you." Using the term implies a willingness to adopt an Anishinaabe concept, one that is so fundamental to the culture that it appears as frequently in prayer as it does in everyday life.

Referring to a decline in his people's ability to pray in Anishinaabemowin, one of Erdrich's characters, Lipsha Morrissey, says: "To ask proper was an art that was lost to the Chippewa once the Catholics gained ground. Even now, I have to wonder if the Higher Power turned its back, if we got to yell, or if we just don't speak its language" (*Love Medicine* 236). Although he uses "Chippewa," the government term for the Ojibwe or Anishinaabe, Lipsha places the blame on the people, saying the Anishinaabe spoke more clearly to one another and to *Gichi Manidoo* when Anishinaabemowin was the tribe's primary language. He knows the story of how the traders and settlers came, speaking French and English, wielding their written language as skillfully as any weapon. He knows that when Anishinaabemowin changed and was used less frequently, the balance of power had shifted. It was eventually outlawed intentionally to help erase Native American identity during the creation of new nations in North America. Like Lipsha, Erdrich is focusing on the locus of change, the source of reversal and cultural revitalization that is the Anishinaabe people. Erdrich's books attempt in a very small way both to report on, and to intervene in, the situation. Her characters set in earlier times speak Anishinaabemowin and learn English; then, as time passes, English speakers learn Anishinaabemowin and begin to examine the importance of the language to the survival of Anishinaabe identity.

Nd'Gikendaamin Enji-endaayaang / Knowing Where We Live

Along with echoing the sound and structure of the language, Erdrich's work also traces connections to the land and the history of the community. The woods, the deep and abundant water, and the cold unrelenting plains are all represented in Erdrich's books. She eloquently and specifically sets her stories in the shadow of jack pines, birchbark, and beet fields. The aurora borealis, with its "stabs of ancient glitter, delicate and lonely," dances above her characters the way it always has (*Bingo Palace* 55). In stories of Nanabozho, these are the lights he set in the sky to remind the Anishinaabe he is always thinking of them (Esbensen 27). The title poem of *Jacklight* describes observers at the edge of the woods:

> We have come to the edge of the woods,
> Out of brown grass where we slept, unseen,
> Out of leaves creaked shut, out of our hiding.
> We have come here too long. (*Jacklight* 4)

These could be the words of sentient prey, perhaps the musings of a deer or perhaps the thoughts kept in the back of Anishinaabe minds as they witnessed the invasion of their land and communities. The relationship with nature described by Erdrich is infinite and seamless—the people cannot exist without the land. Yet there is more to her stories than a romantic general understanding of nature. She makes it clear that the Anishinaabe have come to know the power, unpredictability, and passion of their home. Her characters often explain that among the land, the animals, the people, and the plants there is total interdependence. In *Love Medicine*, Lulu offers the Anishinaabe worldview from her personal perspective.

> No one ever understood my wild and secret ways. They used to say Lulu Lamartine was like a cat, loving no one, only purring to get what she wanted. But that's not true. I was in love with the whole wide world and all that lived within its rainy arms. Sometimes I'd look out on my yard and the green leaves would be glowing. I'd see the oil slick on the wing of a grackle. I'd hear the wind rushing, rolling like the far-off sound of waterfalls. Then I'd open my mouth wide, my ears wide, my heart and I'd let everything inside. (276)

In *Birchbark House*, Omakayas is similarly attuned to the details around her. At the end of the novel, she has lost a brother and learned much about life. Walking alone one morning, she is drawn to the song of the white-throated sparrows of spring.

> She walked toward the strongest center of their music, and then, on a patch of thawed grassy ground, she lay back in the sun, her head against the bark of a fallen log. The birds, the whole earth, the expectant woods seemed to wait for her to understand something. She didn't know what. It didn't matter what. Drowsily, she whistled along with the tiny sparrows. *Ingah beebeebee. Ingah beebeebee.* Those

sweet, tiny, far-reaching notes were so brave. The little birds called out repeatedly in the cold dawn air, and all of a sudden Omakayas heard something new in their voices. She heard Neewo. She heard her little brother as though he still existed in the world. She heard him tell her to cheer up and live. "I'm all right, his voice was saying, I'm in a peaceful place. You can depend on me. I'm always here to help you, my sister." Omakayas tucked her hands behind her head, lay back, closed her eyes, and smiled as the song of the white-throated sparrow sank again and again through the air like a shining needle, and sewed up her broken heart. (238)

For both of these Anishinaabe women, nature is a part of their being in the world. It is not something outside them to be felt or captured but rather something to absorb. Erdrich's characters find in the grass, the logs, the leaves, and the birdsongs a source of peace, a voice that answers questions and satisfies needs. Lulu finds rapture and freedom. Omakayas finds a plane in which her brother can still exist.

Much has been written about the mystical, spiritual union Indians are reported to have with nature. Yet when reading the story of one tribe as written by one author, we find there is no magical, predictable method of becoming "one with nature." Not only is there no single, pantribal approach, there is not even a single way that nature will affect members of one gender or one generation let alone one tribe. For example, it is clear that the birds and trees are important to both these characters and that these images are also found woven into the stories shared by their tribe, but it is also clear that the only secret is that there is no secret. Each person must find her (or his) own way to belong to this earth and eventually to move into the dreams of life beyond it.

This connection was disrupted by manifest destiny and the creation of reservations. One of Erdrich's central characters, Nanapush, says:

> We never had a name for the whole place, except the word *ishkonigan*—the leftovers. Our words for the place are many and describe every corner and hole. We are called Little No Horse now because of a dead *Bwaan* and a drenched map. Think of it *nindinawemagonidok*, my relatives. (*Last Report* 360)

The *ishkonigan* is the "*ishkwa* (after) *ni* (there) *gan* (thing)," something elsewhere and after, something left over. Most reservations were established when the language was still strong, so it is possible that Nanapush might also call Little No Horse *Bezhigogazhiins-Gaawiin-Aayaasiid*, but he uses *ishkonigan*, the generic, sarcastic reference to identify the place the Anishinaabe were assigned. On the other hand, his term for those he speaks to is one of ceremony and significance. *Nindinawemagonidok* is possessive; it is a verb, it is plural, it speaks of being related in specific and powerful ways. It identifies connections between people despite the fact that their physical center has been forcibly changed.

Another way Erdrich writes to identify the place of the Anishinaabe is by tracing their history. Many of her books outline Anishinaabe history and explore how that history subsequently shaped the community. She recounts the history of how they fought with their neighbors, the *Bwaan* (the Anishinaabe term for the Dakota and Lakota nations), how they dealt with traders and Jesuits, and how they now adjust and readjust to one another. Her novels are collections of characters speaking about, listening to, fighting over, and falling in and out of touch with their Anishinaabe identity.

Her histories begin before the Anishinaabe were defined by the *ishkoniganan*, when they were originally people of the woods and lakes, the rivers and prairies. Although she writes these stories in English, Erdrich includes several references to stories of origin that provide an example of early Anishinaabe literature and can also be read as echoes of identity. She preserves the moments in Anishinaabe history that stretch from "the beginning," as the Anishinaabe community has defined it, right up to the present. In some instances her characters speak of a time before human memory, recalling the raw genesis of landscape. This is the science and the fiction of the Anishinaabe; where scientific description and conjecture are melded into a narrative. In the last paragraph of *Love Medicine*, Lipsha Morrissey drives across the Midwest and says, "I'd heard that this river was the last of an ancient ocean, miles deep, that had once covered the Dakotas and solved all our problems" (367). Lipsha is specifically referring to what is now known as Lake Agassiz, a glacial lake of the Pleistocene epoch extending over present-day northwest Minnesota and northeast North Dakota, southern Manitoba, and southwest Ontario. Lipsha knows the Anishinaabe and Lakota have long lived with shifting borders, making both enemies and relations across the nations. For centuries each community had a distinct identity and history; certainly there were problems, but in recent times the problems and the identities have blurred. One of the ways the communities differ is in their stories of origin.

Stories of primordial waters have long existed in the reservoir of Anishinaabe tribal memory transmitted through oral traditions. In 1620 Jesuit Jacques Buteux asked an "Algonquin" where God was before the creation of the earth and was told "he is resting in a canoe that floats on primordial waters" (Thwaites, vol. 9, 127). This "primordial lake" and the one that followed the great flood are familiar features of Anishinaabe creation stories. In the Anishinaabe cosmos the "earthly plain" is surrounded by a realm above and a realm below (Coleman, Frogner, and Eich 12). In addition, each of these plains is divided into four layers (Barnouw; Benton-Banai). The balance, tension, and energy of chaos and cosmos, water and land, spirit and form, are always a part of Anishinaabe creation and re-creation stories (Barnouw; Booth; Chamberlain; Coleman, Frogner, and Eich; Dundes; Jones, *Ojibwa Texts Part 2*; Kohl; Vecsey, "The Ojibwa Creation Myth"). By including origin stories within her novels, Erdrich helps define Anishinaabe literature and culture. When young Omakayas hears the creation story in *The Birchbark House*, she learns to see herself and her people in an Anishinaabe context, at a moment when *Gichi Manidoo* decided he needed to purify the earth because people had chosen to live against the laws of nature. He caused rain to fall for so many days that the earth was covered by a *mushkobewun* (flood). This is one of the first stories to feature Nanabozho, who is sometimes an animal, sometimes a man, and at all times infused with more spiritual power than any other human (Minnesota Chippewa Tribe 3). When the rains ended, Nanabozho was seated on a huge log with several animals. He sent various animals to the bottom of a vast sea to get dirt to make an island. Many animals attempted to complete the task, but it was the *wazhashk* (muskrat) who came up with dirt on his fourth attempt, yet died as soon as Nanabozho took the dirt and placed it on the back of a *mishiikenh* (turtle) to create an island (Benton-Banai 33). Erdrich's version of the story in *The Birchbark House* matches all the other versions and is told because Omakayas begs Nokomis to tell a story before the arrival of spring. She knows that when the days grow longer "there will be no stories until next winter" (171). For her last story of the season, Nokomis chooses what she calls "an important teaching story, or *adisokaan*," the story of how Nanabozho and the muskrat make earth, the story of how the Anishinaabe have lived in the place of lakes since the lakes began (172). It is also a story left open to interpretation by listeners depending on their concerns and interests.

Erdrich's stories of the place that creates Anishinaabe identity are not only anchored to the long-ago past, they also show how the early 1900s marked a time of political resignation and change on the Anishinaabe landscape. The government continued the process of allotment, which was an attempt to "turn Indians into farmers" by forcing them to become stationary farmers rather than wandering agrarians harvesting various plants in the wild (*Love Medicine* 12). For many of the Anishinaabe, "the policy of allotment was a joke . . . much of the reservation was sold to whites and lost forever" (*Love Medicine* 12). Her fictional Kashpaw family traces its current landownership back to the time when the government was allotting plots.

> The land had been allotted to Grandpa's mother, old Rushes Bear, who had married the original Kashpaws. When allotments were handed out all of her twelve children except the youngest—Nector and Eli—had been old enough to register for their own. But because there was no room for them in the North Dakota wheatlands, most were deeded parcels far off, in Montana, and had to move there or sell. The older children left but the brothers still lived on opposite ends of Rushes Bear's land. (*Love Medicine* 18)

This is truly an illustration of how the language, the word *ishkonigan* (leftovers) aptly represents the Anishinaabe reality.

The Lamartines, another family in the same novel, offer a different perspective on the same issue. They were never actually given a deed to their land, yet they still claim it as theirs. Lulu Lamartine, who is related to the Pillagers and Nanapush, says:

> I believed this way even before those yellow-bearded government surveyors in their toe boots came to measure the land around Henry's house. Henry Lamartine had never filed on or bought the land outright, but he lived there. He never took much stock in measurement, either. He knew, like I did. If we're going to measure land, let's measure it right. Every foot and inch you're standing on, even if it's on the top of the highest skyscraper, belongs to the Indians. That's the real truth of the matter. (*Love Medicine* 282)

Ironically, their land is eventually threatened by a development backed by their own tribal government, but Lulu maintains the old rules of belonging and fights for her deceased husband's land. Her insistence in combining ideas both of time and tenure with space and measurement is evident in the words for *dibaaganeg* (time), *dibaagan* (hour), *dibaagens* (minute), *dibaabaan* (mile), *dibaabens* (foot). There is an expectation in the language that place, time, and truth are related. Although the words of trade may be recent, they reflect a non-Western connection in their etymology. When Father Damien attempts to explain the concept of metrical, musical "time" and asks how to say the word in Anishinaabemowin, Nanapush considers the question and replies in a way that makes clear the difference between the languages and cultures:

> We see the seasons pass, the moons fatten and go dark, infants grow to old men, but this is not time. We see the water strike against the shore and with each wave we say a moment has passed, but this is not time. Inside, we feel our strength go from a baby's weakness to a youth's strength to a man's endurance to the weakness of a baby again, but this is not time, either, nor are your white man's clocks and bells, nor the sun rising and the sun going down. These things are not time. Time is a fish and all of us are living on the rib of its fin. A moving fish that never stops. Sometimes in swimming through the weeds one or another of us will be shaken off time's fin . . . into something that is not time. (*Last Report* 225)

As Sidner Larson notes in *Captured in the Middle*, the site of Nanapush's power and resistance is language (97).

One of the most insidious forms of measurement that became a part of Anishinaabe reality and identity was the policy of termination, which Erdrich's fiction also includes. Termination through the designation of blood quantum became a legal way for the government to reduce the number of tribal members through biological redefinition rather than killing them outright. By taking care to give all tribal members a "blood quantum," the American government, and tribal governments, can clarify members' status as the "other" in society and within the community, in many cases creating deep schisms between families, clans, and nations. This approach was never approved by the Anishinaabe, or really by any of the tribes across America prior to its inception. It was just another part of the American culture imposed upon them. Erdrich offers one perspective of the process through Lulu Lamartine, who says:

> All through my life I never did believe in human measurement. Numbers, time, inches feet. All are just ploys for cutting nature down to size. I know the grand scheme of the world is beyond our brains to fathom, so don't try, just let it in. I don't believe in numbering God's creatures. I never let the United States census in my door, even though they say it's good for Indians. Well, quote me. I say,

every time they counted us they knew the precise number to get rid of. (*Love Medicine* 282)

Lulu makes a direct jab at the way Euro-American scientists and anthropologists physically measure people. Her defiance and refusal to accept the dominant ideas of family and community are a part of the Anishinaabe means of survival. Erdrich's characters are full-blood and mixed-blood, traditional and modern, living on and off the reservation. She includes them all as members of the Anishinaabe community. This diversity of opinion and genealogy among members of a single tribe gives depth and dimension to the non–Native American interpretation of Native American Indian history and identity. It might be easier to think of the people as a "vanished race," or at best a collection of communities banished to reservations, but Erdrich's books serve as personal testimonies of survival.

Gikenmaagwaa / Knowing Others

Not stopping at simply problematizing Anishinaabe identity, Erdrich often uses Anishinaabe language and literary patterns to explore who is not Anishinaabe. In some instances this is done through simply comparison, a bit like the way Lipsha might think about the difference between Dakota and Anishinaabe culture. In other instances she considers the way Anishinaabe identify themselves in comparison with those who are only sometimes human, part human, or not human at all. These characters appear in her stories and connect her writing specifically to the culture of the Anishinaabe. It is no surprise that two of the nouns used most often by Erdrich are *Nanabozho* and *wiindigoo*, one a half-human teacher, the other an evil, sometimes formerly human, spirit. *Nanabozho, wiindigoo*, and the less often mentioned *michibizhew* and *jibayag* are all part of the Anishinaabe otherworld that often does not translate directly into English. By using Anishinaabe terms for these other-than-human characters, Erdrich transfers these distinctly Anishinaabe concepts to American readers intact. By referring to the times when *manidoog, wiindigoog, midewiwin*, and *mashkiki* were the common subject of stories, her characters bring these spirits, demons, religious leaders, and medicines to life, defining them as a part of modern Anishinaabe culture.

In the poem "Night Sky" Erdrich recounts the tale of a woman who became a bear to make sense of her life as a woman. She chose to shift her identity into a animal of the forest "because her husband had run in sadness to the forest of stars" (*Jacklight* 33). This is an old Anishinaabe tale. A modern version takes place in Gerald Vizenor's novel *Dead Voices* as the protagonist, Bagese, changes from a bear to a woman. For Erdrich and the Anishinaabe the story is a practical, logical description of how reality can become metaphor.

> She soaks the bear hide
> Until it softens to fit her body.
> She ties the skinning boards over her heart.
> She goes out, digs stumps,
> Smashes trees to test her power,
> Then breaks into a dead run
> And hits the sky like a truck.
> We are watching the moon
> When this bear woman pulls herself
> Arm over arm into the tree of heaven. (*Jacklight* 33)

The damp heavy hide and the smashed bark crumbling beneath the weight of desperation are nearly palpable and, like any good storyteller, Erdrich leaves us focused on the moon as the bear-woman is set free in the heavens. The reader becomes the witness, here on earth, to heavenly drama. This could be one person's dream or a story used to explain constellations darkened by an eclipse. This could be a way of relating the science of the sky to life on earth. This could be a discussion of the power of identity. It could be all of this and history too. For an Anishinaabe writer this is an adaptation of a familiar tribal narrative and a lesson in problem solving. Bears, and women who become bears, often appear in the ethnography of the Anishinaabe. As Basil Johnston explains, "there are two kinds of bear walkers—those who practice evil medicine and those who try to help their fellow Anishinaubaek [sic]" (*Bear-Walker* 8).

In *The Birchbark House* bears speak to young Omakayas: "The longer she thought about her encounter with the mother bear, the more Omakayas was convinced that something she did not understand had passed between them" (34). Later, Nokomis tells her to listen to the bears and learn the ways of the forest (104). The Bear clan is one of the original seven Anishinaabe clans, and it is the most common identity for Anishinaabe people to adopt, which is not to say it is easy, but rather the most talked about in stories.

Many nonhuman *manidoog* are mentioned in Erdrich's books, both in English and Anishinaabemowin. According to Erdrich's characters, identifying the *manidoog* and naming them is part of retaining Anishinaabe identity. Lipsha Morrissey explains in *Love Medicine*,

> Now there's your God in the Old Testament and there is [*sic*] Chippewa Gods as well. Indian Gods, good and bad, like tricky Nanabozho or the water monster, Missepeshu. . . . Our Gods aren't perfect, is what I'm saying, but at least they come around. They'll do a favor if you ask them right. (236)

Of course, the implications of forgetting how to "ask them right" are clear. It is this forgetting that Erdrich and other Anishinaabe authors work against. In fact the darkly comedic outcome of Lipsha's love medicine is a parable about how tradition cannot be altered too much. He says of the medicine, "you don't just go out and get one, you should go through one hell of a lot of mental condensation" (241). The secondary moral of the story is that there is a price to be paid for knowledge.

Before the missionaries brought Western religion to the Anishinaabe, the good gods Lipsha refers to were known as *manidoog* (spirits), not to be confused with *Gichi Manido* (the Great Spirit). *Manidoog* can be the smallest part of the world personified or a kind of grand, indescribable beauty. In *Birchbark House*, Erdrich defines them as "spirits or beings who inhabit the Ojibwa world and often communicate in dreams" (243). In *Tracks* one can see the *manidoo* in the face of a beautiful traditional man, not coincidentally named Moses after a man who preserved the traditions of another tribe of people. One can also be blessed, guarded, and shaped by *manidoog*. When Lulu finds Moses on the island, she intends to seduce him but is seduced a bit herself. "He was surprising. . . . His face was closely fit, the angles measured and almost too perfect. My mother's face was like that—too handsome to be real, constructed by the *manitous*" (*Love Medicine* 77). Only a short time later in the same book, Marie Kashpaw describes her niece June "as if she really was the child of what the old people call *manitous*, invisible ones who live in the woods. I could tell, even as I washed, that the devil had no business with June" (*Love Medicine* 87). In these passages, Erdrich teaches that there is sublime goodness in the creation of the *manidoog*. The *manidoog* connect characters to places beyond this world. Both Moses and June narrowly escape death at a young age and go on to lead particularly complex adult lives, but each is set apart and considered special by others in the community. In *Love Medicine*, Rushes Bear tells the history of Moses's real name.

> When that first sickness came and thinned us out, Moses Pillager was still a nursing boy, the favorite of his mother, *Nanakawepenesick*, Different Thumbs, a woman who always had quick ideas. She didn't want to lose her son, so she decided to fool the spirits by pretending that Moses was already dead, a ghost. She sang his death song, made his gravehouse, laid spirit food upon the ground, put his clothes upon him backwards. His people spoke past him. Nobody ever let out his real name. Nobody saw him. He lived invisible, and he survived. And yet, though the sickness spared Moses, the cure bent his mind. He was never the same boy and later, when the coughing sickness swept through, he left us all for good and went to live on the Island, Matchimanito, training some cats he had stolen from the yard of an old Frenchwoman. The next winter he walked across the lake and appeared in town. His clothes were patched with the tanned and striped skins of cats. He walked with a cat's care, only backwards. (75)

While including the history of the smallpox epidemic of the 1830s Erdrich is able to show how Anishinaabe identity is seen in transition from life to afterlife. She talks about the *jiibayag* (ghosts) who come for the dead. She paints a picture of the long narrow boxes, sitting in fields like graves with legs, built by the Anishinaabe to house the dead as they traveled west to the land of the spirits. She tells how food should be brought to the dead as an offering and explains that their names should not be called. Later, Lulu restores life to Moses's spirit by taking down his gravehouse and speaking his name once again among the living (*Love Medicine* 82). Moses's story echoes the old stories of children who came back to life and explains how Anishinaabe beliefs of spirits, graves, and ghosts adapted to the new ways of Christian teachings. For the Anishinaabe living in the nineteenth century, changes in health, economy, spirituality, language, literature, and identity were radical and irrevocable. As Erdrich explains in *The Blue Jay's Dance*, by the late 1800s "most of the Anishinaabe were concentrated on small holdings of land in the territory west of the Great Lakes. The Turtle Mountain people wore trousers and calico dresses, drove wagons, and spoke their own language, but also attended Holy Mass" (*Blue Jay's Dance* 99). In the century that followed these times, spanning roughly from 1870 to 1970, Anishinaabe culture was forced to confront the fact that without the conscious effort of its people, it could face extinction. There was a need to invite the *manidoog* into a new era, to become American without losing Anishinaabe ways.

To contrast the good of the *manidoog* and illustrate the opposite in Anishinaabe culture, Erdrich includes forces like the *wiindigoo* of winter and the *missibizhiw* of the deep water. The preface to her poem *"Windigo"* explains, "The *windigo* is a flesh-eating, wintry demon with a man buried deep inside of it. In some Chippewa stories a young girl vanquishes this monster by forcing boiling lard down its throat, thereby releasing the human at the core of ice" (*Jacklight* 79). The water monster who lives in Lake Matchimanito is known by many characters and has apparently been there as long as memory extends. The irony of the monster living in a lake with Chi Manito (God) in its name is classic Anishinaabe chaos and central tension. Deep in the center of the source of life is something that yearns to take it away—pure Anishinaabe. According to Lipsha,

> That water monster was the last God I ever heard to appear. It had a weakness for young girls and grabbed one of the Pillagers off her rowboat. She got to the shore all right, but only after this monster had its way with her. . . . She still doesn't like to see her family fish that lake. (*Love Medicine* 236)

Fleur is that young Pillager woman, and her power to stand up against evil and the unknown is also demonstrated when her daughter Lulu goes to the Island to love and change Moses—despite the fact that her relatives warn her, "He's too old for you! Too close a relation! . . . Besides he's *windigo*! His grandfather ate his own wife!" (*Love Medicine* 75). "He's *windigo*" might sound to an English-speaking ear as if he's crazy, but in a correct cultural context, it is a verb meaning he is related to one who succumbed to selfishness and greed to the point of harming others. Erdrich defines these characters and brings them into her work, elaborating on the way Anishinaabe identity can be good and bad, human or more than human, in this world or part of another.

Somewhere between the good and bad in Anishinaabe stories is Nanabozho, the Anishinaabe version of a trickster, jester, and prophet—half man, half myth, he is the subject of many old stories. In his book *Manitous*, Basil Johnston describes Nanabozho:

> The youngest son of Aepungishimook, the Western Spirit, and Winonah, a human woman, some Anishinaabe people regard him as a Manitou; others see

him as the archetypal human. . . . Nanaboozhoo represents a caricatured under-standing of human nature. He is not what he appears to be; his real character is hidden. . . . The name derives from the prefix, *naning*, which means trembling, shaking or quivering, combined with *oozoo*, which is the abbreviated form of *oozoowaunuk*, meaning tail. Trembling tail reflects the character of many people. . . . Nanaboozhoo represents that portion of humanity that often gives in to inner weaknesses. (244)

In Anishinaabe stories, Nanabozho is also often called Wenabozho. The vacilla-tion seems capricious to the English ear, but knowing he changes from a *inini* (man) to a *waaboose* (rabbit) helps perhaps explain the two versions, one is "trembling tail" the other is "waab (white) tail." The constancy between both versions, the *bozho*, was once explained to me by Collins Oakgrove as the origin of today's greeting, *boozhoo*" Saying *boozhoo* to someone invokes a shared knowledge, history, and identity. Erdrich introduces Old Nanapush, a version of Nanabozho, in *Love Medicine*, and he returns as a character in *Tracks* and *The Last Report of Miracles at Little No Horse*. While the surname originates with Old Man Nanapush, it is also a name that connects a wider group of people, including Fleur Pillager, Nanapush's surrogate daughter; her daughter, Lulu, who is given the last name Nanapush; Lulu's son, Gerry Nanapush; and Gerry's son, Lipsha Morrissey. All of them exhibit characteristics often attributed to the mythic Nanabozho. They all have an inexplicable power to transform themselves or escape any situation as needed. Fleur, for instance, escapes the water demon, Lulu escapes a fire, Gerry can escape any prison or blizzard he encounters, and Old Nanapush himself is known for having talked his way out of death (*Tracks* 46). They all represent knowledge of "the old ways." Fleur, Nanapush, and Lulu are native Anishinaabemowin speakers, and Lipsha, although not shown to be fluent in the language, has a deep respect for the old ways and is certainly conversant (if inexperienced) in the art of healing (*Love Medicine* 332). Sometimes, however, Nanabozho is up to no good at all. In *The Last Report on the Miracles at Little No Horse*, Nanapush tells the story of how "Nanabozho Converts the Wolves" (85). He converts them only to skin them—a parable not lost on the Anishinaabe living among fur traders, missionaries, and settlers with guns, weapons, and ideas foreign to their society.

Nanabozho's human nature is reflected in has faults and failures, but also in his sexual prowess and teasing sense of humor, which was often part of traditional stories. As Jeanne Rosier Smith says of the Nanapush clan, they are "a family of tricksters and survivors" (Smith 71). From the elders to the youngest generation they are very like the characters found in the stories of Nanabozho in Basil Johnston's *Manitous*, Gerald Vizenor's *Summer in the Spring*, Victor Barnouw's *Wisconsin Chippewa Myths and Tales*, and Alethea Helbig's *Nanabozhoo*, all of which trace back to stories told long before English was the language of Anishinaabe literature. Erdrich also alludes to a modern version of Nanabozho in *Jacklight* and *Original Fire* with several stories about "Old Man Potchikoo." In her modern version of his life, the story begins with a "very pretty Chippewa girl working in the fields for a farmer . . . someplace around Pembina" and ends with him dying, rising again, and spending his "years of quiet happiness" with the patient Josette, who doesn't mind him hanging his hat on the front of a life-size statue of himself with "the fantasy of his favorite part of himself at its most commanding" (*Jacklight* 74; *Original Fire* 52).

Bizindaawaa Midwejig / Listening to Religion

Along with use of the language and references to the oral literature of the Anishinaabe, Erdrich also incorporates into her books considerable information about the structure and significance of the *Midewiwin* religion. Her references to *Midewiwin* leaders offer a view of community identity not always included in historical ethnographies. Through her fiction, Erdrich explores the way the Anishinaabe created a system of community knowledge that was relied upon to improve the health and harmony of the people. Like other authors including Vizenor and Benton-Banai, Erdrich connects the *midewiwin* tradition to specific Anishinaabe identity and cultural survival both in the past and the present (Vizenor *Summer in the Spring*; Benton-Banai 1988). In *Misquonaqueb*, James Redsky, an Anishinaabe and devout believer in *midewiwin* religion, explains its history:

> The *midewiwin* religion of the Ojibways originated sometime during the eighteenth century. Thus it contains some elements of Christian doctrine, while retaining many of the old spiritual values of the Ojibway people. The *midewiwin* was actively performed in all the major Ojibway villages in Wisconsin, Minnesota, Ontario, and Manitoba during the nineteenth century. The corrupting influence of zealous missionaries, however, caused its demise. (Redsky 21)

The demise he mentions is also documented in Ruth Landes's book *Ojibwa Religion and the Midewiwin*, in which she describes a system of religious practice that by the 1940s and 1950s began to center on fees paid for knowledge, initiation, and service. Erdrich and other contemporary writers and members of Anishinaabe communities of course know this is not entirely true. In fact, most leaders of language revitalization are familiar with contemporary ceremonies in their areas; many are practicing members themselves, and there is a recognized difference between services for pay and spiritual ceremonies. Notably, Eddie Benton-Banai, longtime Anishinaabe leader and Anishinaabemowin speaker, can be found on the Three Fires Midewiwin Lodge website, which explains:

> Bawdwaywidun, or Edward Benton-Banai, is an Ojibway-Anishinabe of the Fish Clan from the Lac Courte Oreilles Reservation in Wisconsin. A strong advocate for culture-based education and the relearning of our sacred Anishinabemowin language, Benton-Banai is the presiding Grand Chief of the Three Fires Midewiwin Lodge. He has a Master's Degree in Education from the University of Minnesota. He is a pioneer in culture-based curriculum/Indian alternative education, believing that education should be built on one's heritage and cultural identity, and should encourage spirituality, creativity, and cultural pride. (www.three-fires.net)

Many other Anishinaabe leaders work to support these ideas of Anishinaabe identity, but Benton-Banai is perhaps the most visible advocate for the Midewiwin Society, a group forced into secrecy during colonization. Like other practitioners, he takes care to sort the sacred practices from secular identity and has been known to say that certain rituals can only be performed in Anishinaabemowin. But he is also one to say that these traditions must be acknowledged. These lodges have a place in today's culture, and while not everyone chooses to participate, their very presence is a part of the complexity of Anishinaabe identity.

Midewiwin phrases and stories are infused throughout Erdrich's texts. These practices are what the dominant culture sometimes mistakenly calls shamanism or magic, but they are most accurately translated as "the sound and sensation of a cure or practice intended to preserve individual and community health." In *Midewiwin* stories there is a wealth of information on how to live in the world and make sense of it, to achieve balance and *bimaadiziwin*, a good life. The medicines used in *Midewiwin* tradition supply a practical means of dealing with the unexpected, good, or bad. True to Anishinaabe tradition, the history contained in Erdrich's writing includes ancestors and contemporaries who follow *Midewiwin* teachings and understand the importance of offering *asemaa* (tobacco), *mashkodewashk* (sage), *wiingashk* (sweet grass), and *giizhik* (cedar). Her characters' memories of elders "talking only in the old language, arguing the medicine ways, throwing painted bones and muttering over what they had lost or gained" are one way of preserving the knowledge of these traditions (*Love Medicine* 73). Fleur is lauded because "she knew the medicines" (*Love Medicine* 101). And although the family fears Old Rushes Bear, they are thankful for her blessing on their house:

> One evening, when she raised her feather and her braid of sweetgrass and began to bless the house, I took the children and we slipped off to eat some bannock and grease. Her blessings could hold rocks, we knew. Often she left off with bringing down the good from above and started slinging accusations. (*Love Medicine* 98)

Old Rushes Bear is depicted as a connection to *Midewiwin* world, "bringing down the good."

By contrast, some characters suffer from the tension of religions clashing. In *Love Medicine* Marie Lazarre is "lured like a walleye" to religion. Her visions are portals between worlds. They are maps of the mixed-blood search for identity and safety. In one particular case, Marie stands ready to feed cornmeal to the birds when suddenly:

> I was rippling gold. My breasts were bare and my nipples flashed and winked. Diamonds tipped them. I could walk through panes of glass. I could walk through windows. [Sister Leopolda] was at my feet, swallowing the glass after each step I took. . . . The glass she swallowed ground and cut until her starved insides were only a subtle dust. She coughed. She coughed a cloud of dust. And then she was only a black rage that flapped off, snagged in bobwire, hung there for an age, and finally rotted into the breeze. (54)

Her fantasy or delusion is echoed by *Midewiwin* tales of ancient humans who were covered in glistening scales, but when they changed to live on land, only a few scales were left on the tips of their fingers and toes (Barnouw; Landes, *Ojibwa Religion*; Kohl; T. Smith).

Mashkiki, midewiwin, manidoog, and the *missibizhiw*—medicine, religious practices, spirits, and malevolent underwater cats—are all part of the Anishinaabe identity that changed abruptly when traders and explorers began arriving in the Great Lakes area in the 1600s. Erdrich's fiction offers an Anishinaabe view of the arrival of the Europeans. She provides a cultural and literary dimension to the account given by the contemporary historians Richard White in *The Middle Ground* and Michael Witgen in *An Infamy of Nations*. White's book about "the search for accommodation and common meaning" tells how Europeans and Native American Indians met and regarded each other as "alien, as other, as virtually nonhuman" and how, over the next two centuries, they constructed a common, mutually comprehensible world in the region around the Great Lakes. He notes, "this world was not an Eden, and it should not be romanticized . . . it could be a violent and sometimes horrifying place" (x). White writes about how America created the "Indian" as an exotic creature to be feared, which is a sad, but very true, fact. By contrast, like Erdrich, Witgen offers a view of the New World from a Native perspective. Whenever possible, he includes the Anishinaabemowin found in primary documents, allowing names and places to retain their Anishinaabe identity. As the New World emerged, cultures collided, and this "demanded that Native peoples, like the peoples of empire, reimagine their social identity in the wake of the epic encounter that brought their two old worlds into contact" (19).

This is precisely the project of *The Birchbark House*. In order to elaborate on Anishinaabe shared identity Erdrich provides an alternate account of cultural change and exchange, the version that until recently was left out of the textbooks. Omakayas's father, Deydey, is a trader who eventually decides that the family may need to flee west. Westward flight was historically the first reaction to encroachment. There are not many battles for land on record between the Anishinaabe and the pioneers and voyageurs. The land was so changed by the new inhabitants that flight was preferable by far. In Erdrich's novel the town LaPointe "was becoming more *chimookoman* every day, and there was talk of sending the Anishinaabeg to the West" (*Birchbark House* 77). As the men discuss the future, the children hear them say:

All of the Ojibwa would be safe on their own land farther west. No one would bother them. Yes, there were hazards on the way—Dakota war parties, hunger, the threat of winter's dire weather. He'd rather not go. Still, said jolly Albert, he had moved before when the waves of white people lapped at his feet. . . . We have to stop somewhere, someday. . . . West is where the spirits of the dead walk. If the whites keep chasing us west, we'll end up in the land of the spirits. (*Birchbark House* 79)

The young girls learn the history of their tribe's migration and witness as elders debate the possibilities for the future. Traditional beliefs, such as the notion that the west is the land of the dead, are reinforced, but this happens in the context of a new political history that is seen through the eyes of the Anishinaabe. While Erdrich is obviously not creating a dialogue from written sources, she allows the oral transmission of knowledge to help reconstruct a picture of the past. As Deydey, who is himself a mixed-blood, considers the character of the *Gichimookomaanag*, we see the Europeans through the eyes of several different Anishinaabe, who compare the settlers to hungry, aimless, angry *wiindigoog*, never satisfied with what they have.

> They are like greedy children. Nothing will ever please them for long. . . . Not until they have it all . . . all of our land, our wild rice beds, hunting grounds, fishing streams, gardens. Not even when we are gone and they have the bones of our loved ones will they be pleased. . . . Before they were born, before they came into this world, the *chimookoman* must have starved as ghosts. They are infinitely hungry. (*Birchbark House* 80)

These are not idle mutterings; these are the philosophical and psychological concerns of community leaders who see their values being eroded by a new population. As the Anishinaabe consider moving west, Erdrich describes where the two cultures meet geographically and politically. As her characters compare the Europeans to the *wiindigoog*, she uses Anishinaabe terms to place the immigrants within the context of Anishinaabe stories.

By allowing the Anishinaabe to speak for themselves in her novels, Erdrich forces the readers to see the nameless "Indians" as individuals. Passages such as these, where a general pantribal interpretation would erase specific detail, illustrate how important it is to read Native American Indian authors in the context of their own tribe. Erdrich gives specific voices to Anishinaabe leadership in contemporary times as well. For example, although it was politically important for the leaders of the American Indian Movement to speak with a pantribal unified voice, Erdrich shows with her fiction that it is equally important to allow history to be told from the perspective of particular individuals. The real pantribal American Indian Movement includes Anishinaabe leaders Dennis Banks, Leonard Peltier, Eddie Benton-Banai, and Clyde and Vernon Bellecourt, among others. In Erdrich's novels they are blended in the character of Gerry Nanapush. Incarcerated for crimes he believes to be overrated, he is a symbol of the relationship between the Anishinaabe and federal U.S. authority, specifically those who were members of AIM. Like the real AIM leaders, Gerry learns the nature of the world the hard way and uses every bit of his knowledge to confound and frustrate the judicial system.

> Gerry's problem, you see, was he believed in justice, not laws. He felt he had paid for his crime, which was done in a drunk heat and to settle the question with a cowboy of whether a Chippewa was also a nigger. Gerry said that the two had never settled it between them, but that the cowboy at least knew that if a Chippewa was a nigger he was sure also a hell of a mean and low-down fighter. (*Love Medicine* 201)

Through Gerry, Erdrich confronts stereotypes commonly incorporated into Anishinaabe history. He challenges the common racist assumption that Native Americans and African Americans are members of the same indistinguishable set of less-than-civilized victims. He also challenges the assumption that the Anishinaabe cannot win a battle, and that the United States is built on "justice for all." According to Gerry's story, his people are spirited, sometimes victorious, fighters not given equal representation in the court system. Unlike many nations, whose history and identity include mass removal to unfamiliar landscapes, Anishinaabe reservations are either "unceded" nations on ancient tracts of land or communities formed in and around sites historically used throughout the seasons. Not surprisingly, the language and traditions have remained strongest in sites where the stories connect with the land.

Erdrich uses Anishinaabemowin sparingly, but she consistently addresses issues of identity through language and narrative, and the perspectives she presents connect with ideologies reflected in the structure of the language. She uses Anishinaabe words or their equivalent concepts in English to explore various ways to identify: self and others, the place of the Anishinaabe, the nonhuman identities familiar to the Anishinaabe and the changing Anishinaabe community. She also contributes to the definition of Anishinaabe literature by demonstrating knowledge of traditional narrative patterns.

One of the narrative patterns she employs is planting stories within stories. This could be considered a common technique in modern curriculum, but it is an essential trait of oral stories reminding listeners of the many ways one story, image, or idea can connect to others. In Anishinaabe stories, these connections are often based on networks of kinship, history, the seasons, or other archetypes that might help listeners anchor the story to the Anishinaabe landscape and way of knowing the world.

The Birchbark House includes three embedded traditional tales. One is a ghost story told in *niibin* (summer), and two are told by Nokomis in *biboon* (winter). The stories are told when the family is gathered and the day is ending. Both Deydey and Nokomis fill their pipes with *kinnikinnick*, and the tales begin:

> Omakayas wanted to ask her for a story, but she knew that her Nokomis always refused, no matter how hard they begged, until the last frog was safely sleeping in the ground. Deydey, with his half-white blood, could often be persuaded because the stories he told were different from Nokomis's. Hers were *adisokan* [sic] stories, meant only for winter. Deydey usually talked about his travels, the places he'd seen and the people, the close calls and momentous encounters with animals, weather, other Anishinabeg, and best of all, ghosts. (*Birchbark House* 61)

Nokomis tells her stories at the same time of day, but her tales are not of her own adventures. Her first tale begins with Omakayas saying: "*Weendamawashin, daga,* Nokomis . . . tell me a story" (*Birchbark House* 132). With all the men outside and only women gathered, Nokomis answers, "Now I can tell you an old story about my Grandmother" (*Birchbark House* 133). "Fishing the Dark Side of the Lake," like "Deydey's Ghost Story," is a magical old tale set in familiar Anishinaabe lake country. This story, told when the men had gone, also demonstrates how some stories are kept and handed down by the women, while others belong to the men.

The last tale Erdrich includes in *The Birchbark House* is the origin story "Nanaboozhoo and the Muskrat Make an Earth," which reinforces the educational value of the Anishinaabe tradition of *aadizookanag* and explains the season for this type of story.

> The only thing good about this time of winter was the stories. While the snow and ice still held fast, Nokomis told them tales about the world of *manitous* and *windigos*, tales of *Nanaboozhoo*, the comical teacher. Those last were favorites

of the girls. Maybe because she so often felt small and helpless, Omakayas thought long about one particular tale Nokomis told. She loved to hear it when the flames jumped and the frozen world outside the small cabin was dark. (*Birchbark House* 171)

Paul Ragueneau, who lived among the Anishinaabe in 1645, wrote about elders gathering to tell stories in winter. Although he was not a member of the community, he recognized the significance of the event.

They are accustomed, on such occasions, to relate the stories which they have learned regarding their ancestors, even those most remote, so that the young people, who are present and hear them, may preserve the memory thereof, and relate them in their turn, when they shall have become old. They do this in order thus to transmit to posterity the history and the annals of the country, striving by this means, to supply the lack of . . . books. (Thwaites, vol. 30, 61)

The elders Ragueneau encountered in the 1600s were doing exactly what Erdrich does today. Although her books can be read any time of year, she places the reader with her characters in the midst of winter to hear the oldest and most important stories of the Anishinaabe community. Erdrich also shows how these mythic parables transmit cultural information and become moral fables, in this case teaching the value of determination. "Omakayas knew that her Nokomis told her this story for a larger reason than just because she asked for it. . . . If such a small animal could do so much . . . your efforts are important too" (*Birchbark House* 175).

The numbers that shape Erdrich's stories are four and seven; of all the numbers, these reoccur most often in Anishinaabe stories. By echoing the patterns and numbering she finds familiar to Anishinaabe culture, she shows how these paradigms can be used in literature to make sense of the world. A poem in *Jacklight* alludes to *Gichi Manidoo* dreaming the universe into existence by using the four elements: *aki* (earth), *nibi* (water), *ishkode* (fire), and *noodin* (wind). *Gichi Manidoo* is said to have infused these elements with special powers (83). After that, he made the plants and animals, also in four groups (Minnesota Chippewa Tribe 1983, 3). There are many versions of this story, but the significant feature that remains the same is the division by four. Erdrich uses this pattern of four overtly in *Jacklight*, *The Blue Jay's Dance*, and *The Birchbark House* when she sets her narrative against the backdrop of the seasons. Quarterly divisions are common enough and may not seem uniquely Anishinaabe to many readers, but Erdrich's use of this narrative framework in several books supports the concepts of balance and the importance of cycles. For her stories to be complete, they must move her characters through at least one year, one set of four seasons, often summed up as surviving one winter.

It is no coincidence that the way to indicate your age in Anishinaabemowin is to count the number of times you have seen *biboon* (winter). Just as time and space are divided into four by seasons and cardinal directions, the language is also divided by four types of action. Erdrich is aware of these divisions. In her poem "Turtle Mountain Reservation" she writes:

Its heart is an old compass
pointing off in four directions.
It drags the world along,
with the world it becomes. (*Jacklight* 82)

The circling of time in Erdrich's stories is dictated by the needs of the story, not the conventions of logic or chronology.

Another significant number is seven, recognized by speakers of Anishinaabemowin as the number of possible pronouns. Again, like four, seven is significant in other cultures and systems of knowing, but for the Anishinaabe it represents the number of ways to specify who is present as speaker, audience, initiator, or object. People pray to seven grandfathers, have seven main teachings, and the seventh generation is the one that must be kept in mind when making any decision (Benton-Banai 61).

The Birchbark House begins in 1840, when a baby girl is abandoned. Smallpox killed her family, and only Old Tallow, the wife of one of the voyageurs, will go to the island to save the baby. Seven years later, as that little girl is confronted with death again, she remembers her story, and the story of the Anishinaabe continues. To find the truth in a child's seventh year fits perfectly into the Anishinaabe lexicon of understanding. The seventh prophecy of the Anishinaabe, made by the seven grandfathers, foretells a rebirth among the people.

The seventh fire foretold the emergence of a new people, a people that would retrace their steps to find the sacred ways that had been left behind. The waterdrum would once again sound its voice. There would be a rebirth of the Ojibwe nation and a rekindling of old fires. (Fox 27)

Omakayas narrates her people's story from a fresh and unburdened perspective. She is young enough to still be learning the story of her people, and her youth affords Erdrich the opportunity to explain and present many details of Anishinaabe life that might be taken for granted in the context of an adult world.

Erdrich is an integral part of her family's and her community's past, present, and future. Her stories contain traces of the windswept prairies of her own youth as well as the birdsongs of her great grandmother's days on the shores of Lake Superior. The history she has made part of her poetry and prose helps to define an Anishinaabe version of events. The object of her work is to bring the stories of one place, one people, to life on the page. In doing so she touches on pantribal, even universal, subjects, but her tales are made more powerful by local details. Her use of Anishinaabemowin and the way she echoes patterns of Anishinaabe storytelling teach readers that there was, and still is, a highly developed culture of the Great Lakes that cannot be completely melded into the wider landscape of America. For fellow Anishinaabe readers, these stylistic traits supply familiar markers. Winter tales, the circle of seasons, patterns of fours and sevens, even visions, dreams, and journeys to the other world are commonplace in traditional Anishinaabe storytelling. But more than simply structuring her work in a familiar way, she marks it as distinctly Anishinaabe by including details that would not be recognized by any other tribe. Neither the eastern Iroquois nor the western Lakota nations speak of *wiindigoo* dogs or the way life is shaped by lakes and pine trees. Many tribes have similar oral traditions, and even place importance on vision quests and a relationship with nature, but Erdrich's characters inhabit a specifically Anishinaabe world.

CHAPTER FOUR

Zhaabwii'endam: Conscious Survival in the Writing of Jim Northrup

In Sawyer, generations of relatives are buried
The air hasn't been breathed by heavy industry
The colors of blue and green rest the eyes and spirits
The quiet makes it easy to hear the spirits and their messages.
In Sawyer, the values and traditions of the people are held
Sacred.

—Northrup, *Walking the Rez Road*

In Anishinaabemowin, the way to say "holy" or "sacred" is *chitwaa*, which is also the equivalent of "fancy." Another option is *manidoo*, which often becomes a prefix to emphasize the spiritual nature of something. For example, a "sacred song" is a *manidoo-nagamon*, and God, the Creator, is *Gichi Manidoo*, the Great Spirit. One natural translation of the last lines of Northrup's poem might be:

In Sawyer, the values and traditions of the people are held sacred.
*Kina goya nagadawendaamowaad ezhi-Anishinaabemaadiziwaad
    Gaakaabiikong.*

All those living have respect for the way they live an Anishinaabe life in Sawyer.

In Anishinaabemowin being sacred is a verb of thought and motion, a way of living recognized by a community. Centering sentiments on actions rather than adjectives, creating such long words as *ezhi-Anishinaabemaadiziwaad* to say "the way they live an Anishinaabe life" requires knowing Anishinaabe patterns of language and style. These ways of thinking and viewing the world are reflected in the work of contemporary authors. Jim Northrup writes sometimes in Anishinaabemowin, but most often in English. What his English can teach us is not only how to see the reservation he calls home as part of America, but also how to recognize Anishinaabe language and narrative patterns, how to think about literature and living from an Anishinaabe perspective. Northrup's poem about his hometown, Sawyer, contrasts the pure air of the reservation with the industrial air of cities nearby. He offers an honest and complete view of modern reservation life. For those living there now and the generations of relatives buried there, it remains a place where Anishinaabe values and traditions are "held sacred" and kept alive. He explains how it is "easy to hear the spirits and their messages" when listening in an Anishinaabe way. This is not just something to watch him do, it is something one might want to learn how to practice.

Jim Northrup is by reputation a comedian, a truth-teller, a survivor, a journalist, a *weweniganawaabinini* who watches the world carefully. Gerald Vizenor has said he is "an imaginative listener; his direct and humorous stories are inspired by the rich language that people speak on the reservation. The wild and wondrous characters in his stories are survivors in the best trickster humor, no one is a passive victim (*Touchwood* vii). Northrup jokes, "I write because it's quicker than printing," but he also acknowledges a deeper need to tell stories (Interview). "I write because I've got stories people want to hear; that's what it's really about. You go for a walk in the woods and you realize that the deer flies don't care if you won a book award." Beneath the sharp wit, soft touch, and painful memoirs is a *manidoo-nagamon*. His words carry the Anishinaabe into the future. He drags truths and traditions, as they are gasping for breath, into the next century. He speaks as often of the serenity of his hometown, Sawyer, as he does of contests and politics. One of the profound lessons he teaches is that the loudest, most immediate, most memorable voice may not be the most important. From him, readers learn to listen for the deeper, more unexpected, sounds of a rice pole hitting bottom; the first drop of spring sap; the snap of a snare; or the powerful voice of a poet on stage.

Gaa Ezhi-bimaadizid / Life So Far

Northrup was born in 1943, less than a decade after the U.S. government handed Fond du Lac Reservation a constitution. He jokes he is one-third Chippewa, one-third Anishinaabe, and one-third Ojibwe. He has also said he is: "pure Northrup, a one hundred percent frybread-wild-rice-maple-syrup-propelled, ricing, basketmaking, storytelling Shinnob" (*Rez Road Follies* 14). He uses the term Anishinaabe, but others have used Chippewa, Ojibwe, Native, Indian, redskin, Blanket-ass, and the list goes on . . . Northrup turns the page on these words and invents a few of his own, finding survival in modern times using language as a mechanism of defense and identification.

At the age of six, Northrup was ordered to attend a federal boarding school in southern Minnesota, away from his family. For his secondary education he was sent to a Christian boarding school in Hot Springs, South Dakota. Ironically, a mission school stands a short walk from his home, but the policy was to send children as far from their culture and family as possible to more quickly and completely remove all traces of their heritage. Northrup later served in the Marine Corps and completed a tour of duty in Vietnam, leaving the service with two good-conduct medals. He has gone on to hold other jobs for pay, but his writing emphasizes the importance of all work—paid and unpaid. Northrup is Anishinaabe and American; he is what he calls an "American American." His writing demonstrates how being Anishinaabe in the twenty-first century requires a keen awareness of two cultures and the cracks between them. He discusses the challenges of surviving attempted assimilation, broken treaties, war, and life as a cousin, husband, father, son, brother, and "grampa." Readers come to understand him as a passionate storyteller who takes time to share what he knows about life, *ezhi-minobimaadizi*.

Northrup began his writing career while in reform school in Red Wing, Minnesota, where he wrote short articles and published questions and answers, a prelude to his current column. In the late 1980s he began to write *The Fond du Lac Follies*. *The Follies* has run in *The Circle*, a Native American Indian newspaper based in Minneapolis, for more than twenty years. Although Northrup's work appeared in other publications prior to the start of *The Follies*, the column is his defining work.

It should be noted that I have cared about Jim and his words for over three decades. He was the only Anishinaabemowin speaker on hand when I earned my PhD, and his wife Patricia and I were north and south beside him at the ceremony when he was granted his PhD. I may not be the most objective source of information about his life and ways, but I would argue I am the truest editor he will ever have. My account of his writing is no less than a representation of the blend of our thinking and in that way perhaps not what critical readers expect, but also so much more.

Gaa Ezhibii'iged / Writing So Far

Northrup's fiction first appeared in 1987 in *Touchwood: A Collection of Ojibway Prose*, edited by Gerald Vizenor. In the early 1990s, stories also began to appear in a number of collections including *North Writers: A Strong Woods Collection* and *Stiller's Pond: New Fiction from the Upper Midwest*, two multiethnic collections dedicated to a sense of place in the contemporary Midwest. He has also written a stage version of *The Rez Road Follies* that appeared in Kim Blaeser's *Stories Migrating Home*, and his play *Shinnob Jep* was published in *Nitaawichige*, a collection edited by Marci Rendon and Linda LeGarde Grover. Written in 1987 and first performed at the University of Minnesota in 1994, *Shinnob Jep* confronts cultural stereotypes among the Anishinaabe themselves. Structured as a game show, the play quickly refutes the myth that all Indians are alike by showing that not even all Anishinaabe are alike.

Walking the Rez Road, his first book, was published in 1993 and won a Minnesota Book Award. Through a combination of stories and poems, the main character, Luke Warmwater, records his modern Anishinaabe life. Both Northrup and Warmwater take seriously the responsibility of being a storyteller in a culture that values the ability to tell a story more than the ability to sell one. Warmwater's name is a play on the stereotype of Indian names in America, but it suits the character well. He is a careful man, neither hot nor cold, and intent mostly on living from one day to the next despite the challenges that come his way as an Anishinaabe man living on the rez and a Vietnam vet who long ago gave up trying to make sense of the war. The name Luke Warmwater is also an echo of Anishinaabe wordplay, which often involves taking words apart and manipulating meaning to surprise as well as inform.

Northrup's second book is *The Rez Road Follies: Canoes, Casinos, Computers and Birchbark Baskets*, published in 1997. Compared to his first book, *The Rez Road Follies* is like a river widening. The second book takes more risks, includes more from the best of the newspaper column, and is more complex both politically and personally. Written as a memoir, the voice is Northrup's directly; the stories are more passionate; the humor more pointed; and the cultural criticism more evident. It is clear in this book that Northrup has defined his audience and intends to teach them what he knows.

Anishinaabe Syndicated: A View from the Rez is his third book and summarizes the first decade of his column. More than just a reprint of every article, it is an edited stream of news and humor with new material inserted to make connections across time. *Anishinaabe Syndicated* includes more Anishinaabemowin and much discussion of language preservation and the connections between language and culture. Northrup's ability to cross contemporary lines of genre is obvious, and he has recently published several poems separately including "Dash Iskigamizigaaning," a poem about sugar bush season written in Anishinaabemowin.

The second decade of columns was published as *Rez Salute: The Real Healer Dealer*. In it Northrup uses more Anishinaabemowin than any of his previous books. Whole passages appear in the language, and throughout the book he comments on how some parts of the culture are retained more easily than others. Some parts of the book are familiar accounts of seasonal activities; in other places he documents the innovation required for a culture to remain vital and relevant to future generations. When he notices more people are interested in buying or making traditional ricing baskets than conjugating eloquent sentences, he combines language with the living arts and hosts a Language Camp where students can learn the *waaginoogan* way, under the bent boughs with their hands busy (122). He also speaks of a time when the community gathers for storytelling: "That showed me the power of stories and storytellers. It also showed me the people are thirsting for the oral tradition of storytelling" (129).

G'Gikenidizomin / Knowing Ourselves

Northrup is clear in his opinion about the language of his ancestors and the importance of narrative as a means of preserving Anishinaabe identity.

> Long ago we didn't send our children to another tribe to raise; we did it ourselves. Just as we are asked to share our history with other people, we need to remember to pass it on to our own children. Anishinaabe children should know their own history and language along with their ancestors' contributions to the present. In the Great Lakes area, just learning the language teaches all the children about the presence of the Anishinaabe. (*Rez Road Follies* 66)

His first book, *Walking the Rez Road* (1993), incorporates several important Anishinaabe words into the text, which, at the time, was unusual for a book from a non-Native publisher. A few years later *The Rez Road Follies* (1997) emphasized his conviction that the language must survive. In it, he introduces readers to the cadence and complexity of the language by including several short stories in Anishinaabemowin. In the story of his grandson's first rabbit trap, he explains, Ezigaa's "education was lacking until today." Or, as he says in Anishinaabemowin, *ogikendaasowin o'o keyaa ji maajiishkaamagadinig azhigwaa* (*Rez Road Follies* 54). In *Anishinaabe Syndicated* he includes a wide range of everyday phrases he is working to share with the next generation, but he also includes several *akiwenziiwag-mindimooyewag baapiwinensan* (old man and old lady jokes), which really are best left untranslated so as to not deny the reader the reward of working through them, or the delight of knowing instantly what they imply. When the text crosses cultures into Anishinaabemowin, readers of his books who know the language will slow to the familiar speed and intonation of a fluent speaker. Readers not familiar with the language will at least have a sample of the multisyllabic pattern of sounds. By including Anishinaabemowin in his books he demonstrates his belief that it is central to Anishinaabe culture.

In *Rez Salute* Northrup recalls introducing himself in Anishinaabemowin over 20 times, and those are just the instances mentioned in his columns. He makes the point that the language needs to be used and Anishinaabe people need to feel comfortable using it. Although the Fond du Lac Reservation Business

Committee passed a resolution stating Anishinaabemowin is the official language of the nation, too many instances reveal its tenuous status. At an elders' dinner with 700 attendees the prayer was offered in English, prompting him to ask, "Are we so far gone we don't need white people to assimilate us anymore, we do it ourselves?" (169).

Like Erdrich, Northrup has consciously spent time as an adult learning Anishinaabemowin. He and his family have organized the annual Nagaajiwanaang summer language camp for several years. The camp is an amazing blend of language and culture held beside the lake where he can set up basket making, canoe racing, and storytelling simultaneously. In each book he has increased the number of words in Anishinaabemowin with the difference being only 39 words used in his first book and over 500 used in each of his subsequent books. Most importantly, the way he uses the language becomes increasingly complex. In early works, individual words were signifiers of identity. Later, phrases and paragraphs contain both literal meaning and subtle humor. He has said the change in his use of Anishinaabemowin is the result of his own continuing education and the renewed interest in the language that he sees in his community and the broader Anishinaabe diaspora. Many colleges in the Great Lakes region have indigenous language classes, Head Start programs offer Ojibwe for preschoolers, several immersion schools have survived over a decade, numerous teaching tapes and workbooks are available, and there are a growing number of interactive lessons on the Internet (*Rez Road Follies* 67). All of these resources are powerfully important, according to Northrup. His own experience of being sent to boarding school nearly robbed him of the language. He is eager to see future generations avoid the same fate. "When I was a young boy in boarding schools, the use of Ojibwe was discouraged. We had Ojibwe pounded out of us and English pounded in" (*Rez Road Follies* 66). The result was that friends who could still speak the language made fun of him when he returned to the reservation:

> I couldn't answer because I was too busy learning English. Somewhere along the way, I started to feel the impact of my loss. I no longer understood what the elders were saying. . . . There were times when it seemed like the older generations were ashamed of speaking it. They never used it when white people were around. For the most part, Ojibwe went underground and stayed there for a long time. (*Rez Road Follies* 67)

Northrup and other Anishinaabe authors are attempting to keep it above ground now. He recalls the way most of today's Anishinaabe people have learned the language.

> Most of us learned a few phrases because we were around Ojibwe speakers. We learned a little but not enough. We mostly learned the command words: don't, be quiet, sit down, don't cry, eat, or go to bed. It is hard to carry on a conversation using only command words. A cousin said for the first eight years of his life, he thought his name was "*gego*," the Ojibwe word for "don't." (*Rez Road Follies* 67)

This haphazard way of picking up language leaves many modern Anishinaabe with no choice but to insert it into the context of an English sentence. Stories with older characters might represent a choice of language, but for most contemporary characters there is no reason to write their dialogue in Anishinaabemowin. These characters use the language in a different way. For them, it is not a tool for carrying on complete conversations; instead, it serves as one way to identify members of the same community, to mark the conversation as Anishinaabe, or confer meaning intended only for one another. The language can also be used to represent an image or idea that does not translate easily into English.

In his writing, Northrup deploys language in ways that are easily connected to patterns of word-building, which requires a focus on action and an emphasis on observing events accurately while still leaving meaning open to individual interpretation. He also relies on time-honored techniques of Anishinaabe storytelling by connecting his stories firmly to the place of the Anishinaabe and paying attention to the patterns of narrative. Not only is it clear that the Anishinaabe language and culture are connected, it is also obvious that in the patterns of speech and story developed by a connected society are ways of understanding the world that offer value not only to that community, but to anyone making interpretive comparisons in world literature. Jim Northrup's dominant perspective is one of survival through observation. Some of the techniques found in his writing are small cultural markers, while others offer more expansive models for interpretation. For example, Northrup continually deconstructs and reconstructs words in ways that allow for more clarity regarding action and possible humorous interpretation. Certainly all languages change, and speakers are constantly creating words to reflect culture. However, Anishinaabemowin is a language that depends on word construction more than sentence construction to create meaning. Adding parts to words is necessary, and a high value is placed on an ability to repeat and rearrange words within a conversation or narrative event. Additionally, the center of construction is the verb, the action, not the subject, or the object, or the order in which they appear, but the action itself and how clearly it can be described. The result is a shared belief among speakers of Anishinaabemowin that one must "look in all directions." The directions might be cardinal points of navigation; they might also be temporal indications of past, present, and intended or certain future. The directions might also be seasons flowing across the pattern of seven pronouns to describe the world, oneself, and others. Furthermore, to speak of anything in Anishinaabemowin requires use of one the four verb forms, each with potential exponential variation based on combination with seven pronouns. All of these directions and possibilities for observation can be viewed as related to a fundamental perspective on life and language that takes shape in Jim Northrup's work as "the observation of survival." His use of language, both English and Anishinaabe, consistently represents an idea of centering oneself in order to observe, to survive by describing and understanding. In his stories his words record survival from both a personal and community perspective, first in boarding school and Vietnam, then in Fond du Lac and on the global stage as he takes his Anishinaabe way with words to an ever widening audience.

Mashkoendamo / Strength in Knowing

Northrup's most emblematic theme is one that ties him directly to his Anishinaabe literary peers. Like Erdrich, Johnston, and Vizenor, his works assert that the Anishinaabe are still here. In poetry and prose, Northrup's contribution to Anishinaabe literature is his testimony to survival. He speaks of the survival of a generation sent to boarding school, the return of a veteran from the war zone, and the survival of traditional Anishinaabe culture and values. He writes about these topics from personal experience, but it is evident from his writing that he is very aware of his audience. Although he jokingly denies it at the end of his editorial each month, he speaks for many people. He gives a voice to all the children who feel torn from their culture. He finds words for the veterans who dance when they return to the reservation, and for their families who must still find a way to dance when they don't. And he echoes all the relatives who shared their stories with him over the years as he learned to record the stories of the Anishinaabe.

Northrup's story begins with the survival of his childhood. Born during World War II on the reservation, like many other children and adults of the time he was exposed to tuberculosis. The history of the Anishinaabe includes many periods when the people fought invisible enemies carried to North America by the immigrants. Like the illness of the tribe in Erdrich's *Birchbark House*, the epidemic of Northrup's childhood affected the entire family. While his father was hospitalized, Jim and his sister Judy were sent to a sanitarium at Agwajiing. They eventually returned to the reservation, only to be sent away again after the war ended, this time several hundred miles south to a federal boarding school in Pipestone, Minnesota. Northrup alludes to this event in the poem "Ditched." He speaks of being in first grade at Pipestone Federal Boarding School, and in part of the poem recalls when he "Said '*anin*' to the / first grown up. / Got an icy blue-eyed stare / in return" (*Walking the Rez Road* 72). As the conclusion affirms, he "toughed it out" and survived, but the poem leaves a bad taste in your soul. Short, direct lines, delivered in the style of a first-grader, but with all the power of a grown man, bring the memories to life. "Ditched" is a poem about knowing who you are, but not knowing who the "others" are, or who they think you are. Too young to read or write, he first learned lessons that were physical and emotional. His record of this period in American history is important. He documents not only the inhumanity of a colonizing nation, but also the sheer will of the Anishinaabe to survive. In the poem the verb "survived" has one full line to itself, which is a powerful act in this context. It is a harsh, inhospitable environment he describes. The poem speaks only of the "first grader" and "first grown up"—which is an interesting parallel. The only adjectives in the poem's stark environment describe the "icy blue-eyed stare" of that mute "other," who may or may not be any wiser than the young child in his or her custody. Even the other students are so intent on their own survival that the only advice they have is to toughen him by offering further beatings. There is no dialogue other than the innocent, polite, Anishinaabe greeting *aniin*, which is met only with punishment. The entire encounter works as a metaphor for the conquest of the Americas. Not understanding the intentions of the colonizers, a few Native people offer greetings, only to be misunderstood and punished for their differences. In Northrup's work, historical theories become very real. The children he describes have faces, bruises, and scars. Escapees are young Anishinaabe boys and girls. Their emotions are more easily understood than vague references to nameless students of unspecified tribes. Notably, buried in this poem in English is an echo of Anishinaabe repetition and observation intent upon survival: "Got an icy blue-eyed stare," followed by "Got a beating," and again "Got an icy blue-eyed stare" followed by "Got another beating." Boarding school is not an experience exclusive to the Anishinaabe, and many poets repeat lines for effect, but it is worth noting that this poet is Anishinaabe and chose to write in a way that echoes the short, repetitive, verb-centered healing songs of former generations.

Northrup speaks again about boarding school in *The Rez Road Follies*. The description in his chapter "*Nindanawemaaganag*" (families) includes his sister Judy's presence and his descriptions of the nature that surrounded him but went mostly unnoticed by the school staff. The period is still described through the eyes of a child, but Northrup addresses some of the political questions that many Anishinaabe of the time may have had.

> I do remember wondering why just Indians went away to school. I asked Ma why the white kids didn't have to leave home when they were in the first grade. She couldn't answer; she just looked away, but not before I saw the pain in her eyes. (4)

The act of sending children away from their families, away from their language and culture, was so blatantly heinous that his mother couldn't come up with a plausible reason. Like an implied subject or a rhetorical question, the unspoken becomes the loudest, most essential sign in the equation. If you were Anishinaabe, you were less American. To survive, you had to become more American, become less Anishinaabe. In short, to live, you had to let a part of you die. Even a small child could see this killing for what it was.

In the midst of this childhood experience, Northrup begins to define himself as an Anishinaabe storyteller. He developed an Anishinaabe storyteller's interest in detail and observation.

> I would find something to look at directly in front of me. It didn't matter what it was. Outside it was a blade of grass, or a stick. Inside, I learned to study the cracks in the concrete floor or the pattern of the wood grain. I would pretend great interest in the object, poking at it with a finger. Then I would have a look at it from another angle until I was up on my knees. Finally, I would get to my feet, still looking. (*Rez Road Follies* 6)

On the surface, this is a young boy's way to trick his mind into forgetting the tears, for saving face, for getting up, and walking away with dignity. This is also an incredible insight into the art of observation. Northrup shows readers how a "place" is located in our minds as much as it is defined by cartography. When his literal home was taken from him, he began to redefine home and find comfort and safety more figuratively. By training his mind to take him away from the painful reality others were imposing on him, he could forfeit their interpretation of events and move into a place that they might not even have within their range of vision. His survival was dependent upon his ability to observe. While his foes delighted in their definition of victory, he moved to another plane by having "a look at it from another angle." Northrup continues to do this throughout his work—to offer us the view from another angle. At boarding school, in Vietnam, or back home, he always offers an alternative to the mainstream American view.

The skills of observation, first honed at boarding school, were definitely called upon in Vietnam. It was his duty to be like the Anishinaabe warriors, his grandfather remembered, the *ogichidag*, who bravely fought the Sioux. "While standing on his cut-off feet, one warrior pulled the stake up out of the ground . . . That's the kind of warrior that used to live around here" (*Walking the Rez Road* 150). In "Shrinking Away," Northrup explains: "Survived the war, but was / having trouble surviving the peace" (*Walking the Rez Road* 8). The poem continues as he describes how he later went to a psychiatrist to help him get over needing a gun to feel safe, to get over the "nightmares and daymares." Unfortunately, the sophisticated, expensive "shrink" committed suicide. It was then that Northrup realized "surviving the peace was up to me."

He plays with the word "shrink," empowering both veterans and Anishinaabe to see the representative of the dominant culture as a "shrink," a disappearing entity that, in this case, eliminates itself. Changing the noun to a verb, the "shrinking away" of the title refers to the point when Northrup's fears and dependence on the answers of the dominant culture began to lessen. This conversion of nouns to verbs and shift from one meaning to another is a typical word-building strategy in Anishinaabemowin.

Echoes of Anishinaabe language and narrative can also be found in other war stories. Just as elders tell stories of children and adults who die and return, or animals who accomplish the impossible while time stands still, Northrup describes the way time loses meaning in the face of great loss. Holding a dressing on a wounded door gunner, Luke recalls: "Something happened to time. It no longer flowed. Time slowed down and the grunts were no longer aware, but their eyes, ears and minds kept absorbing things" (*Walking the Rez Road* 13). As it does in the traditional Anishinaabe tales of Nanabozho, time becomes irrelevant. When Nanabozho sends various animals to the bottom of a vast sea, gathering dirt to create the earth, the time required to complete the task becomes unimportant. Survival can become all that matters. The animals and Nanabozho survive the great flood by trusting the smallest of their number to succeed. Northrup writes about the ability of the Anishinaabe to survive centuries of colonial abuse and of his comrades' survival of only seconds in a minefield.

In both his fiction and his memoirs, Northrup combines his distinctly Anishinaabe background with his description of life as a veteran. When he writes specifically about Vietnam, he mentions how his view of events is influenced by his background. When Hollywood star John Wayne visited An Hoa, Vietnam, and refused to walk with the grunts, it wasn't just a movie star refusing to lower himself to the level of the fighting men, it was "John Fucking Wayne, who killed / Indians by the dozens / with his movie sixshooter" (*Rez Road Follies* 176). For the Indians in the company, it was acknowledgment of the ethnic and economic divisions in America. Speaking specifically as an Anishinaabe ricer, he is aghast that so much killing would take in place in rice paddies that in times of peace are harvested by other indigenous people, people who look like his relatives. Northrup's stories of Vietnam are carefully aimed literary grenades that explode a reader's ideas about what it is to be a veteran of modern American wars, what it means to come home to a war that follows you in your mind, and what it means to be the object of attempted cultural genocide.

The poem "Walking Point" and the story "Veteran's Dance" echo one another in an interesting way. Each of the titles connects the experience of being at war with others to the experience of being at war with oneself. In this case, perspectives collide in an attempt to get over the trauma of war. The titles also connect the spirit of dance to a warrior's survival. At most powwows today, veterans play an integral part in the grand entrance of all dancers, and one of the first dances is often a dance for the veterans. Just as the warrior of his poem stepped lightly and carefully to survive, the Anishinaabe still consider the steps one takes to be important. Dancing is a spiritual, healing act. "Walking Point" is a powerful poem sketched by memories that assault the readers as if in a dream.

> The marine was walking point.
> He was hunting men
> Who were hunting him.

> . . . He sang to himself as
> his senses gathered evidence
> of his continued existence.
> His eyes saw, his ears heard
> his heart felt a numb nothing
> His mind analyzed it all as
> He studied the trail. (*Walking the Rez Road* 20)

Notice the way the verb turns, as it would in Anishinaabe, a single word moving from something one does, to something one does to others, to something done to one by others; the repeating recombination of the possibilities echoes the way words work in Anishinaabemowin. Notice too the multiple viewpoints: he sang, he saw, he heard, he felt, he analyzed, he studied. To sing and sense the world on many levels is to survive through observation, a skill that Northrup connects with his Anishinaabe culture and demonstrates in his writing.

These raw images are the exact memories that haunt the main character of "Veteran's Dance." The story recounts Lug's return to the reservation for a veteran's dance. With no real plan in mind, he watches "snaggers eight to sixty-eight cruising the river of Shinnobs" and takes in the sights, sounds, and tastes of a powwow. Later, talking to his sister, he tries to tell her what it was like in Vietnam. It is here that Northrup offers yet another way of presenting the subject. Unlike the cinematic realism of his poetry, in the context of a story, Northrup concentrates on what the experience has done to his characters. It is clear, as Lug tries to tell his sister what he has seen and felt, that the war has scarred them both.

> Lug stood up to show his sister what it was like standing in the dark. He leaned forward trying to see through the night. His hands clutched an imaginary rifle. Lug's head swiveled back and forth as he looked for the hidden rifleman. He jerked as a rifle bullet came close to him. He turned his head towards the sound.
>
> Judy watched Lug. She could feel her eyes burning and the tears building up. Using only willpower, she held the tears back. Judy somehow knew the tears would stop the flood of memories coming out of her brother. She waited. (27)

As memories flow, like blood from a wound, Judy understands this catharsis is necessary, but it clearly pains her to watch. As the story unfolds, we find that she lost her husband to the fields and paddies of Vietnam. Northrup's gentle narrative about a simple veteran's dance takes on greater significance for his characters when placed adjacent to the realism of his poem. He writes of the experience in a way that can be understood by many because it is the truth of one. He is not a soldier, he is a marine. He is not a veteran, but a survivor of the 19-year and 180-day Vietnam War. He not an American Indian, but an Anishinaabe ricer and storyteller sent to defend a nation with which his nation still has a complicated relationship and a land that has been home to his ancestors since before it was land.

Gikendaan Enji-endaayaang / Knowing Where We Live

Learning to live with the land, to survive the seasons as a steward of *Anishinaabeaki-ing* (Anishinaabe country) is another main theme of Northrup's writing. The same patterns of verb use, wordplay, repetition, and observation are found as he writes about following the seasons with respect. In the poem "Barbed Thoughts," he declares, "I am Anishinaabe . . . we thank *Manidoo* for fish, for life, as we praise our grandfathers and their generational wisdom . . . we do what has been done since there have been Anishinaabe" (*Walking the Rez Road* 136). Using the untranslatable term *manidoo*, he writes about his connections to the past and the place of the Anishinaabe. He also notes that, according to his teachings, it is essential for a traditional Anishinaabe storyteller to have tales to tell and ways to be a part of each season. "We know who we are from the seasons" (*Rez Road Follies* 37).

For the Anishinaabe, each season brings its own activities. Each action is tied to the land and reaffirms the relationship of the Anishinaabe to their northern Great Lakes homeland. This is where pantribal interpretations fail. Four seasons are essential to the cultural perspective of the Anishinaabe who harvest seasonal gifts from the Creator. Certainly, the Hopi and Inuit have different worldviews, philosophies, and relationships with the land as a result of their endless days of sun or long winter nights filled with snow. Northrup's work demonstrates how Anishinaabe culture is shaped by a relationship with the lakes, the loons, the birches, and beds of rice that are unique to the geography of their tribe.

Biboon, winter, is the primary time for storytelling among the Anishinaabe, which is why a seasoned storyteller like Northrup says:

I am glad to see the occasional snowstorm. When it falls, it covers up the old, used-up snow. I used to think snow only came in one color. As an adult, I look around and see all different colors. I see brown snow where it has been salted and sanded. I see the almost blue of the fresh new snow and the gray of snow at dusk. I like the diamonds that sparkle when the sun hits the snow just right. I am glad we have the changing seasons so I can recharge in winter. This is the storytelling time of the year. (*Rez Road Follies* 51)

He tells us how storytelling fits into the Anishinaabe calendar and how the stark shift in seasons has been incorporated into the culture. His first winter tale, presented exactly as it might be told aloud, supports an understanding of differences between tribes that existed before the colonization of America. For centuries, numerous tribes coexisted, peacefully or fitfully, but fully aware of their differences. The tale he inserts in his memoir is one he says "might explain why Shinnobs are known among other tribes as 'rabbit chokers'" (*Rez Road Follies* 51).

The story begins, "Winter was here" and tells how he passes on the tradition of *waaboozoog genagwaanindwaa*, rabbit snaring. In telling the story, he preserves the tradition of snaring, storytelling, and cultural education. Grampa and young Ezigaa set out to catch some rabbits, but they also "went out in the woods to snare our own stories" (*Rez Road Follies* 53). They study tracks, set traps, and share memories: "Just being in the woods with the little boy brought back memories" (56). By telling one of the stories central to Anishinaabe tradition within his own story, Northrup emphasizes the way narrative tradition has been attached to the seasons in Anishinaabe country. "I remembered walking behind as Grampa or some older relative broke trail for me. It felt good to be breaking trail for my grandson" (56). Northrup speaks again of survival and demonstrates how each person can be responsible for his own survival, his families' survival, and the very survival of the cultural continuum.

Later, in *The Rez Road Follies*, Northrup includes a spring story of tapping for sap. "Once again it was a learning experience for our grandchildren. They helped us gather sap from the trees. They are too young to help with the boiling so they just watched and listened when we told sugar bush stories" (72). Again, the stories are tied to the woodland seasons. The lessons elders and children share in this setting are best understood against the backdrop of their geography. Northrup's direct, autobiographical style, occasionally more dramatic, is perfect for stating the strings of facts he tosses readers. The connections to the earth are not fuzzy, indefinite secrets. They are real sensations.

When we say we are of the earth, it is true. I think there is something in the maple syrup I need. It makes sense, countless generations of my ancestors depended on the syrup for food. I will continue to make syrup every spring. (*Rez Road Follies* 75)

The first line above is one that might be found in any modern American's imagination of how Native Americans relate to their surroundings. It is the very specific, very Anishinaabe, second line that crystallizes the philosophy. More than just saying "we are of the earth," Northrup describes how he needs the sweet sap of the sugar maples in spring. To love something from afar, and to need to drink it, are two entirely different relationships. His stories give shape and specificity to the distinctly Anishinaabe relationship with the land.

Each season is part of the puzzle, but Northrup writes most about *dagwaaging*, or fall, the season of the *manoomin* harvest.

According to the old stories, the Anishinaabe would migrate west until they came to a place where food grows on the water. . . . It feels right to go out on the lakes to gather our share of the harvest. Ricing is hard work but we feel connected to the old days, the old ways when doing it. (*Rez Road Follies* 38)

It is important to note that he says "we feel connected to the old days" in the present tense. The past is not being relived as a separate time. It is part of the present. There is no illusion of escape to the past or attempt to re-create it. Ricing can be done by Anishinaabe in aluminum canoes, wearing camouflage from Wal-Mart, just as well as it was once done by Anishinaabe in birchbark canoes, wearing buckskin. Northrup shows how the Anishinaabe continue to value an understanding of nature as interconnected with human life. His poem "*Mahnoomin*" is an eloquent lesson in why ricing continues to be an Anishinaabe art that remains key to the survival of the tribe.

Tobacco swirled in the lake
as we offered our thanks.
The calm water welcomed us,
rice heads nodded in agreement.
Ricing again, *miigwetch Manidoo*.
The cedar caressed the heads
ripe rice came along to join us

in many meals this winter.
The rice bearded up.
We saw the wind move across the lake,
an eagle, a couple of coots,
the sun smiled everywhere.
Relatives came together
talk of other lakes, other seasons
fingers stripping rice while
laughing, gossiping, remembering.
It's easy to feel a part of
the generations that have
riced here before.
It felt good to get on the lake.
It felt better getting off
carrying a canoe load of food
and centuries of memories. (*Walking the Rez Road* 98)

Scientific and anthropological details are embedded in the poem. The rice is only harvested when the *ogimaa-manoomin* says the beards are ready. Communities care for the rice and pay attention to its cycle so that it will be there for generations to come.

What Northrup does in this poem that echoes Anishinaabemowin is related to the two classes of nouns. In Anishinaabemowin nouns are either animate or inanimate, with the difference being the way a speaker can talk about what they do. Wind moving across the lake would require a different verb in Anishinaabe, although it sounds fine imagined as animate or inanimate in English. However, a number of "characters" act in ways that are not typical English usage: water welcomes, cedar caresses, sun smiles. Very poetic, very Anishinaabe. The use and manipulation of these classes is part habit, part intent. Many of the nouns are typically classified one way or the other, but one of the most difficult concepts for students of Anishinaabemowin to grasp is the loose nature of these categories. As with many other concepts in Anishinaabe culture, the paradigm allows for slippage and shifts in identity. There is always the possibility that something normally seen one way will appear different the next day, and therefore need to be discussed in a new way. Fluent elders do this all the time, especially when telling stories. Here in this poem, Northrup speaks in English, which has no animacy applied to nouns.

As a student of the language he knows tobacco, the sun, and cedar are naturally animate in Anishinaabemowin. As a poet, he pulls the water and rice into the poem as animate nouns. In his story "the rice nodded," "bearded up," and "came along to join us." Northrup paints a picture of a ceremony, a celebration of the Anishinaabe relationship with nature. Certainly the *manoomin* itself is tangible and valuable as sustenance, but it becomes much more than a grain. The act of finding it, recognizing it, and knowing to thank *Manidoo* with an offering of tobacco is key to actually ricing. Writing about the rice in an Anishinaabe way, Northrup offers poetic support for efforts against genetic modification of wild rice. The "Keep It Wild" campaign led by Minnesota's Anishinaabeg works to remind those who are not Anishinaabe of the impact of industrial agriculture. As Winona LaDuke has said, "In the end this rice tastes like a lake, and that taste can't be replaced" (LaDuke, "Maps, Genes and Patents"). Northrup's subtle message is the same; far more than simply a love of nature, he asks readers to read the environment in an Anishinaabe way, to consider the possible relationships with the landscape and acknowledge the way those complex relationships lead to sustainability, to that taste of the lake. As the poem says, "it's easy to feel a part of the generations that have riced here before." Ricers leave carrying a "century of memories" as lightly as the wind moves across the lake or the sun smiles on the day. Northrup speaks of ricing as only an Anishinaabe ricer could.

The same poem has also appeared in the anthology *Voice on the Water: Great Lakes Native America Now* (Chaillier and Tavernini). In that collection it appears in two languages so that all of the animacy can be fully enjoyed and a few untranslatable concepts can be seen. "Talk of other lakes, other seasons" becomes *dibaajimonid gaa ezhiwebag zaaga'iganag*, which makes a more explicit connection to *dibaajimo*, the verb for storytelling. Best of all, "carrying a canoe load of food" literally becomes *miijim oondoondanid jiimaaning*, which invites thoughts of the way *jiimaa* can mean "canoe" or "kiss."

Northrup also takes time to let readers know not all is serious with ricing season. Ricing becomes a reason for Luke and Almost Warmwater to be released from jail on their own recognizance (*Walking the Rez Road* 102). Ricing season sparks memories of an old joke about traders who pay by the pound for rice, and along with traditional wild rice, get "half a muskrat house, wet blue jeans, and some rocks with zero nutritional value" at the bottom of at least one bag (96). Cognizant of his multiple audiences, in *The Rez Road Follies* Northrup discusses a variation of the ricing sale joke.

One of my favorites is the time some people sold a rice buyer something other than wild rice. They added a couple of big rocks to increase the weight of the rice sacks. The next day, the rice buyer came back and sold the people some groceries. The people found the rocks in their flour. (42)

As Northrup explains, "the power of the story comes from our reaction to it" (42). He gives us six ways to read the story. It could be a fable with a moral; a lesson in what won't fool the white man; a simple ricing memory; an old familiar joke; a business recommendation; or a memory passed down by a relative who might have been there in the 1930s when it supposedly happened.

The *waawiyeyaa*, or circle, of the seasons and the attention it must be paid is referenced throughout Northrup's writing. He teaches that things are done best at the right time. Unlike the larger American culture, where all fruits are on sale all year, and where people never ask where fruits or people come from, Northrup teaches the universal lesson of time and the seasons from an Anishinaabe perspective. Winter is a quiet time for resting, reviving, and telling stories. Occasionally, trips are made into the snowy woods to set a trap line to snare rabbits. When the world wakes up in spring, it is time for spearing and sugar bush. Summer is a time for powwows and basket making. Autumn is time for ricing. Many stories begin by stating the season. This, according to Northrup, is the natural way to begin almost any tale.

Seasons are questions and answers, patterns and surprises. Traditional Anishinaabeg life follows nature's changing cycles. From harvest to hibernation, sweet spring, to summer wandering. We know who we are from the seasons. When living with the seasons, we don't get worried about time as measured by the clock. (*Rez Road Follies* 37)

Except for the culturally specific references to harvesting *manoomin* and gathering *ziinzibaakwadwaabo*, Northrup could be waxing eloquent along the shores of Walden Pond.

Like other Anishinaabe authors, Northrup explains how he likes to measure time, saying, "time is measured by the sun, not quartz on the wrist" (*Walking the Rez Road* 90). Certainly, he arrives on time to meetings, book signings, and classes in the wider world, but he shares an alternative idea of time that he explains still has relevancy. He begins his poem "*Weegwas*" with the line, "Time to gather bark, another gift from the Creator" (*Walking the Rez Road* 78). Time, counted as one of the many gifts from the Creator, cannot be bought or sold. Certainly many tribes have similar, cyclical approaches to time. What Northrup makes clear, however, is exactly how one particular tribe, the Anishinaabe, lives with the seasons and has adapted to their surroundings. Through his description of the Anishinaabe worldview, the philosophy of the Anishinaabe becomes evident. There are a great many things man cannot control, and therefore, it is perhaps best for man to simply control himself. Starting with his emphasis on the unalterable gifts from the Creator, and including his scorn for modern American holidays, Northrup, like some of Erdrich's characters, offers views alternative to those held by the dominant culture.

Northrup offers a clear view of how Anishinaabe families and communities continue to live within the northern woodlands of the Great Lakes region. Each of his books includes mention of the "rez" in the title. The notion of home and place is central to his writing. He wants readers to see what he and his relatives have seen along the "rez road." He wants readers to note the fact that the Anishinaabe are still walking—on narrow dirt footpaths lined with agates, on paved Sawyer streets surrounded by jack pines; on highways that wind from Minnesota's north shore of Lake Superior to the Twin Cities; and on runways that have taken them everywhere from Vietnam to Scotland.

According to Northrup, part of cultural continuity, cultural survival, is knowing the history and stories of the land. These are the issues that inspire anger when argued and misunderstood. In the poem "1854–1988," Northrup explicitly states that the Anishinaabe right to live with the land cannot be sold. Even those Anishinaabe who choose to be lured by money are scorned. The faceless "State" is the ultimate, unnamable "other." And the bottom line is defined as the bottom line of a document; a living man's last offer; an outline of the graves that will embrace those who failed to understand the essential. The poem begins, "We told them not to sell, but *boochigoo* / They had to do it anyway. / The bottom line is the bottom line" (*Walking the Rez Road* 48). Not all Anishinaabeg agree and not all Anishinaabeg care, but as the end of the poem points out,

Anishinaabe have survived
Missionaries and miners,
Timber barons and trappers,
We'll survive the bureaucrats

And policy makers.
Bury the sellouts deep, their
Grandchildren will want to
piss on their graves.
The bottom line is the bottom line. (*Walking the Rez Road* 148)

From the first *boochigoo* to the repetitive refrain and play of words throughout, the poem relies in part on recognizable Anishinaabe language and narrative to make its point. Northrup makes clear he is not speaking for all Anishinaabeg; in fact he is speaking directly to other members of his own community. It is as important to diversify national identities as it is to have them. Not every Anishinaabe person will choose to use the linguistic structures that are available; not everyone will have the same connection to the environment or knowledge of history. It is the way these commonalities form a recognizable whole, and the way they are also still a web with space for differences that is worthy of examination. Northrup's "bottom line" is the difference between the traditional Anishinaabe perspective and capitalist Anishinaabe perspective; between the Minnesota Chippewa and the State of Minnesota; between Native and non-Native Americans; between poets and politicians . . . the list could go on, and in each instance, Northrup will have a view that is his own, but one that shaped by the life he has inherited, the language he has heard and learned, and the stories he creates for this and the next generation.

One of the stories he often shares is about the importance of clearing your mind and moving on. To do this, he once moved into a tipi. "Grandpa called it *bajeeshkaogan* and knew all about it before I was born." The word for tipi in Anishinaabemowin means something pointed, and it can carry "your eyes, thoughts and prayers to the sky and beyond" (*Walking the Rez Road* 60). Northrup includes the Anishinaabe word and uses it as both an adjective and verb. The teepee is pointed and it points. The Anishinaabe word also explains the Anishinaabe habit of never pointing at someone with your index finger. You will see people use a nod of the head, a quick pursing of the lips in a particular direction, but never use of something actually "pointed." *Gegwa bajiishkigawke*, "Don't point," in many dialects also means "Don't chop." Although many Anishinaabe no longer use the word this way, most will still avoid pointing directly at one another. In this poem Northrup references tribal diversity by using a tipi, which is a design borrowed from the Dakota, rather than a more traditional Anishinaabe wigwam. But this is the kind of intercultural competency that existed for centuries as nations altered boundaries, married across tribal lines and learned from one another. Living in the tipi, he found a way to connect the Anishinaabe past and present. "Sitting around a fire eating / freshly roasted meat / it could have been yesterday / or eons ago" (61). He found a way to carry his identity with him from the reservation to the city. "The smell of wood smoke / clings to me when I have to / go to the city, it is a / reminder of where I come from / and where I am going" (62). He concludes with a positive thought, a gift to all readers. "How many men have stood / where I stand, thinking / what a fine place to live" (62).

Northrup's focus on survival starts with his personal perspective and radiates out to include family, friends, the broader Anishinaabe community, and then the circles of people outside the definition of Anishinaabe.

> Most people know who they are because of their parents and grandparents. Some might even know who their great-grandparents are. In our family oral history, I can tell you who my relatives are going back to about 1740, when Mikinaak, my great-great-great-great-great-great grandfather, was living his life here with the seasons. I teach my children so they will have something to teach their children. (*Rez Road Follies* 132)

By working to keep the stories in his circles alive, he sets an example for members of any community. His main point is that speech and story are methods of sanity and survival.

Northrup shows how dialect and word choice reflect the way we maintain our relationships. This is true in any community, but what Northrup does is show how it works in his world. There are several words that still circulate among Anishinaabe, even those who no longer speak Anishinaabemowin. They are words that say more than is possible in English and allow people to connect in ways not easy in the dominant culture. For example, the word *niij* means friend, but is also a prefix that connects people, as in *niijinini* (my fellow man) or *niijibimaadizijig* (my fellow ones moving along living). The word appears in Northrup's fiction when Ben Looking Back says, "*Boozhoo neej*, did I wake you up?" (*Walking the Rez Road* 155). Only by reference to the glossary on page 6 would a reader who is not Anishinaabe know the phrase means "Hello, friend." Only an Anishinaabemowin speaker would recognize the word as one used only by men. However, this same example also relates to the second reason Northrup inserts Anishinaabemowin into his texts. Sometimes there simply is no easy English equivalent. A *niij* is only male. It would sound awkward to say "Hello, my male friend," "Hello, brother," or "Hello, buddy," but *"boozhoo neej"* is perfect. It's likely that Ben did wake up his friend, or is in the process of doing so. The *niij* adds a bit of apology and camaraderie to the act. One of the comments critics often make about Northrup's work is that it is wonderfully realistic. Numerous Native American stereotypes exist: the pantribal view of missionaries and anthropologists; the demeaning caricatures of Hollywood; the "new age" shaman stereotypes. Northrup's portrayals of modern life as a member of one particular tribe are wonderfully redolent in all the idiosyncratic behaviors of real Anishinaabe people and contrast sharply with idealized, poorly defined images. Translation: the men care about each other and need a way to show it that is culturally acceptable.

One of the most common words heard among relatives is the particle *gaawiin*. In some homes it is the last bit of language to leave. As only one word, and only half of the grammar required to actually say something is not happening, it does not really represent linguistic continuity on its own, but it is one of the first and most common words used in Anishinaabe-English conversations. In *Walking the Rez Road*, the word *gaawiin* is used often by Luke Warmwater and other characters. In most cases, the word is exchanged only by members of the Anishinaabe community and, in addition, often denotes a stronger negative than just a simple "no." In the story "Goose Goose" it is used when Louie Wise Owl asserts he can indeed return to Bob's Tavern. Luke Warmwater assumed he was still barred from there for fighting, to which Lou replies, *"gaawiin*, I can drink there again" (*Walking the Rez Road* 107). It is used a page later when Dunkin Black Kettle shows up and the friends ask if winter on Perch Lake has frozen him out yet. *"Gaawiin*, I've survived over forty of these winters. I just wanted to see people again" (108). The word also slips into the story "Bingo Binge" when Luke asks his cousin, Sarge, if he is having any luck. Sarge replies, *"gaawiin*, just donating tonight" (127). Later he asks if his wife was the one "hollering bingo" in the back of the hall. She replies, *"gaawiin*, that was Nita, she hit on the picture frame" (127). In these instances *gaawiin* performs three distinctly different functions. It serves as a way for members of the Anishinaabe community to identify one another and recognize their shared culture. It is also a way to answer a question in a way that only friends and relatives can understand. Finally, it replaces the superlative English adverbs writers might choose to indicate strong emotions attached to the reply. Northrup simply writes, "he said," "he replied," or nothing at all. But, in each case, when *gaawiin* is used, the reply is actually emphatic. Put plainly, *gaawiin* is a darn good word to haul out when you need a strong negative that might not be intended for everyone in the room, or bar, as the case may be.

Gikenmaagwaa / Knowing Others

As mentioned during the discussion of Louise Erdrich's work, part of cultural survival is an ability to discern and describe the other. To do this in his writing, Northrup often relies on Anishinaabe words and wordplay. The entire Warmwater family, for example, admits they like to "watch *chimooks* on the tube" (*Walking the Rez Road* 166). I suppose this is the equivalent of all the children and anthropologists over the years who constructed and admired dioramas. *Chimooks* is slang for *Chimookomaan*, American, a term derived from early observations that Americans as enemies carried long knives on their bayonets or at their sides. Nowadays, most Americans are not enemies in combat, and few actually have large knives with them as they go through the day. Northrup knows this is a stereotype and he uses it as a way to bring up racism on both sides of the fence. As he says, "racism is not easy to discuss."

> I've been called a racist myself. I write occasionally for area newspapers. Many places in my writings, I use the term "white man." Someone who lives near the rez wrote to accuse me of being racist. I was going to ignore it but decided to explore the issue in my column. I tried to think of some alternatives to "white man." How about *gichimookomaan*, our word for the Americans encountered by our ancestors? In our language it means big knife. When they first met us, these colonial Americans had swords and bayonets. But who would want to be known as a "big knifer?" What about Caucasian? Call them Cauky for short? Maybe a term like European would work, but I'm not sure the pale-skinned Irish or Scots ever wanted to be part of Europe at all. I got it, we'll call you Invaderman. I'm at a loss here but am taking suggestions. (*Rez Road Follies* 122)

Anishinaabe is another word Northrup interrogates. As noted previously, it is the correct term for the Anishinaabe-speaking people who live in the Great Lakes region. It means "first people" and is the name chosen and used originally by the people themselves. It is used by the Ojibwe, Potawatomi, and Odawa in most areas.

It is a testament to modern Anishinaabe people that the word is beginning to be the correct and recognized term for the affiliated tribes. Northrup's vernacular abbreviation, *Shinnob*, further emphasizes the use of the word that has come to include at least this one slang derivation.

At the heart of racism is misunderstanding, and Northrup often tries to use Anishinaabe paradigms to make sense of American traditions. For example, he notes how commercial the holidays have become, explaining that in his house there is no tree. "We leave them outside where they continue to grow" (*Rez Road Follies* 68). He goes on to say the frenzy of shopping is completely ignored. "When we want to give a gift, we just do it regardless of the season. It is a year-round activity for us" (69). He says, "I am still confused about who we should be honoring at this time of year—Santa Claus or Christ" (69). Easter is even more indecipherable. Having attended Christian boarding schools, he notes that he is well aware of the purported reason for the season. He remains confused, however, because

> It all begins with a pre-Easter sale in the retail stores. An unusual rabbit lays and delivers paste-colored chicken eggs. The *wabooz* also lays chocolate eggs. The gender of this strange critter is never mentioned. Green plastic grass is part of it somewhere. The kids are teased by hiding the food. They look for and collect the bunny's leavings. Each year the pastel-colored eggs are rolled down the White House lawn. (*Rez Road Follies* 69)

Put that way, it is clear the American tradition of marking the seasons with holidays and sales can be confusing, especially to people whose cultural hero, Nanabozho, can shift his shape into a rabbit. Northrup points out that very little logic remains once the holiday has been spun through the melting pot and made secular enough for common consumption. This is exactly what most Indians would say about "The Song of Hiawatha." Northrup illustrates how general assumptions about a wide range of people and behavior can leave the observer understanding very little about any of the people counted as part of the culture.

Readers learn from Northrup's observations of America how strange it feels to be misunderstood, mocked, and considered illogical, which is exactly the way many missionaries, explorers, and early politicians treated the Anishinaabe and other tribes. In the story "Looking with Ben," Ben Looking Back tells his cousin, Luke Warmwater, about his visit to the Smithsonian Institution, which has a collection of Indian remains. There are "over eighteen thousand bodies there, all tribes" (*Walking the Rez Road* 158). Since the Smithsonian collects Indians, Ben decides to chip off pieces of brick from the walls of the "castle-looking" building and bring it back to Luke. He jokes that if they take enough chunks, one day, they could build their own museum. The story pokes fun of the notion that museums are always right and able at all to contain the true essence of what they "collect." Once again, Northrup questions the dominant view of how people and ideas can be owned.

Inside the museum, Ben sees a group of dioramas in the midst of being changed and decides to offer his own interpretation. He steps over the velvet rope and displays himself with a sign reading "Contemporary Chippewa." He charges tourists to take pictures of him. He also has a bit of fun by claiming to be "half Chippewa and half Ojibway." Then, just to really test their credulity, he tells them he is Sioux and Comanche (*Walking the Rez Road* 159). The story is humorous, but the message is clear. Tribal distinctions are important to the members of various nations, but they are something most tourists will not even notice.

The processes of observing and being observed have always contributed to the dynamic of the relationship between indigenous cultures and arriving immigrants. Northrup refers frequently to the way an ability to observe relates to survival. First, a community must see that it is being watched, and then it must find ways to watch when others are not looking. According to Northrup, the power lies in the ability to watch out for yourself, as well as learn how to interpret the acts of others. This is something all children come to realize, but when applied to the circumstance of an entire community attempting to understand another, it does not always meet with success. He points out that few of the visitors to his reservation realize they are not only learning how to live life with the seasons on the rez, they are demonstrating how to be unaware of nature and live in the city. Perhaps he is influenced by his years as a marine, but often Northrup's characters survive by seeing without being seen. This is how Hary escapes from the white judicial system long enough to spend an afternoon with his uncle (*Walking the Rez Road* 119). This is also what Ben Looking Back did when he watched the reaction of tourists at the Smithsonian. Northrup himself observes the world that surrounds him. He watches it, steps into it on occasion, but for the most part, he is content to be in a primarily Anishinaabe world. But he reminds readers, "We have TV, that window to America, we see you, you don't see us" (*Walking the Rez Road* 104).

Northrup warns that bloodlines and fluency cannot predict a person's perspective. In the short story "Jabbing and Jabbering," two groups of Anishinaabe are described quite differently. Tuna, Luke, and Sonny sit carving rice knockers, looking ahead to the year's rice harvest:

> The warm southerly breeze was shrinking the remaining snow. The crows were back; they could hear them cawing in the distance. It felt good to be sitting in the warm sun after the usual long, cold winter. Sugarbush was over so they were getting ready for ricing. There is always something to do to prepare for the next season, Tuna thought. (*Walking the Rez Road* 138)

A group of men with opposed opinions are on the same rez not far away:

> Ten miles east of the carvers, five other Shinnobs were sitting at shiny conference table. It was the regular Tuesday morning meeting of the reservation Business Committee. The Chairman was sitting at the head of the table. He was sipping hot coffee. . . . The thick turquoise chunks on the watchband caught the morning sun. (*Walking the Rez Road* 138)

These are the men Northrup accuses of selling the children's future. Sitting at their "shiny conference table," they represent the greed of modern society. With "thick turquoise chunks," not in any way indigenous to the Anishinaabe, they perpetuate the pantribal stereotype of the American Indian. Northrup demonstrates the importance of diversity for survival, both among the Anishinaabe and among the nations. Telling stories about the life of a "Shinnob" on the rez, he makes the point that tribal distinctions have not been erased. And in his opinion, these cultural distinctions are no less important than those he was asked to risk his life for in Vietnam.

To assure that at least some Anishinaabe maintain and renew old ways of thinking, Northrup uses Anishinaabe words, wordplay, and narrative patterns when writing books predominantly in English. He has infinite patience with both the students and the children in his own community and with curious members from other cultures. To ensure that the lessons about the connection between language and culture are clear, in *The Rez Road Follies* several short stories are written entirely in Anishinaabemowin, and *Anishinaabe Syndicated* contains several jokes and numerous everyday phrases. For Anishinaabe readers, these paragraphs are reminders, or teachers, but Northrup recognizes that most of his readers do not speak the language. He writes in Anishinaabemowin "to preserve the language" and "to show how expressive, how complex the language can be" (*Rez Road Follies* 51). He proceeds to tell the story in English, then tells the same story in Anishinaabemowin. The translation is not intended to be exact, but he does provide short definitions for many of the words used so that readers can follow the Anishinaabemowin version better. He certainly accomplishes his goal of demonstrating the range of complexity of the language. "Winter was here and my grandson and I went out in the woods to see if we could choke some rabbits" becomes *Biboon. Ninoozhishenh miinaawaa gayeniin nindizhaamin iwidi megwayaak nandawaabamangwaa waaboozoog genagwaanindwaa* (*Rez Road Follies* 51). Later, in a story about sugar bush time, when maple syrup is gathered, sentences undergo similar transformations. "As I travel around Indian country, I see more and more Indian people going to the sugar bush" becomes *Babaa-izhaayaan Anishinaabeg odenawitoowaad, niwaabamaag eshkam nawaj niibowa Anishinaabeg izhaawaad iwidi iskigamizigaaning* (*Rez Road Follies* 70). The Anishinaabemowin versions are close equivalents but contain some information that the English do not. *Biboon*, for example, is a lovely way to begin the story of a grandfather and his grandson. It not only means winter, it connotes age as well. In Anishinaabemowin, the way to ask "How old are you?" is *Aanii ezhi-boonigiziyin*, literally "How wintery are you?" The answer, *Ingodwak nd'ensa boonigiz*, would be like saying, "I am a count of 100 winters." Nowhere in the question or the answer is the winter ever turned back into a noun, nor does the adjective *gete* (old) ever come into play. The cycle to count is the survival of seasons, and to do so in Anishinaabe sounds a bit like becoming the season, which is a familiar sensation to anyone native to the Great Lakes.

Readers could learn *bangi* (a little) Anishinaabemowin reading Northrup's work, but more likely, they will discover a new way to think about and talk about the world they share with him. Due to efforts of language leaders like Northrup, Anishinaabemowin is slowly gaining ground, but the possibility of losing the language is very real. Northrup addresses the issue in several of his poems. "Ditched" and "Lifetime of Sad" capture the pain of losing Anishinaabemowin. One poem describes the day a young boy realizes he cannot speak the language of his home, and the other records the memories of a grown woman who has "pride in her language, but no one to talk to" (*Walking the Rez Road* 84). At the other end of the spectrum are his poems about *weegwas* and *manoomin* and the way they fit into the life of at least one contemporary Anishinaabe writer.

Jim Northrup continues to practice what he preaches. He lives a life that ensures at least some of the Anishinaabe traditions are being carried into the future. He freely shares all the wisdom of survival he has earned. He is one "Shinnob" changing the perception problems of the past.

> As long as people see us as barely human, nearly extinct relics not worthy of a proper burial, we have a problem. Racism could be defined as a serious image problem. In my lifetime, I have dedicated a lot of hours to changing the perception of us. I am one of the modern Anishinaabe men, the contemporary Chippewa, the omnifarious Ojibwe, the savvy Shinnob. I'll tell you one thing we are not. We are not at the end of the trail. (*Rez Road Follies* 116)

By projecting a sharper image of one distinct culture, Northrup not only offers readers ways to understand Native American life but also hear the language of the Anishinaabe and view the world through the patterns of Anishinaabe narrative. Readers adopting Northrup's Anishinaabe perspective see the United States in a critical light not otherwise available to them. In the 1990s, the Minnesota Department of Energy made a proposal to store nuclear waste in the Great Lakes area "because the geological formations were ideal." Writing about the idea, Northrup does not wax poetic, nor does he invoke the image of a Native American romance with nature. He makes it clear that everyone concerned about the continuity of his or her tribe, be they Anishinaabe, Irish, or Sudanese, could make only one logical choice:

> We don't have to worry about damaging the earth, air, and water. The earth will still be here if we poison ourselves out of existence. The wind doesn't care if it is blowing radioactive dust. The rivers will flow even if they are glowing, even if there is no one here to see them. It is not too far from casks to caskets. (*Walking the Rez Road* 233)

By knowing who he is, and standing at the center of his own culture, Northrup maintains he is able to see the world and his place in it more clearly. Northrup gives readers the truth about Anishinaabe life as he has seen it thus far. He shares his solid sense of being a part of, not owner of, his surroundings. He shares his ability to see beyond some of the myths marketed in America, his lifesaving sense of observation, and his belief that life does not begin or end with birth and death, but instead connects us to all the lives that come before and after. As he says in his poem "End of the Beginning," "everything happens in cycles" (*Walking the Rez Road* 68).

CHAPTER FIVE

Giizhigomaadiziwin: Universal Life in the Writing of Basil Johnston

> Words are but sounds, stories a series of sounds, articulated they pass into space and echo into eternity as messages to be heard only by the spirits. For a person to see or to perceive the inner meanings of sounds is a gift. For a word to reveal its souls and spirit and heart is nothing short of revelation.
>
> —Johnston, *Anishinaubae Thesaurus*

Speaking of a time when Anishinaabemowin was the primary language of the Great Lakes and stories were the best and only means of transferring them from one generation to the next, Basil Johnston has said that "words and stories carried meanings and teachings drawn from Mother Earth and meant to instruct, entertain, and guide along the Path of Life" (*Stories* 2). Johnston's reverence for the word could be considered religious, aboriginal, ancient, or modern. His stories can be read from many angles, but when they are examined as part of the Anishinaabe literary canon, they are foundational and informative. In his literature he explores an Anishinaabe way of being in the world. Connected to a language based on action, reinvention, and constant imaginative redefinition, Anishinaabe stories offer a view of life as conscious change. Through the words he chooses and the stories he tells, Johnston explores the way an Anishinaabe worldview teaches us how to change while staying the same; how to connect multiple times, places, and ways of being with a self that is centered and observant.

As Johnston himself often says before he begins, all of this would be much easier to convey in Anishinaabemowin. The word he offers for what might be considered Anishinaabe philosophy is *kiki-inoomgugaewin*. In English he explains this word represents "what men and women teach" to "prepare the minds of their youth to look for and to see relationships between insects, birds, animals, fish, the land and the seasons; their spirits to reach out to the spirits and the Spirit World; their hearts to take up compassion, selflessness, courage, love, respect, honesty, tenacity and all their kindred attributes; and their inner senses to perceive things that are beyond the reach of their physical senses" (*Stories* 1). He doesn't say "knowledge," which is the translation most dictionaries offer, but the way he sets the word on the page says a great deal. *Kiki-inoomgugaewin* contains *kiki*, which connects with *maashkiki* (medicine) and *aki* (earth). Reading across the syllables, it also contains *kino* or *kina* (everything), and at its core is *kinomaage*, which is the verb for "teach," a word related to *gikendaan* (to know) and *kinowaabmaa* (to observe). The *win* ending is a removable part often used in Anishinaabemowin to turn a verb into a noun. All of this is a longer, less direct way of saying the words of stories are medicine of the earth, information about all that can be observed, parts of universal understanding that are essential for living according to the Anishinaabe people. This has been Basil Johnston's lifelong message. Sometimes with great seriousness and sometimes with sneaky humor, Johnston has worked not only to urge that the Anishinaabe regain use of their language and traditions, but also that these ways of understanding be understood as powerful, still relevant, and connected to their place of origin. When he advises modern Anishinaabe to "take up again their ancient way of believing," he is not asking them to live in an idealized past; he is asking them, and anyone who wishes to understand the culture, to live with more awareness of both the past and present. Through his dedication to the language and history of narrative, in his explanations of the universe, and in his focus on the Anishinaabe concept of *minobimaadizi* (living a good life) he teaches "*kiki-inoomgugaewin*."

Gaa Ezhi-bimaadizid / Life So Far

Johnston is known throughout Anishinaabe country as a linguist, lecturer, storyteller, and speaker of Anishinaabemowin. A member of the Cape Croker First Nations Reserve in Ontario, he was born in 1929 in Wasauksing First Nation (formerly Parry Island First Nation), which is an Ojibwe, Odawa, and Potawatomi First Nation located near Parry Sound, Ontario, Canada. When he was ten, an Indian agent came to take him from his mother's single-parent home. This fate was common for children of his generation. Fathers were often forced off the reservation because of poor economic conditions, and Indian agents took children from their mothers because, in their opinion, children should not live in a "broken home." Both Johnston and his younger sister were placed in Jesuit boarding schools in northern Ontario. In his memoirs Johnston records his years at St. Peter Claver's School. After high school, Johnston studied history and English at Loyola College in Montreal, and then attended a teacher's college.

Recording and perpetuating the stories and language of the Anishinaabe is his life's work. Johnston's career as an author is one of many links in the chain of reclamation begun in the 1970s. His stories, set in a number of different communities, are familiar from Ontario to Minnesota. A mermaid, "scaled from the waist down," is the one "they used to see over at Little Wikwemikong on Manitoulin Island" (*Tales of the Anishinaubaek* 27). He tells of a woman at Cape Croker in Georgian Bay "who never failed to offer tobacco when it thundered" (*Tales of the Anishinaubaek* 43). In his book *The Bear-Walker*, an old man has visions of "the place before Toronto was there" (62). Another story takes place quite far from Johnston's home, but still Anishinaabe country, in Mille Lacs, Minnesota (*Manitous* 231). By noting the origin of each story, he follows Anishinaabe storytelling protocol and makes clear the wide range of real communities where these stories still circulate. Unlike Erdrich, who centers her fiction on one imagined place that could be anywhere, or Jim Northrup, who writes about the world from his place on one reservation, Johnston has worked to collect words and stories from many communities.

Johnston lived 35 years of his life in Willowdale and Richmond Hill, north of Toronto, where he worked. He notes, however, that "to live in a city was a question of expedience, not choice. I had to live and work somewhere. The glamour and the glitz, the zip and the schmaltz did not appeal to me; I much preferred the serenity and the beauty of my village and its people" (Johnston, Letter). In recent years he says he has been "teaching language and heritage in the community . . . to lure Nanaboozo back into our midst" (Letter). His many publications, vast knowledge of Anishinaabe narratives, and use of Anishinaabemowin show that Johnston has been "luring Nanaboozo" for many years.

Gaa Ezhibii'iged / Writing So Far

Johnston began publishing his writing in 1976. His books mix mythical narratives, history, memoir, and lessons in the language. Looking back to the beginning of his career, he recalls:

> Like many other North American Indian people, I became drawn even more closely into North American affairs, especially into the cultural and educational spheres, by the continentwide American Indian awakening and rediscovery of the "Indian" in the early 1960s. (*Manitous* xii)

Johnston has put into print both the serious *aadizokaanag*, the teaching stories that were originally reserved for winter times, and the *dibaajimowinan* that reflect the culture in less ceremonial, but equally important ways.

His first book, *Ojibway Heritage*, published in 1976, was intended to furnish students and their teachers "with what they could not derive from the available texts. . . . I was invited to tell stories to native and non-native audiences alike. Following these presentations I was frequently asked to explain the meaning of the stories and the *manitous*" (*Manitous* xxii). In 1982, he published *Ojibway Ceremonies* to continue his explanation. Reviewing the book, Carol Miller said, "much has been written about the sacredness of language among Native American people, but here Johnston provides an uncommonly concrete and succinct explanation of the logic which accounts for the reverence" (2). In *Ojibway Ceremonies*, Johnston says:

> I learned that the words in our tribal language had meanings more fundamental than the primary ones that were commonly and readily understood. To know this character of words is crucial in understanding how the tribe perceived and expressed what they saw, heard, felt, tasted, and smelled in the world, what they thought and how they felt about the world of ideas. (6)

Although he focuses on only a few ceremonies and sometimes writes with a tone that suggests little variation is acceptable, his work has been praised by members of the Anishinaabe community for careful and respectful representation of spiritual events. Keewaydinoquay Peschel wrote, "This is the first time I have seen *mide* information publicly printed by a native author. No one could accuse Mr. Johnston of excesses. The Anishinaubeg have a great diplomat in this man" (43).

In 1995, Johnston published *Manitous*, which began to thread these traditional tales and ceremonies together for readers, filling in gaps and making connections between stories. He dedicated *Manitous* to "the recovery of the Anishinaabe language and the restoration of spiritual and cultural traditions in Anishinaabe family and community life" because, as he explains, the *manidoog* are central to the Anishinaabe culture.

> Stories about the *manitous* allow native people to understand their cultural and spiritual heritage and enable them to see the worth and relevance of their ideas, institutions, perceptions, and values. Once they see the worth and relevance of their heritage, they may be inspired to restore it in their lives. Perhaps other people will find worth in our understandings as well. (xiii)

In *Manitous*, Johnston begins with the importance of one Creator, *Gichi Manidoo*, who represents the greatest power and mystery. He takes time to ensure that every possible nuance of the concept is translated. He then introduces other *manidoog* "according to the sequence in which they appeared and performed services in the development and growth of the nations" (xiii). These heroes, especially Nanabozho, represent larger-than-life goals and ideals combined with human weakness and limitations. Johnston's desire to elaborate and redefine the stories of the Anishinaabe emphasizes the importance of understanding each tribe in detail as part of the larger indigenous whole. What Johnston does with his book *Manitous* is to invite one group to remember a shared heritage. As he introduces the myriad of *manidoog* that surround the central *Gichi Manidoo*, he readjusts the lens through which the Anishinaabe have been viewed.

At the same time he was beginning to record many of the important teachings in the 1970s, Johnston was also gathering the stories elders still told in Anishinaabemowin, the memories, fables, and humor of long ago and recent times. He described his first collection of stories, *Ojibway Tales*, as "a kind of history although it is not intended to be such . . . it is intended primarily as an amusing account of Indian-white man relationships" (9). In it, he tells the stories of the imaginary Moose Meat Point Reserve, a place "like many other Indian reserves; neither prosperous nor severely impoverished; westernized in outward appearance but in soul and spirit very much still Ojibway" (7). He describes numerous attempts made over time to change the people of Moose Meat Point. Education, integration, assimilation, grants, and government programs had little effect.

> While many aspects of Indian life changed over the years, the basic nature of the Ojibway of Moose Meat Point remained essentially the same. They were individualistic, resourceful, informal, proud, impulsive, imaginative, practical, independent, perceptive, patient, and above all, possessed a wonderful sense of humor. As long as they retained their language, they retained their sense of fun and wit. (9)

Johnston is more than an ethnographer or anthropologist. He is a descendant, passing the stories and the language to the next generation. He is adept at inserting Anishinaabemowin into English stories as needed, and his command of both languages is evident. He also obviously enjoys the same subtle game of naming that both Jim Northrup and Gerald Vizenor employ. In *Ojibway Tales*, for example, Johnston introduces Corporal Don Key, an obnoxious representation of local law enforcement; Father Curser, whose homilies live up to his surname; and Sergeant Goodenough, who really isn't. At the end of *Ojibway Tales*, Johnston reminds readers that the stories are based on true events. "If the accounts sometimes appear to be far-fetched and even implausible, it is simply because human beings very often act and conduct their affairs, and those of others, in an absurd manner" (187).

A more serious book, *Tales the Elders Told: Ojibway Legends*, published in 1981, is a compilation of traditional tales told to Johnston by various elders and family members. The primary characters are those of the Great Lakes area; some are the emblematic creatures that have come to define the region. For example, Spirit Woman knows many creatures; but the ruffed grouse, the rabbit, and the whitefish are the only ones content to stay near her. *Maang* (the loon) and *Kakkak* (the hawk) challenge one another to a game of lacrosse. Even the simplest stories, for example one recounting the day Nanabozho creates butterflies by tossing pebbles to amuse children, serve as examples of how Anishinaabe natural history, etymology, and spirituality come together in traditional tales.

Tales of the Anishinaubaek, The Star-Man and Other Tales, and *The Bear-Walker* further explore the landscape of Anishinaabe narrative. Tales entitled *Nebaunaubbaequae* (mermaids), *Mashk-aki-quaewuk* (medicine woman), *Animikeek* (thunderbirds), *Mishibizhew* (the underwater lynx), and *Gaupoonikae* (wintermaker) reflect the distinctly Anishinaabe combination of inland seas and a cycle of four seasons. Like the oral stories gathered in other volumes, these tales have survived many generations. Images of the *michibizhew* (the underwater lynx), for instance, are among the ancient petroglyphs along Lake Superior's shores, on medicine bags from the eighteen century, in the dreams of Johnston's characters, and in the stories still told by the Anishinaabe today. Johnston does not stray too far from the original format and content, but he tells each story as if it is set in the present.

> It is through stories that the knowledge and understanding of one generation are passed on to the next. Although the themes are far-ranging, and often deep and serious, the storytellers could always relate the stories with humor. If these stories do no more than give some idea of the scope of the Ojibway imagination, and perhaps bring a smile, they will have fulfilled their purpose. (*Tales the Elders Told* 7)

In *Honour Earth Mother*, he includes his own lyric poetry as an epigraph to some of the traditional tales, often making the point clear in two languages. After sharing stories of fishing in both the distant past and recent memory he offers a poem titled "Sole Trout" that concludes with a lesson of thanksgiving.

> *Meegawaetchiwi-audauh gayay*
> *K'bim-gaedauguninaunik*
> *Waesseehnuk, benaessiwuk, geegoohnuk gayae*
> *W'gee pagidinumaukooying w'bim-audiziwiniwauh*
> *Tchi ishko-nae-ing keeyaubih ningo-geezhig.*

> Let us give thanksgiving
> To our co-tenants upon this earth
> The deer, the geese, the fish
> Who gave their lives so that
> We might live to see another day. (143)

These are the lessons of the Anishinaabe literary canon in prose and poetry. They are the classics often referenced by contemporary Anishinaabe authors.

Johnston has also published nonfiction in the form of two memoirs and a collection of essays. *Indian School Days* has a surprisingly humorous edge and offers an alternate reading of the boarding school era. Although it addresses the painful transition of young boys from their homes on the reservation to residential school, it also demonstrates the use of humor as a survival tool. *Indian School Days* differs from other accounts of Anishinaabe children at boarding school because it covers a span of time when attendance was voluntary, which is when Johnston chose to attend in order to complete his degree. Johnston was lucky enough to encounter a group of Jesuits who truly attempted to give their students what they might need to survive. Although it contains passages about running away, the book also details the efforts of the missionaries to understand the boys and their needs. There are difficult passages of cultural genocide, when the Anishinaabe language and religion are cast aside. But there are also accounts of learning that hold up even to today's most ideal standards. Eventually, Johnston left school as valedictorian of the first secondary class to graduate.

Crazy Dave, which came out in 1999, is autobiographical, but it is also a tragicomic story that needed to be told. The subject of the book is David McLeod, Johnston's uncle, who was born with Down's syndrome. He was sheltered at home by his mother for many years, and the struggle of Dave's family to raise him on Cape Croker Reserve in the early 1900s reflects the aboriginal struggle in Canada, the struggle of all children with Down's syndrome, and a lesson in humor and humility. Although Johnston says it took him a long time to figure out how to write about his uncle, in the end he was able to show how Dave taught everyone who knew him some of life's most important lessons. Dave's exploits often centered on his inability to play by the rules and be serious. He was often cussing in his own blended dialect of English and Anishinaabemowin. One of the most significant characteristics about Dave was his ability to talk to "the little people," the *memegwesiiwag* who live in the woods, which was acknowledged by everyone who knew Dave. Johnston writes, "I looked on David not as someone odd but as someone special, possessing something ordinary people didn't have" (*Crazy Dave* 240). "There are lessons to be learned from this story about people's attitudes," says Johnston (St. Germain 3). Johnston admits he focused on the humor more than the tragedy but explains, "that's the way life should be . . . I think there's a helluva lack of humor in a lot of writers . . . funny things are part of this life" (St. Germain 1). A third work of nonfiction, *Think Indian: Languages Are beyond Price*, is a collection of the essays Johnston has written over the years. It includes memories of his first public speeches as well as a chronology of his theories about language and narrative.

A completely different, but extremely important category of publishing for Johnston is the work he has done creating language resources over the years. Like other Anishinaabe authors, he uses Anishinaabemowin in his English-language publications for a range of important reasons, but in some cases, he writes stories, grammars, and reference books for the primary purpose of teaching the language. His *Anishinaubae Thesaurus* is divided into five parts to help students of the language recognize patterns of meaning: (1) nouns, (2) adjectives, adverbs, conjunctions, prepositions, and pronouns, (3) suffixes, (4) verbs, and (5) prefixes. It is organized according to the standards of a verb-centered language with categories that reflect the way words are constructed. Although it may not seem intuitive to someone whose first language is not Anishinaabemowin, it has the advantage of teaching students *ezhi-Anishinaabendamo*, how to think Anishinaabe. Along with the thesaurus, Johnston has published *Anishinaubaemoowin: First Year High School Curriculum, Dibaudjimootaudiwin, K'd'Inawaewininaun: Our Language,* and *Verbs: Ae-idumoowinuguk Doodumoo-kittoowinun* through his own publishing company, Winter Spirit Creations. Johnston's journey as an author, born of a need in the 1970s, continues to play an important role in the Anishinaabe community. His experience working to revitalize the language and bring back the stories teaches many lessons about the way Anishinaabe writers use both Anishinaabemowin and English to tell stories. He offers readers new ways to view a landscape previously undefined, or sketched only in loose stereotypes.

Raised on the reserve by elders fluent in Anishinaabemowin, Johnston's experience includes the attempt of "educators" to cause him to forget the language of his tribe.

Johnston comments frequently on the attempt of the Jesuit missionaries in Canada to assimilate children from various tribes, including the Anishinaabe. His description of the way Anishinaabe children learned English shows exactly how the languages differ.

> No matter where the students came from, they all had difficulties with the correct
> pronunciation and enunciation of the English language. The tribal language
> operated quite well without the letters "r," "l," "f," "v," "x," and "th." Thus, when

the boys attempted these strange sounds they stuttered and muttered and made substitutions . . . "never" became "neber," "Virginia" became "Bayzhinee." . . . And having at the school German and French priests and brothers who also had problems pronouncing the ubiquitous "th" did not help. From the tribal tongue and from the influence of the French teachers, the boys developed their own slang and dialect with a strong Gallic bias and flavour. (*Indian School Days* 9–10)

He also notes that the boys had trouble learning to use nouns and pronouns, which have very different rules in English. Examples of the transitional challenges he mentions are found in more than just his memoir. His stories of the Moose Meat community include many characters who speak English with a strong Anishinaabe accent. They frequently drop the unfamiliar consonants, leave out pronouns, or conjugate incorrectly. For example, when accused of eating bologna on Friday, Kitug-Aunquot says, "I got nutting else Fauder" (*Ojibway Tales* 83), which gives a sense of the sound speakers retained. A tendency to misuse nouns is obvious when the Moose Meat Point chief declares, "If you're satisfaction, I'm satisfaction too" (*Ojibway Tales* 177). By including these phrases in the story, Johnston offers clues to understanding Anishinaabemowin. In Anishinaabemowin, "satisfied" should be a verb, and one would have to specify who is satisfied, or who might be satisfying who, but the word repeated in English as a noun, with no clarifying prefixes or suffixes, leads to confusion.

Like other Anishinaabe authors, Johnston often examines the meaning of names. Names in Johnston's stories offer insight into the language culture; sometimes they give evidence of colonization as records change traditional names to English versions or substitutes. Sometimes they reveal characteristics about people and communities that should not be ignored. Naming in some cultures equates with possessing. Johnston and other Anishinaabe authors write about naming and use names in a way that reveals names to be stories, if they are thought about and understood.

In "They Don't Want No Indians," Johnston shows how English names and Anishinaabe sounds collide, causing shifts in individual and community identity. The story begins when "Zubyaeh barked in his ordinary gruff voice." Later, "Zubyaeh reflected on the mortality of men." Yet when Sergeant Goodenough calls, he asks for "Mr. Xavier McMac" and Zubyaeh answers. This example of there being more than one way to say a name marks the period when members of the First Nations in Canada began to see themselves as belonging to two worlds. Initially, the cultural exchange was more equal; missionaries and settlers were forced to learn Anishinaabemowin, but over time the language was discouraged and began to disappear from mainstream culture. Zubyaeh likely says his name that way all the time, but there is no longer any effort on the part of others to learn the sounds of Anishinaabemowin. Elders become concerned and wonder what else is being lost when the Anishinaabe accent, intonation, and pronunciation are no longer familiar outside of the community. Through proper nouns and dialect variation Johnston traces the loss of the language.

Johnston attempts to reverse this situation by using Anishinaabe names in his own writing, partly because they have an etymological background that provides cultural insight, and partly to insert the sound and tempo of Anishinaabemowin back into modern life. For example, the names of the *manidoog, Maudjeekawiss, Pukawiss,* and *Wauboozoo,* could have been translated to First Son, Unwanted One, and Rabbit, but that would not afford Johnston the ability to emphasize the cultural importance of these names. As he notes, the name *Maudjeekawiss* was a traditional name for the eldest child and carried with it the responsibility of an elder sibling entering the world first. *Pukawiss,* because his older brother was most loved, was called by the word meaning "forsaken, disowned, or unwanted." The third brother was given the name of an animal, a *wabooz* (rabbit), as a young boy because the elder who named him was hoping he would do great things for the tribe. In just these three names we learn a great deal about variations for naming in Anishinaabemowin. These brothers offer a wide variety of naming scenarios: a name based on the verb "*maaj*" (to begin), an adjective, and a totemic animal. Of course, these are mythic *manidoog,* not real people, but the many nouns that Johnston uses in his books illustrate similar diversity in naming. His use of these names renders them more common. In some cases, as in the work of other Anishinaabe authors, the word becomes the standard English term.

Aanii dash Anishinaabemoyaang / Why Speak Anishinaabemowin?

The ability to use and understand Anishinaabemowin is central to the view of the world that Johnston tries to share. Sometimes it seems as if the language is a place, and perhaps for some it is. Some characters leave the land, language, and traditions of the Anishinaabe, while others fight to protect it and remain within it. Johnston offers an example of this in *Indian School Days*. Not only do the boys in school frequently make up Anishinaabe names for each other, outside of class they exchange greetings with relatives and members of their tribe.

When he arrived at school, Johnston was greeted in Anishinaabemowin by an older boy prepared to cut his hair. *"Numudubin! Aneesh abi-ondijibauyin,"* says the older boy, asking him in Anishinaabemowin to sit down and tell where he has come from, not just the town, but the community of people he calls home (*Indian School Days* 23). When the priest returns, the older boy quickly switches back to English, saying to the priest, "Don' hurry me up. Take my time if I wan' to. No white man's gonna make me hurry" (23). At school, Anishinaabemowin goes underground. The exchange of words between the priest and the boys and among the boys themselves can be interpreted several different ways. It is clear that, to get by, they must use English, but not perfectly and not always. Some of Johnston's characters present the possibility that their use of imperfect English has more to do with defiance than intellect. In the example above, Eugene Keeshig could be dropping consonants and using nonstandard contractions on purpose, the way many teenagers do, or he could be refusing to learn the subtleties of English.

Anishinaabemowin can provide a way to work together against the dominant English culture. For example, in the short story "The Power of Prayer," four members of the Moose Meat Point Reserve are falsely imprisoned and charged with drunkenness and disorderly conduct. To plan their trial, they need to compare strategies, so they take advantage of their right to "pray" on a Sunday. As they kneel together they say:

> *Aungwaumzik* Amen *naunigotinong kidook* (Be careful to sometimes say Amen).
> *Aubidaek tchi naussaubaudjimowing* (We all must tell the same story).
> *Kaween k'miniquaemissimnaubum shkotae-waubo* (We were not drinking liquor).
> Amen! They responded. (Johnston, *Ojibway Tales 94*)

The use of Anishinaabemowin gives readers a sense of what the guards actually heard and how different it would have sounded from their own native English. The story these men tell is certainly not an *aadizokaan* of ancient significance, but the verb they use is *dibaudjimo*, marking this as more than conversation—it is a story shared for a reason, among members of a community of Anishinaabemowin speakers. Through stories like these, Johnston offers both comic and real reasons to return to the place of Anishinaabemowin.

Perhaps it is unfortunate that the men use prayer as a ruse for conversation, but the relationship between the Anishinaabe and representatives of Christian religions has been complicated. Without judging the value of any particular theology, Johnston often comments on the cultural and linguistic misunderstanding between the Anishinaabe and the missionaries who settled in the area surrounding his reserve. He does this because it relates directly to the reason the language and stories "went away." Until now the Christian and traditional Anishinaabe religions have most often been described as opposing. Some ethnographers have offered apologies for the missions (Bowden; Zanger), while others give scathing summaries of injustice (Devens; Hallowell, "Ojibwa Ontology"; Tinker). Yet the cultural curiosity and concern of such people as Bishop Baraga in the 1840s and more recently such elders as Larry Cloud Morgan, who lived until 1999, have not been adequately studied. Traces of these attempts (and sometimes failures) to understand one another can be found in the language and stories of many Anishinaabe authors. The common word for Sunday in most places is *Anamae-giizhigad*, or "prayer-day," which indicates one point on which it was easy to agree. But how converted a community is can be determined by the word for Saturday. In some communities it is *Maanii-giizhigad* (Mary's Day), while in places where the missionaries arrived later it is *Giziibinigezaganige-giizhigad* (Clean the Floors Day). Johnston offers another example of cultural intersection in religion when he tells how the Anishinaabe were scandalized by the missionaries' habit of continually erecting wooden memorials. What the Jesuits saw as a crucifix was thought to be a *dodaem-wautik*, or funeral totem, by the Anishinaabe. Another problem was the term *manidoo*. The settlers interpreted this term to mean only "spirit." They assumed the primitive mind and language were incapable of more complex or abstract morphology. As Johnston explains,

> Thereafter, whenever an aboriginal person uttered the word manitou, Western Europeans thought it meant spirit. When a medicine person uttered the term *manitouwun* to refer to some curative or healing property in a tree or plant, they took it to mean spirit. When a person said the word *manitouwut* to refer to the sacrosanct mood or atmosphere of a place, they assumed it meant spirit. And when a person spoke the word *manitouwih* to allude to a medicine person with miraculous healing powers, they construed it to mean spirit. (*Manitous* 2)

People who did not speak Anishinaabemowin took it for granted that the Anishinaabe used the word in only one way and saw spirits everywhere when, actually, the Anishinaabe understood many abstract meanings of the word and used it to indicate any number of spiritual or transcendental concepts, including a view of *Gichi Manidoo*, as the center of existence and creation. In the previous paragraph Johnston uses the word three ways: as the description of an atmospheric condition (*manitouwut*), as an inanimate object with spirit (*manitouwun*), and as a complex spiritual relationship (*manitouwih*). In these few examples Johnston is able to at least allude to the way linguistic misunderstanding contributed to spiritual stereotypes of both Christians and Anishinaabeg and why maintenance of Anishinaabemowin helps us understand the history of cultural change and the complexity of cultural exchange.

Like other Anishinaabe authors, Johnston encourages the use of Anishinaabemowin, if not as the vernacular language of the home at least as the language of story and ceremony. For example, when prayers or stories begin, Johnston frequently switches to Anishinaabemowin. He explains:

> "*Ahow, n'gah auttisssookae*" was a sacred invocation that was performed only in winter, when the *manitous* were abroad in the physical world and were proximate to humankind. Once brought into being, the *auttissookaun* became an *awaetchigun*, a story akin to a parable that could be told anytime it needed to be told. Most narrators prefaced their stories with "*Ahow, n'gah dibaudjim*" meaning "well the time has come for me to tell a story . . . to tell what I know of such an event." What followed was more than a story; it was a lesson in the art of storytelling, language, and drama, meant to waken and enlighten. (*Manitous* 172)

It is clear this is the model of storytelling Johnston strives to follow, one in which the language and stories are connected.

Johnston works to intervene in the process of assimilation by bringing the language and stories back, especially those that were replaced by colonial interactions. His view of both languages is complex. He recognizes the contemporary need for English, but he attempts to share what it can and cannot do. "Even though a large number ceased speaking Ojibway for the sake of English, they were not invited to white homes; despite forsaking their own religious practices and beliefs and embracing several shades of Christianity" (*Ojibway Tales* 73). It is fine to consider the song and spirit of another culture, but Johnston and his characters show how acculturation is healthier than complete assimilation. When Steamboat hears a hymn he remarks, "how beautiful it sounded in Ojibway! He listened, remembering how, in days past, the old people talked in Ojibway" (*Ojibway Tales* 97). The implication is that the hymns may have use, but sound best in Anishinaabemowin.

Furthermore, English can't always get a person the job. In the story "Can I See the President" the grammar of an out-of-work Anishinaabe man is so embellished that it serves as a hindrance rather than a help in seeking a job. He practices, saying, "Mr. President . . . I am desirous of obtaining a position in your Personnel Relations Department and becoming a member of your esteemed organization which I know by reputation to be the kind with which I would be proud to be associated" (*Ojibway Tales* 143). For all his practice, he is greeted by a receptionist with "whadayawan" and eventually, an interviewer who opens with "yeah?" (147). Like other Anishinaabe writers, Johnston uses English to call attention to its limitations and point out how fluency in any language is relative to shared understandings of use.

Johnston maintains that a strong cultural identity and sense of well-being is related to use of Anishinaabemowin. In describing the real people who inspired the stories contained in *Ojibway Tales*, Johnston notes that "as long as they retained their language, they retained their sense of fun and wit. . . . Unhappily the language is vanishing" (9). The language of Nanabozho not being recognized by the people could be considered linguistic impoverishment because, as Johnston pointedly states, "the limits of translation act as an effective bar to a fuller exposition" of many stories (*Ojibway Tales* 188). In his opinion, the ability to communicate in Anishinaabemowin is essential for the survival of the culture. In *Think Indian* he recalls, "To instill respect for language, the old counseled youth 'don't talk too much' (gegoh zaum-doongaen) for they saw a kinship between language and truth" (90). As the movement to regain the language has gained ground, thanks to Johnston and others, it may be possible for the culture to take back a language in written form that was essentially lost in an oral state. There is no way the Anishinaabemowin of the future will be the Anishinaabemowin of the past, but change is a defining characteristic of a living language.

Dibaajimowinan miinwaa Aadizokaanag / Stories and Stories

Anishinaabemowin is the matter that makes up many of the narratives indigenous to the Great Lakes. Its sound gives speakers a recognizable identity. Its rules of engagement reflect ways of thinking that have become the words and phrases of stories. Some Anishinaabe authors focus on ways to create variety in words, while others weave narratives of their own invention. Basil Johnston collects stories like stones on the shore, fallen stars or healing spheres of basalt. He sees purpose and origin in them that others miss. He shows readers a world where all possibilities are considered, where the gods of other religions are invited to fall through a hole in the sky and learn Anishinaabemowin.

> "Now, I'm going to tell you a very different kind of story. It's not really a story because it has not yet taken place, but it will take place just as the events in the past have occurred." *Daebaudjimoot* paused to fill his pipe. "And even though what I'm about to tell you has not yet come to pass, it is as true as if it already happened because the *Auttissookaunuk* told it to me in a dream." (*Manitous* 178)

According to Johnston, listeners or readers of Anishinaabe narrative need the ability to distinguish one story from another. There is a difference between the careful reporting of *dibaajimowinan* compared to the soul-searching, far-reaching parables of the *aadizokaanag*. Although often translated as the nouns "story" and "myth," *dibaajimo* and *aadizoke* are verbs that describe the way a narrative is told. Constructing a *dibaajimo* is like being a witness while awake. Telling an *aadizokaan* is like steering a story through dreamtime so that the correct meaning will be visible just below the surface. Johnston does both, *dibaajimo* and *aadizokaan*. He writes about his own experience, and he brings the spirits of the Anishinaabe, the *manidoog*, to life. The word *dibaajimo* is related to the verbs "*debwe*" (to tell the truth) and "*dibaadaan*" or "*diba'ige*" (to measure something or someone). Both *dibaajimo* and *aadizokaan* relate to a person's ability to describe his or her perceptions of a subject. As Johnston explains, "there is no absolute truth, only the highest degree of accuracy" (*Manitous* 241).

> Because each story may embody several themes and meanings, time and de-liberation are required for adequate appreciation. There is no instantaneous

understanding. Anishinaabe stories are as broad and deep in meaning and mystery as are the tales, legends, and myths of Greek, Roman, Egyptian, and other peoples, and just as difficult to understand as are the parables in the Bible. (*Ojibway Heritage* 7)

Just as Western notions of fiction and nonfiction have become fixed as binary options, Johnston suggests that the determination of true or untrue is not as important in Anishinaabe literature. Instead, all stories are a kind of truth, and it is important for the storytellers and listeners to understand what kind of truth a story contains. It could be the kind of truth that operates in dreamtime and moves between the past and future. Or it could be the kind of truth that makes elders laugh after dark. And of course, in many cases it could shift smoothly from one kind to the other.

This ability of stories to shift from serious to bawdy, from ethereal to physical, is common in old stories. One of the ways Johnston draws the old traditional tales into the present is by restoring the original *bgoji-dibaajimo*, the wild, or natural Anishinaabe narratives. For example, he exposes the emotions of a *manidoo* when he describes how it came to pass that Winonah got pregnant. True to tradition, the young girl was warned not to urinate facing west, and that's when it happened:

> When Ae-pungishimook saw Winonah's little moss-covered cleft, the coals of lust glowed in his loins, and without prolonged foreplay, or the recitation of sweet nothings, he cast his loincloth aside and humped the girl then and there. When his fire had petered out, Ae-pungishimook put his loincloth back on and staggered away, leaving poor Winonah to manage for herself and to face the future alone. (*Manitous* 17)

This may not be the traditional Native American Indian myth readers expect, but it is true to Anishinaabe style. From the taboo concerning the god of the west to his all-too-human reaction, it is told with the traditional bawdy humor. Johnston makes a point to relieve readers of any sentimental or romantic notions about Anishinaabe stories.

In another instance of honest representation, Johnston recalls his own graduation when Mishiminoauniquot, Joe Peter Pangwish, Chief of Wikwemikong, gave a speech in a mix of English and Anishinaabemowin:

I hope you don' min' my English . . . I never learn . . . not like youse. *Aupitchi dash igoh nauh n'kitchi-inaendum gee abi izhauyaun.* (I am exceedingly glad that I came.) I wasn't goin' come; too busy on the farm; can' leave an'mals jis' like that . . . *Nongom dush aeishkawau-nauwiquaek mee gee aundaukinigaeyaun. Ah nindowautch n'gah zauh.* (But this afternoon I changed my mind. In spite of all the work facing me.) I decided to come, see what I miss. (*Indian School Days* 240)

The struggle for an English reader to read even this short introduction gives a sense of the way the Anishinaabe of this time period struggled to be understood in an English context. It also demonstrates how a leader esteemed by his tribe felt he had to apologize for his command of English. Unfortunately, no one asked the English speakers in the audience to recognize that the word he used for "happy" is made of words that literally mean "great thoughts." *Gichinendam* implies that intellectual activity and reflection is "happiness." People still use this word when greeting someone by saying, *nd'gichinendam waabaaminan* (I'm "happy" to see you). In small exchanges like this one, meaning can be lost.

The primary lesson of Johnston's work is that all of life is related and that there is an Anishinaabe perspective on life and the universe that must be maintained for cultural continuity. Every story, every life, is dependent on a web of relationships that must be acknowledged to fully appreciate the view from a center that is alive with possibilities. All of his stories, his own or his retellings, are about the relationships of Anishinaabe with the universe itself, the sky, the earth, the plants, animals and humans, and the *manidoog*. To live, *bimaadizi*, is to experience presence and be in motion. The word *bimaadizi* itself signals these concepts. Interpretations will always vary, but any speaker will hear similar networks of meaning in the word. Most often cited are the words for moving oneself forward, *bimode* (to crawl), *bimose* (to walk), *bimipto* (to run), *bimishkwan* (travel by canoe). The *bi* can also indicate immediacy, as when one says, *n'wii bi dagooshin waabang* (I will arrive here tomorrow); the *bi* changes to *ni* if one were to say "arrive there." A closer look will also connect the word with *maada'ado* (to follow something), *maada'azha* (to follow someone), *maadookii* (to share, collaborate), *maadakamigad* (to start). The *zi* at the end of the word indicates it is a verb, typically one that reflects a personal state of being, as in *giinaadizi* (crazy), *zhiingizi* (naughty), *akozi* (sick), *ayekozi* (tired), in short, a matter of health and balance. How does one make an equation of all these factors? Putting these ideas into an English sentence is not easy. One might say that life is the process of moving along a path while collaborating and sharing, but any attempt to lock these ideas into a single phrase limits them. Basil Johnston constantly reminds readers that the *Midewiwin* traditions evolved specifically for these reasons, but that those who speak Anishinaabemowin carefully and proficiently will find their own interpretation of life and how to improve the experience for themselves and others. His definition of *Midewiwin* is "a society of medicine men and women dedicated to the study of the curative properties and attributes of plants, healing, and the relationship between living and upright life (walking in balance) and well-being, derived from the term *mino-odae-win* good-hearted or *medaewaewin* (sound)" (*Anishinaubae Thesaurus* 19). The lesson on the surface is one of etymology; the lesson just below the surface is that an Anishinaabe linguist, fluent in his own language, after a lifetime of listening to his own elders, resisted selecting a single interpretation of *Midewiwin*—it could be related to the center of human energy, the heart; or the center of ceremony, the drum, and in the word for drum, *dewegan*, we hear both.

> Learning comes not only from books but from the earth and our surroundings as well. Indeed, learning from the mountains, valleys, forest and meadows anteceded book knowledge. What our people know about life and living, good and evil, laws and the purpose of insects, birds, animals and fish comes from the earth, the weather, the seasons, the plants and the other beings. The earth is a book; alive with events that occur over and over for our benefit. Mother Earth has formed our beliefs, attitudes, insights, outlooks, values and institutions. (*Honour Earth Mother* vii)

There is always one more way to view any word or world, one more secret from the past that is unseen, one more possibility about to unfold. Johnston carefully never claims his stories are the stories told in the *Midewiwin* lodge; what he tells are the stories one might need to prepare to understand those stories or to simply live each day in an interconnected universe.

The Anishinaabe cosmology presented by Johnston begins much like many other creation stories. First, there was nothing and then there was life. According to the Anishinaabe, this happened when *Gichi Manidoo*, who has no beginning and no end, "created the world, plants, birds, animals, fish, and the other *manitous* in fulfillment of a vision" (*Manitous* xi). This world then flooded, and, while all of life was under water, *Giizhigoikwe*, Sky Woman, conceived with another *manidoo*. Noticing her condition, a giant turtle offered her his back, and while specific accounts vary, in Johnston's book it is *Giizhigoikwe* who creates the earth anew by breathing life into a scrap of soil carried up from under the water by a muskrat. The monotheism, the flood, and the miracle of life brought forth from dust are elements shared across parts of the human family. The involvement of *Giizhigoikwe* and a turtle, combined with the fable of a muskrat bringing dirt up from a vast body of water, is specific to the Great Lakes and part of all Anishinaabe origin stories.

Giizhigoikwe created the world from a speck of dirt, and it is re-created later by the half-human, half-*manidoo* character Nanabozho. One reading of this act is to recognize the importance of creation that comes from within the individual. According to Johnston's interpretation, the story of *Gichi Manidoo, Giizhigoikwe*, and Nanabozho represents the imperative of the individual to act in accordance with spiritual and natural guidelines.

> Every person is to seek a dream or vision within the expanse of his or her soul-spirit being and, having attained it, bring it into fulfillment and reality. . . . Furthermore, every person is endowed with the gift of a measure of talent or aptitude to enable him or her to bring the vision or dream to reality, to shape his or her own being, as it were, and to fashion an immediate world and destiny. But finding this substance deep within one's innermost being is not an easy task. One must descend to the depths or ascend to the very heights of one's soul-spirit being, by means of a vision or a dream, to discover and to retrieve that morsel of talent or aptitude. (*Manitous* 3)

This story also forges the connection between life and the earth as a life-giving entity made of light and dark, land and water. The sun is often depicted as a man and nature. The earth, sometimes literally named *Muzzukummikquae* by Johnston, is female. Although Johnston always translates *Muzzukummikquae* as Mother Nature, the meanings in the word could be heard more literally as "image-making sea woman." This is one of the proper nouns that Johnston simply moves into English, making the term a part of both languages. Some Anishinaabe question the use of the term "Mother Earth" as a recent anthropomorphic lapse, but all authors agree that the origin stories call life out of cosmos and water. Whether or not that force has a face or gender is a matter for further debate.

Many of his stories record the connection and interdependence between the Anishinaabeg and the universe in practical, tangible ways. When Johnston describes young boys sent to the remote corners of nature in search of visions, they find *manidoog* in the elements. Storytellers are inspired by the *aadizokaanag*, the muses, who dwell at the earth's four cardinal points. And it was at the place of the "*kikinoomaukaeassin*" or "*kikinoomaukaewaubik*" (teaching rocks) that the young students of Anishinaabe culture, the next generation of storytellers, were taught by their elders. Throughout all of his books, Johnston incorporates the Anishinaabe belief that the relationship with *Gichi Manidoo* and all the *manidoog* depends on being capable of finding them within nature.

> Besides beauty, Mother Earth also had a spiritual presence, an aura of mystery that imparted a sacred character to certain places. What conferred this sacredness on a pinnacle of rocks, or a glade in the forest, where one ought not to be, was the presence of *manitous*. For the most part, men and women, as bidden, left these places undisturbed. . . . But it was in these places, or nearby, that men and women came to quest for visions and dreams and to talk to the *manitous* directly, to gain entry to the world through dreams. (*Manitous* 14)

To make the stories more real, Johnston shares examples from his own life, and the life of the tribe as a whole. When the boys in boarding school were allowed to spend the summer on a nearby island, he notes:

> There may not have been much on Aird Island, but the boys took what little there was and what little they had, and made it into something bigger, and finer, and stronger than they had found. No one could see it, but it was there; no one could express it, but it was there. It was in each boy. With every renewed attempt to achieve, the resourcefulness grew, and as the resourcefulness increased so did the spirit of independence and the passion for personal freedom. (*Indian School Days* 101)

The sense that each person has a connection to an array of options could be related to the more complex system of verbs used in Anishinaabemowin. As he writes about this in English, that link is less evident, but his stories in Anishinaabemowin reinforce the way the language allows for broader interpretation. For example, in "Medawaewaeigun: The Story of the Drum" Wauboozoo asks Nokomis about *manidoog, chechaukoom,* and *chiboom,* which are the other spirits and the spirits of oneself. Telling Wauboozoo why he has them, she says in English: "Everyone and everything needs a spirit to look after them. Everyone has a spirit that looks after them, keeps them alive." In Anishinaabemowin the same line says, *Kauween k'dauh bim-audizissee keeshpin ayauwausseewudoowauh. K'bim-audizee-ikook.* A literal translation of the Anishinaabemowin version would be "You can't live if you don't have them. They enliven you." It's an awkward, inadequate summary of a very big idea. The word *bimaadiz* is so much more than "to live." And then *bimaadiz* is turned around as a verb and used in a way that says these spirits are doing it for/with/to you. These are the phrases that would leave a listener thinking long after the story ended.

Animals and nature are also part of *bimaadiziwin.* The Anishinaabe have long relied on the animals and plants in their northern surroundings for inspiration and information, and there is an implication that they have their own "language" or system for understanding the world that the Anishinaabe can hear if they listen. One might suppose this is a bit like what an environmental biologist would still tell us. Information is coded into the environments in ways we can understand if we try. Johnston writes:

> From infancy, children were taught that the sudden calls or unexpected shadows of animals, or birds, meant no harm, that these calls were talk in the animals' and birds' own language, and that all creatures had their own purpose and affairs to conduct. (*Manitous* 116)

Johnston's stories of relationships between the various animals and humans demonstrate the strength of the connection between the Anishinaabe and their surroundings.

> Human beings had special regard for certain qualities and virtues of the animal world. To possess and exercise comparable qualities and virtues would exalt and dignify the human spirit and soul, and men and women aspired to deeds that would make them proud. . . . Men and women especially valued attributes that would enable them to achieve their dreams and visions more readily; to carry out their duties and responsibilities more easily, and to safeguard their lives and health in times of great need. They wished they had been as endowed and favored by *Gichi Manidoo* as were the eagles, sparrows, bears, deer, turtles, butterflies, and sturgeon. (*Manitous* 119)

A system of *doodemag* (totems or clans) was created to associate families with specific animals and give the tribe a way to ensure that various members were striving to provide leadership, protection, food, education, and healing. *Tales of the Anishinaubaek, Tales the Elders Told*, and *The Bear-Walker* all contain references to animals and their specific characteristics. Johnston uses the word *doodem* for clan because, as in other instances, its etymology is important. The word for heart, *ode*, is the central part of *doodem*, and typically when one speaks of clan identity, one uses the verb *dibendagozi*, which is typically translated as "to be a member of" but comes from the set of words that start with *diben* and indicate who has control, who participates or has ownership of an idea, group, or thing.

Johnston often tells stories that reach far back in time to an unnamed past. For example, he retells the story of four young men who go off in search of "the land of plenty." They find an old woman, actually *Muzzukummikquae*, who needs their care to survive. After they provide for her and nurse her back to health, she reveals herself as a *manidoo* by causing the branch of an apple tree to burst suddenly into bloom. She tells them she can grant them heaven on earth, gives them medicine bundles, and sends them home. Back among their people, the young men begin to doubt her, but they mix the medicine as she told them. All of them die within days of one another. However, out of each of their graves springs a tree, stone, or plant that changes the life of the tribe forever. This is how the land of the Anishinaabe came to be covered in pines and birch; how they first found flint; and how *asemaa*, the tobacco-like herb used in pipes, was found (*Manitous* 97). This a wonderful example of how Johnston blends the old legends with his own words to create philosophical parables specifically related to the surroundings and culture of the Anishinaabe.

Dreams, visions, and transformations are some of the ways Anishinaabe stories present possibilities. Stories are not always composed carefully for large audiences; they are sometimes given to Anishinaabe people individually in dreams, through visions, or as part of an epiphany. Later, these personal stories become part of other stories, but they often begin when one person listens to the universe. One of Johnston's examples shows how his relationship with trees led to a story he needed to hear when thinking about his own life.

> On this particular night I dreamed of the bush, of maple, oak, ash, ironwood, birch, and hemlock. As I stood next to a birch, sizing up where best to sink the blade of the axe, the nearby trees began to whisper. "He's going to kill the birch!

He's going to kill the birch!" And their whispers beat upon my ears like hail. I planted the blade deep into the flesh of the birch, which shuddered and gasped in pain. The other trees hissed. . . . At last the birch toppled to the ground, where it convulsed for a few moments before lying still. . . . Appalled by what I had done and mortified by the accusations of the trees, I coiled and then uncoiled to cast my axe far from me, but the axe clung to my hands. It was bonded to my being. (*Indian School Days* 179)

This passage contains numerous lessons. It explains why he went back to school rather than becoming a logger or entering the army. It speaks of his personal and cultural values regarding nature and violence. In the dream, he did not thank *Gichi Manidoo* before felling the birch, and he suffered bad consequences. The trees themselves are embodied with a spirit that, in this case, can speak and chastise him for taking one of their kind. He is forever connected to his act and cannot be separated from his fate. One might even guess that he dreamed of the birch because the white tree, called *wiigwas* in Anishinaabemowin, is the tree that gave its bark to homes, containers, and scrolls. The few written records known to exist prior to encountering the English alphabet were pictures on either rocks or birch bark scrolls. Elder women in many Anishinaabe communities still chew thin pieces of birch to "write" stories and pictures of the tribe. As it turns out, Johnston awoke and has gone on to honor the stories that might have been lost. He has kept the stories, possibly symbolized by the birch, alive. However, all of that is easy to say from the vantage point of looking back on Johnston's career after many decades. The important note is that he includes these learning moments in his stories. In fact, he includes them without interpretation, true to tradition, leaving the meaning open to speculation.

Manidoog minwaa Wiindigoog / Spirits and Unspirits

Another element of the universe Johnston highlights through language and story is the relationship between the *manidoog* and the Anishinaabe. Johnston is likely the person most responsible for making "manitou" an English word. By using it as a title and consistently using the word in all his works, he successfully moved the word from one language to another, allowing it to keep all its varied meanings without being reduced through translation to the image of another culture. For centuries, translators wrote "god," "God," "Creator," "Great Spirit," and all of these are still correct, but as soon as one is chosen, the meaning becomes limited. By leaving the word in Anishinaabemowin Johnston allows even more potential definitions to be associated with the word. Johnston speaks about his initial desire to find the stories of the elders and set them down and how that quest became a search for stories of *manidoog*. As Johnston learned, *manidoog* serve many purposes in Anishinaabe stories. They represent the best and worst of man and animals. They are not limited by the bounds of reality and are memorable and compelling characters. In *Manitous*, Johnston explains that he "tried to keep with the practice of setting down the stories as they were in the old days, allowing the stories to speak for themselves" (*Manitous* xiii).

Johnston carefully arranges his stories to introduce readers to a wide variety of *manidoog*. Unlike his own early works and the many ethnographic surveys that have been done over the years, Johnston describes and connects the most important *manidoog* as if they were an ancestral family. He notes the relationships *manidoog* have with the people and also explains the relationships among the *manidoog* themselves. The most important of this group is *Gichi Manidoo*, the Creator, or the Great Mystery, the one who infused all other life on earth with spirit. *Gichi Manidoo* never appears directly in any of the stories, but is constantly referenced.

The four other *manidoog* who often appear in stories are the sons of Aepung-ishimook and Winonah. Aepungishimook is the *manidoo* of the west, destiny, old age, and death. Winonah, an Anishinaabe human, was only a girl when she gave birth to the first of her half-*manidoo*, half-human, children. Later, as the other boys appeared, over a succession of generations, she inherited the fertility and longevity of a *manidoo*. Each of her sons also came to represent a necessary element of the community. In *Manitous*, Johnston eloquently tells the story of each son. For someone who has read and heard many short versions of these tales, it is a wonderful surprise to find that he creates an elaborate narrative from the many snippets that must have been given to him throughout his life. The four sons of Winonah are distinctly Anishinaabe characters, which Johnston explains as he tells the story of each son's gift to the community. *Maudjeekawis*, the eldest, "typifies men and women of deed and accomplishment. . . . He serves to inspire people and instill pride in the Anishinaabe" (*Manitous* 25). The second eldest, *Pukawiss*, represents "a love for drama, dance, festivals, elegant attire, and a disposition for practical joking" (*Manitous* 35). *Cheebyauboozhoo*, the third son, became the *ogimaa* (chief) of the underworld and is "credited with bequeathing music, dream quests, chants, and belief in the supernatural to the Anishinaabe" (*Manitous* 49). The last, and most well known, son, is Nanabozho. Nanabozho "represents a caricatured understanding of human nature" (*Manitous* 244). He is not always what he appears to be, and he does not quite understand his own power. At times, he is a hurt and very human son, searching for his father; at other times he is a *manidoo* stealing fire from the sky.

Johnston mentions other *manidoog* in his books, but more often by category than by name. There are the amazing *animikiig*, the thunderbirds, thought to be related to eagles; the *maemaegawaehnse* (little people), who protect the Anishinaabe; and the *nebaunaubaequewak* (mermaids), who rise from the depths of the lakes.

Johnston also includes the frightening *michibizhew*, a dangerous *manidoo* who dwells beneath the water, and the evil *wiindigoos*, who smell of death and blizzards. Like the *manidoog*, these creatures represent more than entertainment. They inhabit the periphery of the known and understood world. Their very existence could spark an allegorical debate about how to survive. Stories of these threatening *manidoog* are more appropriate now than ever. For example, the tale of the flesh-eating *wiindigoo* unfolds much like a classic morality play:

> A *weendigo* gorged itself and glutted its belly as if it would never eat again. But a remarkable thing always occurred. As the *weendigo* ate, it grew, and as it grew, so did its hunger, so that no matter how much it ate, its hunger always remained in proportion to its size. The *weendigo* could never requite its unnatural lust. . . . It could never stop as animals do when bloated, unable to ingest another morsel, or sense as humans sense that enough is enough for the present. For the unfortunate *weendigo*, the more it ate, the bigger it grew; and the more it grew, the more it wanted and needed. (*Manitous* 222)

The *wiindigoo* represents not only the worst that can be done to a human, but also the worst a being can do to itself. The term *wiindigoo* echoes undesirable characteristics, derived from *wiin dago*, meaning "solely for oneself," or from *wiinin n'd'igoo*, meaning "fat" or excessive."

One of the most powerful combinations of ancient Anishinaabe narrative with modern literary and cultural criticism is Johnston's story "Modern *Weendigos*," in which he reclaims the Anishinaabe character the *wiindigoo* and uses it to critique the current culture of capitalism. There was a time, he explains, when the mythical figures of Anishinaabe stories were thought to have truly disappeared into the category of "superstition" imposed by assimilation into a culture that did not recognize them. "Actually," he says, "the *weendigoes* did not die out or disappear; they have only been assimilated and reincarnated as corporations, conglomerates, and multinationals" (*Manitous* 235).

A second important example of *wiindigoo* behavior involves linguistic racism and shows how a dominated culture will often turn on someone else. "Don't Call Me No Name" begins when two World War II veterans, just back from a tour of duty, try to buy a drink. They are told, "Indians ain't allowed in here . . . Forget the war. It's over. Indians is Indians. An' the law says you Indians can't drink." Eventually, one says to the other, "You know, you look kinda Chinese." To which the immediate reply is "Don't call me no names!" However, they hit upon a solution. When the next waiter tells them "We don't serve Indians," one of them replies, "Don't caw me no name. I not Indian. I Chinee" and orders "two Blue Libbons" (*Ojibway Tales* 124). Shocking to any modern, politically correct reader, the story shows the effectiveness of the law against "Indians" drinking. The punch line is funny at the expense of the Chinese, opening up opportunity for an even more complex discussion of racism. The two Anishinaabe veterans live up to the stereotype by lying to get alcohol. They become they worst kind of *wiindigoog*, buying their satisfaction at the expense of their self-esteem and someone else's identity. They leverage their knowledge of linguistics to imitate an "other" they don't understand, and ultimately, the story shows how racism swells to the size of a *wiindigoo* gorged on misunderstanding. What Johnston doesn't mention is that the Anishinaabe term for someone of Asian descent is still *Niibiishabo-inini*, which means "tea drinker." Perhaps it is not the most offensive term possible, but it reveals a lack of depth in understanding a culture. Surely the Ojibwe, Odawa, and Potawatomi who insist they are Anishinaabe could learn more about the Han and Tang people of Zhonghua.

Johnston reaches back into the memory of his tribe and sees the faces of the hungry *wiindigoog* in the "self-serving, gluttons" who cannot control their cravings, have no respect for others, and are willing to survive through consumption, greed, and dishonesty. His modern narrative, like so many of the stories of Gerald Vizenor, proposes that the survivors of the American holocaust have the right to reclaim and rebuild their distinct cultures as they see fit, not as they are seen by others to fit in.

Like the term *manidoo*, *wiindigoo* is used by both Anishinaabe and non-Native writers. Perhaps this is because it offers a universal message. Old people warned against *wiindigoo* behavior: "Not too much. Think of tomorrow, next winter. *Kegoh zaum! Baenuk!* Think of others! Balance, moderation, and self-control!" (*Manitous* 222). These sentiments echo the traditional concept of *bimaadiziwin* in Anishinaabe culture but apply to humanitarian ideals in general. The balanced relationships of *bimaadiziwin* are the counterpoint to stories of *wiindigoog*. The beliefs he asks contemporary Anishinaabe to once again embrace are the tenets of *minobimaadiziwin*, "the good life." It is also important to note that Johnston is one of several scholars who currently write about this idea and one of many elders who hold to this belief. Hartley White says in *Living Our Language*:

> Apegish gashkitooyaan ji-daanginangiban ji-izhi-inigoondebinagiban a'aw be-maadizid ji-booniikang o'ow isa gegwaadagitoowaad gegwaadagii'igoowaad gaye wiinawaa sa ji-nandawaabandamowaad aandi o'ow dibendaagoziwaad o'ow dibishkoo omaa akiing. Niitaa, akina endaso-bezhigooyang ingii-miinigoomin, ingii-pagidinigoomin gaye giinawind. Gaawiin igo gidayaasiimin gegoo gomaa. Ayaamagad gigii-izhi-miinig a'aw manidoo gaye giin ge-bima'adooyan ge-ani-waabanda'ad sa Anishinaabe bemaadizid miinawaa a'aw wiijabinoojiinyiimag. Miish i'iw apane, gaawinn noondawidawaa bizindawagwaa wewini ongow chi-Anishinaabeg, chi-aya'aag gaagiigidowaad. Mii go gaye wiinawaa ge-izhi-in-aaboo'iwewaaban ongow.

> I hope I'll be able to reach them, to convince the people to start over, to abstain from this suffering, from that which makes them suffer, and they will look for their real place of belonging here on earth. Niitaa, we've all been gifted, every one of us, and we've been put here ourselves. We're not here for very long. But there is something that Spirit gave you to carry with you so you can show the living Anishinaabe and their children. Although not all the time, they do hear me, just as I listened to these elders in a good way when the old people spoke. And they will echo those thoughts themselves. (219)

There is no doubt that a system of belief centered on *bimaadiziwin* could benefit anyone living today, Anishinaabe or not. The question Johnston has asked, with the leaders of his generation, is whether the language and narrative structure that supported the concept can be restored and transmitted to future generations. He acknowledges a common linguistic heritage as a way to explore cultural identity and talks about the broader group of related nations.

> The Anishinaabe nation lived in relative peace while occupying such a large territory. Such good fortune may be attributed to the size of its population and the preoccupation of all its neighbors with survival, the primary goal of life; and in having neighbors who were kin in language and in many cultural respects: the Cree to the north; the Naskapi and Addikumaek to the east; and the Shawnee, Kickapoo, Sauk, Fox, and Menominees to the south and southwest. As neighbors, and sometimes as foes, were also people of different stock and culture such as the Huron, Mohawk, Seneca, Onondaga, Oneida, Cayuga, and Tuscarora to the east, and the Winnebago and Dakota to the west. (*Manitous* xvii)

In this passage he mentions eight tribes of similar background, yet sufficiently unlike the Anishinaabe to be considered different communities. He also mentions nine tribes "of different stock and culture." This comment is only a small aside in his book about *manidoog*, yet it is an important clue to the Anishinaabe self-image as a large nation aware of both neighbors and enemies. Part of Johnston's objective is to broaden the image of the "Indian" in the Americas or to at least require non-Indians to think from an indigenous perspective. By making clear that he is speaking only about one tribe, and noting the many tribes who contrast with his own culture, Johnston contributes to a more complete recognition of the ways Anishinaabe *bimaadiziwin*, or way of approaching life, relates to the broader history of diplomacy and social development in the present. His depiction of Anishinaabe culture and the surrounding communities shows that the early immigrants and explorers encountered people who had a complex system for understanding the world that was reflected in their language and stories. Perhaps if this reality had been recognized and cultural and language barriers had been bridged, North American history might have turned out differently.

The people of Moose Meat Point Reserve, who comprise the characters in *Ojibway Tales*, are often caught between cultures trying to find Anishinaabe *bimaadiziwin* while surrounded by a very different culture. Some characters have no interest in changing. Ben Cabooge learns English only when forced.

> He did not consider English often. He did not need it; he did not want it. As a fisherman, hunter, trapper, and gatherer of wild rice on Moose Meat Point, Ben

got along well enough in Ojibway. On the few occasions that he had to consort with white people, they were forced to deal with him on his terms. He liked that just fine. (*Indian School Days* 113)

Others find themselves unable to move forward in either world. Yellow Cloud was an older man of sixty or so who avoided the white community in part because he was naturally shy and in part because he did not speak English. Yet because he was assured that *wiindigoos* and the *makwabimose* (bear walker) do not exist, Yellow Cloud converted to Christianity. His conversion, however, was not so complete as the converter might have imagined:

> Having embraced such beliefs and taken part in the ceremonies for sixty years or more, Yellow Cloud found it difficult to abandon them. Even more difficult was the espousal of new beliefs and attendance at new ceremonies. Accepting the Ten Commandments was easy enough, but trusting in angels, saints and guardians was, he felt, not much different from invoking his own traditional patrons. He became a Christian in name but not in conviction. In fact, old Yellow Cloud was confused, and in his confusion he became a skeptic believing in neither his tribe's beliefs, nor the tenets of Christianity. (*Ojibway Tales* 58)

The tale goes on to recount Yellow Cloud's frightening nighttime encounter with a terrifying monster, roaring toward him, lit by two bright lights. He is convinced, in a flood of incomplete memories, that this is the *makwabimose* described in tales of his youth, and he smashes what we later find out are headlights. Of course, the sermon the next day at mass focuses on the wrath and results of irresponsible drinking. It would not have occurred to any of the whites to ask if there were a reason for Yellow Cloud to have been afraid. He might have saved himself some trouble by recalling that the *miskobimossae* sometimes hover above trees, but in the confusion of conversion this fact was lost on him. Johnston's story shows how this inability to believe either in the traditional tales or in the new religion of the missionaries causes the erosion, the forgetting, of traditional Anishinaabe *bimaadiziwin*.

While his short traditional tales are intended to keep the language and narrative tradition alive, most of Johnston's stories of modern life document the erosion of Anishinaabe culture. In a few cases, characters fight to uphold traditional beliefs, even dare to tell the whites of their own failings. The final story in *Ojibway Tales*, "A Sign of the Times," recalls a special meeting of Ojibway and Cree chiefs with the Department of Indian Affairs. The meeting was called to mark "the inception of a new and exciting relationship and partnership" between the federal government and the Native peoples (*Ojibway Tales* 169). After several hilarious linguistic misunderstandings about such words as "arbitrate" and "emasculate," the government prepares to offer various social services to the Ojibway and Cree communities. Big Flossie, an elder in the Moose Meat group, sees this as a new way to tell the Anishinaabe they are not good enough, and starts to question the panel in unanticipated ways. Big Flossie is a bit of a *manidoo*; she is larger than life, and too real for some to believe. First, she questions Miss Olga Shaposhnikoff, who offered to assist in matters of family planning and diet. When Miss Shaposhnikoff refuses to note her own marital status and number of children, if any, Big Flossie insists:

> Look, Miss whatever your name is . . . Don' git smard wid me. Maybe old me, but I kin skin you any day. Jis remember dat. Always de same. White peoples come 'ere tells us poor Indians what to do, ast us questions. An' when us Indians ast questions, youse neber answer. Dis time youse gonna answer . . . Youse ain't married; youse ain't got kids; youse don' take pills; youse don' hab a house. How you gonna teach dem things? Eh? Eh? Eh? . . . Well, me, I don't hab no education. I raisit ten kids. I keep house. I keep clean. I feed my husband. I happy me. You happier, you, wid no kids? . . . Is dat de bes' your department can do? If dat's de bes,' den we don' need you damned help. (*Ojibway Tales* 175)

Big Flossie then offers to speak Anishinaabemowin to another woman prepared "to assist in developing language curriculum" and finds out that the professor does not speak either Ojibway or Cree, but only reads a limited number of words. The real issue at hand is finally revealed when everyone gets down to business to vote on whether or not to construct new homes on the reserve. Much discussion ensues on the merits of progress, but once again, it is Big Flossie who raises the difficult issues:

> Youse young peoples, alls you tink about is progress. You tink we nember heard of dat, us, eh? Well, Indians tought about progress long times ago; before youse was borned. Married the whites, dem; moved off de reserve, dem. Got Metis kids. Didn' do dem any good. Jis ast de Metis. Don' eben talk Indian youse. Dat progress

eh? Do you any good jus' to speak English? Eh? Eh? Like you any bedder, dem? Eh? (*Ojibway Tales* 179)

In the end, they vote to build the houses. When the materials arrive, they decide instead to build ice-fishing houses, which the government then tries to remove from the lake. thinking they are outhouses. A sad comedy of errors, this story is based on real events. Although the jokes are everywhere, they can't cover up the harsh reality. Big Flossie puts it plainer than most Anishinaabe or whites might have. The truth is that there is no turning back. Yet Big Flossie clings defiantly to her language, her culture, and her happiness, her *minobimaadiziwin*.

Johnston's writing makes the case that there is good reason to believe ideas of Anishinaabemowin and *bimaadiziwin* will be relevant throughout time and should be part of both the present and the future. Clearly, everyone in the Great Lakes would benefit from a better understanding of nature and how to protect its interdependent support of all life in the region.

Johnston's use of Anishinaabemowin and introduction of traditional mythic characters can also be applied to many of the relationships still part of modern life. His stories include spousal disputes, maternal adoration, and brotherly competition—all of the same dramatic points of interaction that the literature of any complex culture would include. At these times we see exactly how the Anishinaabe narrative heritage can influence the course of human lives. For example, in *The Bear-Walker*, a young man goes out in search of answers. "He wanted to learn what you might call medicine. Actually, he really wanted to learn all kinds of things. Besides, he wanted to understand himself" (8). He found a teacher willing to help him, but the teacher asked him to get wet and dirty and look for long periods at nothing. He gave up too soon. Later, in winter (a time of stories and reflection), "when he was sitting at home in the big city," he realized the lesson the teacher had been trying to teach him:

> If you were to help your fellow Anishinaubaek, or your fellow human beings generally, what you must do is already set. However you may hate it, however unpleasant it may be, you must work at it. It is not always beautiful. . . . To get to the source of beauty you must dig deep. (*The Bear-Walker* 15)

This is a story Johnston wrote after hearing it told in Anishinaabemowin by Frank Shawbedees, who noted, "this is a relatively new story." And yet, in the context of all that Johnston presents to his readers, it is also a very old story. The lesson is to recognize it as both old and new, and to allow both views to influence relationships of the present.

Another story set in both the long ago and the right now is the story of Nanabozho and his grandmother, Nokomis. As people stop using the language in the community, Nanabozho gathers his worldly possessions and leaves in a canoe with Nokomis.

> He does not want to leave, but he must, for he is no longer welcome in his ancestral home. Still, he tarries and looks longingly in hopes that someone will notice and bid them to stay. But no one gives Nana'b'oozoo and his grandmother a second glance, and they pass beyond the horizon and out of the lives of their kin.
>
> No one in the village misses them; no one mourns their passing. No one cares enough. Perhaps, no one will ever care enough to call them back.
>
> But should enough people care, and recall Nana'b'oozoo into their midst by learning their ancestral language and espousing their old traditions, giving them new meanings and applications in the modern age; the spirit of Nana'b'oozoo and the Anishinaubae people will be restored to its rightful place in the lives of the Anishinaabe nation. (*Manitous* xxiii)

Through his stories, Johnston calls to Nanabozho and Nokomis. Whether he knew of other Anishinaabe writers calling with him when this was written, I cannot say. But Johnston is not alone. He and other literary members of the Anishinaabe nation are giving new meaning to old stories. They are forming new relationships that define Anishinaabe culture as distinct in North America and well worth preserving. Johnston teaches his readers:

> If the Native Peoples and their heritage are to be understood, it is their beliefs, insights, concepts, ideals, values, attitudes, and codes that must be studied. And there is, I submit, no better way of gaining that understanding than by examining native ceremonies, rituals, songs, dances, prayers, and stories. For it is in ceremony, ritual, song, dance, and prayer that the sum total of what people believe about life, being, existence, and relationships [is] symbolically expressed and articulated; as it is in story, fable, legend, and myth that fundamental understandings, insights, and attitudes toward life and human conduct, character, and quality in their diverse forms are embodied and passed on. (*Ojibway Heritage* 7)

Johnston teaches without being didactic or determinate. He would rather teach the importance of listening and thinking than give the answer too easily. He is like the elder in his story "The Bear-Walker," who says to his student, "Try to remember! Think! Why did you do what you did?" (*The Bear-Walker* 14). He is not as concerned with finding one true ending as he is with encouraging readers to become engaged with the text and think about their own stories. Often he includes a variety of optional twists and turns in the plot of a single story. For example, when Nanabozho finds out that his father is Aepungishimook, a *manidoo*, he decides to confront him and punish him for leaving his mother to raise her sons alone. But how can a young man, only part *manidoo*, take on the *manidoo* of death itself and live to tell about it? Johnston offers several endings to this somewhat unreasonable quest. In one version of the tale, Nanabozho finds an old man in the forest, tells him the story before realizing it is Aepungishimook, and reconciles with him before any battle begins. In another version of the same story, Nanabozho treks all the way across the plains. At a point near the mountains, a flicker appears to him in a dream and tells him how to take advantage of his father's weakness. In the heat of battle, however, Nanabozho is so overwhelmed that he forgets how to win. Eventually, his father offers him a *pawaugun,* or pipe, which they smoke together. Some say this is how the tradition of the pipe came to the Anishinaabe (*Manitous* 67–69). Johnston's stories are interactive and offer readers several ways to interpret events. His stories illustrate the power of multiple views of one reality. In *The Art of Norval Morrisseau* he teaches:

> It is through our neighbors, the plants, the seasons, the daily changes that we come to know something of life, being Kitchi-Manitou. That is revelation. Kitchi-Manitou is manifested all about us. Humans need only to watch and listen and they will see and hear The Creator. Before The Book there were only mountains, lakes, plains, forests, fair and cloudy days. (16)

This process of teaching how stories function in life is as important to Johnston as are the stories themselves. He leaves room for many possibilities. He edits scenes and characters to give readers a sense of why storytelling is important. He often comments that the Anishinaabe may have lost some specific traditions, but not their values. He allows readers to determine if the path chosen is good, bad, or merely a step on a trail between good and bad.

Much has changed for the Anishinaabe Johnston writes about and for those who read the stories today. Yet he points out that much has also remained the same. The people still face many of the same issues and, according to Johnston, they will be stronger when they relearn stories of the past and apply them to the present. In my opinion, one of the most profound differences between Anishinaabe and contemporary American culture is that Americans are driven to live for the future, to set goals, to challenge and compete with themselves and others. When balanced with the reality of our temporal impermanence, these are not bad instincts to have and can lead to much success. But when wealth, power, winning, and the future are the center of too much attention, life can be less satisfying and less healthy. These are not surprising or unusual suggestions, and many communities both secular and spiritual urge their members to consider these issues carefully. The point that Johnston makes is that the principles of *bimaadiziwin*, as represented in so many of the traditional Anishinaabe stories, advocate a healthy, balanced lifestyle—a way of life that would serve the Anishinaabe as well amid corporations and casinos as it did in canoes and at campsites. His use of Anishinaabemowin and preservation of Anishinaabe storytelling style can bring *bimaadiziwin* back to the Anishinaabe. He is a skilled storyteller who can be as subtle as the choice of trees mentioned in a dream or direct as the warning:

> The following does not apply to just one Anishinaabe, but to all, every single one. There is no question that it is necessary for them to return to the way they used to worship, to again take up their ancient way of believing. At that time they will survive; they will prosper. (*Tales of the Anishinaubaek* 13)

Combined with numerous admonitions to "return to old ways" is the assertion that these old ways are perfectly modern in their recommendation of balance and shared values. Johnston writes, "It will not be until our grandchildren and their grandchildren return to the ways of their ancestors that they will regain strength of spirit and heart" (*Manitous* 181).

CHAPTER SIX

Waninawendamowinan: Stirred Thoughts in the Writing of Gerald Vizenor

Listen, there are words almost everywhere. I realized that in a chance moment. Words are in the air, in our blood, words were always there. . . . Words are in snow, trees, leaves, wind, birds, beaver, the sound of ice cracking; words are in fish and mongrels, where they've been since we came to this place with the animals. My winter breath is a word, we are words, real words, and the mongrels are their own words. Words are crossbloods too, almost whole right down to the cold printed page.

—Vizenor, *Landfill Meditation*

Like the *jiisakaawininiwag* who built tents of twigs and spirit for their ceremonies, Vizenor builds tents of language and calls forth the voices, words, and stories that others often do not hear. In one of his earliest books, Vizenor writes about the time of night when the shadows fall and "the *jiisakaawininiwag* commune with the voices of the *manidoog* that surround us" (*Summer in the Spring* 83). The *jiisakaawininiwag* learn from nature and careful observation. They find words, images, and meaning everywhere. Vizenor is an Anishinaabe author who tests the limits of the English language, and he strains and stretches the boundaries of traditional Anishinaabe narrative. He invents words, including "holosexual," "crossblood," and "survivance." He gives names like Bagese, Griever, Pure Gumption, and Stone Columbus. He confronts contemporary Native American Indian political issues in sometimes shocking ways. In the novel *Chancers*, he shares the revulsion of the bone repatriation wars by writing a graphic sex scene in the hallowed halls of anthropology, which leaves the reader feeling either as assaulted as the poor skulls themselves or as guilty of visceral voyeurism as the anthropologists. In *Father Meme* he writes of a priest's sexual abuse. Always he reinvents tradition, moves in and out of reality, and writes in a way that is part Anishinaabe, part international intellectual. *Ikidowinan dagonanan*, he stirs words. He mixes thoughts, *waninawendamo*. In his work he shows a reverence for what the Anishinaabe language can represent, a deep knowledge of Anishinaabe storytelling, and a philosophy of *Nanabozhogaazo, Makwabaabaabmose*, and *bimaadizitaage*, the shapeshifters who dream of every day as a new game to play, a new chance to take.

Throughout his career, Vizenor's work has inspired a wide range of reactions. His books have been praised by critics, deconstructed by academics, and in some cases, rejected by readers including members of his own tribe. On the one hand Kenneth Lincoln characterized *Bearheart* as "funny talk, fellatio, cryptic comedy and mindless violence" (Lee 158). On the other hand Barry O'Connell salutes Vizenor as a "master comedian" (Lee 82). Bernadette Pugal-Cellards addresses his cultural critical complexity in her essay titled "A Post-Maodernist Little Red Book of Cocks, Tricksters, and Colonists" (Krupat, *New Voices* 317). Among Native American Indian readers and scholars he also garners mixed reviews. Jim Northrup once joked in conversation, "The only way I'll read Vizenor is if someone held a bayonet to me" (Interview). Nothing could be further from Northrup's casual storytelling style than Vizenor's postmodern fiction. Choctaw-Cherokee professor of literature Louis Owens describes how angry students reported him to the dean when he put *Bearheart* on the syllabus (Vizenor, *Narrative Chance* 141).

Vizenor's stories are not the easily understood echoes of Anishinaabe tradition that readers may expect. They are self-proclaimed postmodern flights of imagination. His books are wordarrows that lodge themselves in the heart of the idea of what it means to be Anishinaabe. Readers are as likely to encounter epigraphs by Samuel Beckett, Maurice Blanchot, and Anais Nin as they are to be told stories of Nokomis and Nanabozho. His books are complex creations that can be traced to centuries-old stories. They are also simple and straightforward in their desire to carry Anishinaabe language and culture into the future and shed the useless "fugitive poses" suggested by the dominant society.

Gaa Ezhi-bimaadizid / Life So Far

To understand how Vizenor's writing fits into the context of Anishinaabe literature it is helpful to review his family's history and the events of his life. His relatives were among the first to see "the white strangers, the French explorers and fur traders at Michilimackinac, Great Turtle Island," which is now a part of Michigan (*Interior Landscapes* 5). When this happened, sometime in the late 1600s, the Anishinaabe had already lived many generations in the woodland area of the Great Lakes. Their oral histories included creation stories, tales of migration, and entertaining parables of man and the *manidoog* with whom they share the earth.

Related to Keeshkemun, Vizenor is grandson of the first leader of the crane families, and recipient of the George Washington Peace Medal (*Interior Landscapes* 4). When asked by a British officer to explain who he was, Keeshkemun replied:

> You ask me who I am. If you wish to know, you must seek me in the clouds. . . . I am a bird who rises from the earth, and flies far up, into the skies, out of human sight; but though not visible to the eye, my voice is heard from afar, and resounds over the earth. . . . You wish to know who I am. You have never sought me, or you should have found and known me. (Warren 373)

It is recorded that the British officer warned the Anishinaabe leader not to join forces with those who fight against the English. Keeshkemun's reply was a powerful poetic image. "You are stronger than I am. You can do as you say. But remember the voice of the Crane echoes afar off, and when he summons his children together, they number like pebbles of the Great Lake shores" (Warren 374). As a descendent of the crane clan, Vizenor is one of those pebbles, and this quote may hold special significance as he now lends his voice to the body of Anishinaabe literature while living far from the land his tribe calls home.

As members of the crane clan, the *ajijaak*, Vizenor and his relatives are expected to be leaders and interpreters in the Anishinaabe community. For this reason, they are also known as the *passwewag*, the echo makers (*Interior Landscapes* 5). The first chapter of Vizenor's autobiographical book *Interior Landscapes* is titled "Families of the Crane" and traces the history of the family from its avian origins along the shores of *Kchi Gaming* to the present. The history extends from Keeshkemun, who guarded the peace of his people in difficult times, through generations of French, Métis, and Anishinaabe traders; to the first settlers at White Earth Reservation; and finally to Clement William Vizenor and LaVerne Lydia Peterson, the parents of Gerald Robert Vizenor, who fell in love in the urban landscape of Minneapolis.

Intermarriage and the adoption of French or English names for religious or business reasons were common among the Anishinaabe of the Great Lakes. The Vizenor family is no exception. Ogemaugeezhigoquae, the granddaughter of Keeshkemun, was baptized Margaret Racine. She married Basile Hudon dit Beaulieu, who was born in 1785, in Quebec. His son, Paul Hudon, was one of the first settlers on White Earth Reservation in 1867. The Beaulieu family also published the first newspaper on the reservation. The first edition of *The Progress* was printed in 1886, but an Indian agent disliked the content and threatened to shut down operations. The matter was settled in U.S. district court by Judge Nelson, who defended the right of any member of a tribe to print and publish a newspaper. Later, the paper was renamed *The Tomahawk*, and its editors wrote articles opposing the Dawes Severalty Act, which parceled out the reservation in taxable allotments. Again, Vizenor's heritage leads back to members of the tribe who were outspoken in their search for peace and justice.

The history of the clan and the lives of his White Earth relatives are the well-documented aspects of his ancestry. Gaps in his family history, however, have played a major role in Vizenor's life. The first unanswered question to arise is the unsolved murder of his father, which took place when Gerald was not yet two, and his father only twenty-six. His mother's inability to raise him on her own marks another early loss, and, as he was shuffled from one household to another, the lack of a stable family became another difficulty in his life. But in all this, Vizenor now finds a lesson in humor, chance, and survival:

> Surely my childhood was more chance than manners, and that memory pleases me now. Even some of the most miserable situations come to mind as humor, and sometimes the memory of my grandmother and the tease of other Anishinaabe relatives is a cue to tricky stories. So, you might ask, why didn't they take better

care of me, and rescue me from fosterage? Well, stories are not a ransom. Luckily, my stories save me from the obvious, and the curse of victimry. (*Postindian Conversations* 20)

Saying this, he makes the point that all the tradition in the world won't heat a house in winter. His grandmother gave him what she could, but her own life after moving from the reservation to the city was difficult, and although he visited her often during his youth, she was unable to take him into her home. Instead she and her brother, John Clement, gave him the gift of storytelling.

Vizenor eventually took control of his own story and enlisted in the army. In 1953, at age eighteen, he set sail for Korea. As Kim Blaeser explains in her biography of Vizenor,

> It was amid military structures that he first experienced a feeling of liberation and promise. Through a standard army intelligence test he was shown to be intellectually gifted, a fact that surprised him so much he insisted the test must be in error. But when a second exam resulted in yet better scores, Vizenor for the first time in his life began to see himself as having potential. (*Gerald Vizenor* 6)

As a result, it was while he was in the army that Vizenor began reading the books he associated with an academic life, including the Japanese poet Bashō, who left an enduring impression on him. After an honorable discharge in 1955 he returned to the United States to go to college. He studied child development and Asian studies and, encouraged by a professor of Asian studies, began publishing short chapbooks of haiku and transcriptions of Anishinaabe tribal history.

In 1965, he became director of the American Indian Employment Center in Minneapolis, where he worked in social services and education to serve the members of the Native American Indian community. He describes the experience as one when he "lived in a world of rage, the silent anger of cures and promises. . . . Radical advocacy demanded more than just a good and worried heart, and street work took much more than compassion and anger. . . . The native street demanded a strategy of rage, an antidote to curses, and clear articulation of situational ethics" (*Postindian Conversations* 36–37). His desire to speak out on Native American Indian issues led him to begin a brief career in journalism writing for *Twin Citian* and the *Minneapolis Tribune*. For several years he worked on assignment. He covered the trial of James White Hawk, a young Lakota man who was tried for murder, and the story of Dane Mitchell, another Lakota, who took his own life after being sentenced to solitary confinement for truancy. He later became an editorial writer offering a Native American Anishinaabe view of the American Indian Movement. Vizenor was one of the few Native Americans willing to critique the politics of AIM. The American Indian Movement brought national attention to pantribal stereotypes in a way that captured the attention of average Americans. By contrast, Vizenor has always been more interested in serious Native intellectual discourse combined with less visible grassroots activism. The stereotypes AIM embraced and used to their advantage are the very aspects of Native American Indian identity that Vizenor rejects. He was a leader of the other AIM, the "Anishinaabe Intellectual Movement."

His career and life changed in 1970 when George Mills, the chair of the social science department at Lake Forest College in Illinois, hired Vizenor to teach because he liked his haikus. After teaching at the Bemidji, Augsburg, Macalester, and Hamline campuses, he ended up teaching Native American literature at the University of Minnesota in Minneapolis. While teaching at Minnesota he was also hired to teach on the Berkeley campus for the University of California. For a time he alternated between the two states. However, in the early eighties the American Indian Studies Department at the University of Minnesota was dismantled by the dean. Vizenor attempted with his colleagues to salvage the situation, but the issues were too complex to unravel in the one year they were given. A story in *Earthdivers* critiques the painful situation and the people involved. In 1983 he moved to California to teach in a large Department of American Indian Studies. The fields of Native studies and American literature continue to change, and he is now Distinguished Professor of American Studies at the University of New Mexico, Albuquerque, but he has not forgotten the early struggles of his career as a new generation of ethnic studies professors attempts to make sense of the social sciences and humanities. In his 2012 novel, *Chair of Tears*, he warns again of those who "flunked as innovative native executives" because "they deserted stories, practices of natural reason, and survivance, and disregarded the very emotive sentiments of a native presence" (24).

Vizenor the writer, like his characters, has several masks. He is a journalist, poet, novelist, and critic. He has poured the politics of Native American Indians onto the pages of major metropolitan papers, written spare and elegant haiku, published fantastic postmodern fiction, shared the language and history of the Anishinaabe, and edited volumes of academic essays. He often weaves fact and fiction into a single volume, and to sort out what is reality by conventional standards can be difficult.

> Maybe my memories are the creation of my chancy presence. Maybe my memories precede me, the very tease of creation, and my stories are the ransom of a presence. Maybe not, but only those who tease memories and create stories come close enough to the ironic humor to know otherwise. Even so, the stories of our presence are the natural tease of memories, and the points of view we create must be chancy. (*Postindian Conversations* 19)

With statements like this one he makes it clear that he is not always trying to present the truth as a perfect snapshot. His own recollections, like the recollections of the Anishinaabe community, are open to multiple interpretations. According to Vizenor, the versions of history most easily presented may not contain the real story at all.

Gaa Ezhibii'iged / Writing So Far

For his first publications, Vizenor was poet and publisher. His haikus were printed by Nodin Press, which he started and eventually sold to a local book distributor in Minnesota. Lee notes in *Shadow Distance* that "haiku, for all its objectivism, has been an especially intimate signature for Vizenor" (xxiii). Describing the change in his verse over time, Vizenor has said, "The haiku in my first three books, *Raising the Moon Vines*, *Seventeen Chirps*, and *Empty Swings*, were common comparative experiences in the past tense. Later, in *Matsushima* my haiku were more metaphorical, concise and with a sense of presence" (*Shadow Distance* 30). In 2006, both *Bear Island* and *Almost Ashore* were published, and each departed from the haiku form in a different way. *Almost Ashore* is a series of short imagistic poems that capture the history and reality of several landscapes. Some of the horizons focus on parts of the Anishinaabe world, while others journey to places far away from the Great Lakes. *Bear Island* is the story of a battle in Sugar Point, Minnesota, in 1898. In epic format, Vizenor describes the "hunted and harried," the sacred *Midewiwin* bundles used for ceremony and survival cut open and destroyed and the decisive victory of the Anishinaabe Pillagers against the Third United States Infantry.

In 1974, Vizenor began work on the first of his novels, *Darkness in Saint Louis Bearheart*, which was published in 1978. Twelve years later, he revised the novel, and it was republished as *Bearheart: The Heirship Chronicles*. Louis Owens has called *Bearheart* "a postapocalyptic allegory of mixedblood pilgrim clowns afoot in a world gone predictably mad" (229). The novel begins in the Bureau of Indian Affairs in Washington, D.C., when an old man, Bearheart, asks a young radical to find the manuscript of his novel in a file. The novel they are trying to locate records the visions of a traveling band of Anishinaabe. Throughout the novel the characters impose an Anishinaabe worldview on modern America, resulting in a rather harsh critique of industrial society. Vizenor calls *Bearheart* "a journey of survivance at the end of a chemical civilization, a wild cut of presence, and the consequences of material failure, long after the waves of righteous immigrants, mercenary settlements, mining, the simulations of postwestern movies, and the exclusion and removal of natives" (*Postindian Conversations* 97).

Vizenor did not start his second novel until nearly a decade after beginning his first. His tenure as a professor at Tianjin University in China led to *Griever: An American Monkey King in China*, which was published in 1987. Inspired by the Chinese opera *Havoc of Heaven* and traditional Anishinaabe tales, *Griever* is a novel of mirror images, cyclical storytelling, and cultural commentary. Linda Lizut Helstern calls it "a cross-cultural re-membering" that conveys Chinese and Anishinaabe cultural legacies (Lee 136). The Chinese legacy is one of an attempt to liberate the people, while the Anishinaabe legacy is the lesson that freedom must sometimes be taken back from colonial powers. The novel is filled with parallels between Chinese and American tribal people, not the least of which is the comparison between the Monkey King and Nanabozho.

One year after *Griever*, Vizenor wrote *The Trickster of Liberty: Tribal Heirs to a Wild Baronage* as "an anticampus novel . . . an academic aversion" wherein "the trickster characters create and reveal the consumer contradictions of institutional education" (*Postindian Conversations* 127). As an "academic aversion" or "episode of confrontation," the novel is an important interrogation of the processes used to transmit and perpetuate knowledge. The "trickster" of the title is an echo of the impetuous Anishinaabe characters in his book, who are very like cunning Nanabozho in the way they find solutions to every problem that confronts them. The members of the White Earth band of Anishinaabe are the "tribal heirs" who confront modern anthropology, technology, and reliquaries. They are the "oshki Anishinaabe," the new people of the woodland.

Vizenor's next novel, *The Heirs of Columbus*, was published in 1991, when the quincentennial of Columbus's arrival in the Americas was being "celebrated" across the country. Reversing the standard explanations of the Age of Discovery, *The Heirs of Columbus* establishes a radically different premise: the discovery went the other way. Long before the rise of European power, inhabitants of the Americas "discovered" Europe and the Mediterranean. In Vizenor's version of history, Columbus's origins were American, and Columbus was not searching for an utterly new world but instead wisely seeking to discover his roots by tracing his genealogy back to the Americas. In the present, his heir, Stone Columbus, returns to be a part of the annual storytelling season, which takes place at the headwaters of the *Michiziibi*, the Mississippi River, in Minnesota. The heirs of Columbus create a new nation dedicated to healing, and that process becomes yet another avenue of exploration for Vizenor.

Vizenor's next three novels continue his pattern of using the perspective of one or more Anishinaabe characters to critique popular culture and politics. In *Dead Voices: Natural Agonies in the New World*, a bear-woman named Bagese tells stories in the framework of a seven-card Anishinaabe game of chance, *wanaki*. *Hotline Healers: An Almost Browne Novel* continued the stories of White Earth crossblood tricksters loose in the world. *Chancers*, published in 2000, includes an Anishinaabe character who is part of an intertribal group of students fighting for bone repatriation in California. In 2003, *Hiroshima Bugi: Atomu 57* kept up with debates of the time in Native studies by examining issues of identity, hybridity, and victimization through Ronin Browne, the orphaned son of a Japanese dancer and Anishinaabe interpreter. His 2008 novel, *Father Meme*, is a *wiindigoo* novel with an evil priest dead center. Banishment, human rights, and the mind of an artist are the subjects of his 2010 novel, *Shrouds of White Earth*. The list of Vizenor's contributions to Anishinaabe fiction continues to grow.

In addition to fiction, Vizenor has published a range of essays about Anishinaabe society and history. His blend of images, the narratives of witnesses, and cultural documents bring together seemingly disparate events and offer a new way to read history and stories. *Escorts to White Earth, 1868–1968: 100 Years on a Reservation*, published in 1968, carries on the tradition of his great uncle, John Clement Beaulieu, who worked to preserve the history of the Anishinaabe families at White Earth Reservation. *Anishinabe Adisokan: Tales of the People* was first published in 1970; it includes numerous traditional tales of the Anishinaabe. *Summer in the Spring*, published in 1965, and reprinted in 1981 and 1993, combines poetry and prose and introduces his opinions about haiku and the Ojibwe dream songs recorded by Frances Densmore. In 1972, Vizenor edited *The Everlasting Sky: New Voices from the People Named the Chippewa,* which gave voice to the Anishinaabe of the present. *Wordarrows: Indians and Whites in the New Fur Trade* is real history told through the voice of Clement Beaulieu, a fictional character named for several of Vizenor's actual relatives. *Landfill Meditation* and *Earthdivers: Tribal Narratives on Mixed Descent* also blend recorded events with narrative imaginings. *Crossbloods: Bone Courts, Bingo, and Other Reports* contains Vizenor's famous postmodern satire on history and sociology, "Socioacupuncture: Mythic Reversals and the Striptease in Four Scenes." Following a quote from Michel Foucault about "the battle for and around history," Tune Browne confronts the subject of history in a way that no passive narrator could (*Crossbloods* 83). He creates a new framework for interpreting the present by dismantling the old stereotypes. The notion of a "striptease" stems from Roland Barthes's writing in *Mythologies* about the "moment of nakedness." Barthes maintains that the spectacle of the striptease is "based on the pretense of fear and ritual," which Vizenor sees as directly parallel to the way Native American Indians are taught to think of their own culture in the context of American society. Vizenor deconstructs the pantribal American idea of Native American Indians by giving voice to one very well read and articulate Anishinaabe professor. His lecture at the "first international conference on socioacupuncture and tribal identities" is a striptease filled with irony and truth. Browne seduces the audience by pretending to be for a moment what they expect him to be. Then he strips them of their racist views by showing he is more than they expected, a gesture that leaves them illuminated intellectually but literally in the dark. He tells his audience: "We lost the election in leathers and feathers, failed and fixed in histories, but through mythic satire we reverse the inventions, and during our ritual striptease the inventors vanish" (*Crossbloods* 92).

Although Vizenor has made it clear throughout his career that his writing relates to one specific tribe, he also uses this base of understanding to contribute to the wider field of Native American Indian studies as an author and critical editor. He has been a collector of and contributor to the canon of the Anishinaabe and a teacher and critic of Native American literature in a national and international context. In 1987 he edited *Touchwood,* a collection of Anishinaabe prose. A few years later, in 1989, he edited *Narrative Chance: Postmodern Discourse on Native American Indian Literatures* for a primarily academic audience. He also edited a pantribal volume of Native American literature published by HarperCollins for a general audience in 1995. In *Manifest Manners, Fugitive Poses, Native Liberty,* and *Postindian Conversations* Vizenor challenges the understanding of identity and nationalism, often using his own Anishinaabe heritage as a starting point, but moving well beyond the boundaries of a single nation. His cultural criticism often focuses on language, story, and the complex dreamscapes of history, survival, and continuance that must be acknowledged rather than blended into the format of the colonizing nation. He wants readers to think beyond their first idea of an Indian, past their second thoughts of specific Anishinaabe culture and use both hindsight and foresight to see how indigenous perspectives have altered history in ways that might be unremembered yet.

At the heart of all of Vizenor's irony, cynicism, and sarcastic wit, beneath even the most violent and titillating passages of fiction, he is a source of hope. Even as he describes the painful need for healing in Anishinaabe society, he writes of possibility:

> Centuries ago the Anishinaabe were one of the most active and significant cultures on the continent. Then colonialism, disease, war, and removal to federal reservations weakened native communities everywhere in the country. In the past generation, however, the Anishinaabe have restored some of their original stature as a visionary culture by the creative work of painters, sculptors, and literary artists. By original styles, imagic scenes, and conceptual art, many contemporary artists have reached beyond the bounds and obvious cues of tradition and culture. (*Everlasting Sky* xii)

This impetus for survival echoes the very heart of Anishinaabe spirituality as it is represented in both oral tradition and the texts of modern authors. The characters of Louise Erdrich, the survival stories of Jim Northrup, the universe as described by Basil Johnston, and the cultural juxtapositions of Gerald Vizenor all represent the central tension of possibility that threads through Anishinaabe language and narrative.

Vizenor's many connections to other authors have been explored in monographs and edited collections including Kimberly Blaeser's book *Gerald Vizenor: Writing in the Oral Tradition* and the multiauthor essay collection *Loosening the Seams: Interpretations of Gerald Vizenor.* Deborah Madsen's book *Understanding Gerald Vizenor* offers an excellent introduction to his world including analysis of his plays *Harold of Orange* and *Ishi and the Wood Ducks.* Vizenor's is a metaphorical *jiisakaawininiwag* whose work shakes the stereotypes of the Anishinaabe and challenges the people themselves to remember and redefine their culture.

Although Vizenor's writing is published in English for modern readers, the sound and meanings of Anishinaabemowin are included in many of his books. In *Chancers,* an Anishinaabe character named Round Dance says, "The Anishinaabe word *wanaki* means to live in a place of peace, and *animishimo wanaki* means to dance away and show me a place of peace" (88). Vizenor offers readers another way to think about peace, as a round dance and a word with the term "earth" (*aki*) built into it. In *The People Named the Chippewa* Vizenor explains why he reaches back to bring these words into the present:

> The Anishinaabeg did not borrow words from other languages to speak about their own dreams and lived experiences in the woodland. The words the woodland tribes spoke were connected to the place the words were spoken. The poetic images were held, for some tribal families, in song pictures and in the rhythms of visions and dreams in music: timeless and natural patterns of seeing and knowing the energies of the earth. (26)

In *The Heirs of Columbus* Vizenor goes on to say, "language is a game, not a rule" (*Postindian Conversations* 133). This combination of reverence and play creates in Vizenor's work the living tension of possibility that connects his work to Anishinaabe culture. As a writer, Vizenor sees how language can be a game, yet he also has strong opinions about language and its power.

Readers of his early works and careful readers of his novels know him as a champion of Anishinaabemowin. Vizenor's subjective bias is obvious as he describes the rich heritage of the language:

> *Anishinaabemowin* is a language of verbal forms and imaginative word images. The spoken feeling of the language is a moving image of tribal woodland life: *nibi* (water), *maang* (loon), *makwa* (bear), *amik* (beaver), kingfishers at dusk, owls at night, and maple syrup in the snow. The language is euphonious: *Anishinaabe nag-amon* (songs of the people), *bibigwan* (flute), *manoomin* (wild rice), *gimiwan* (it is raining), *ziibiwan* (rivers) *memengwaag* (butterflies), *giiweniibin* (late summer), *giiwebiboon* (late winter), *ishkode* (fire), *bapakine* (grasshopper), *waawaatesiwag* (fireflies), *miigwani wiiwakwaan* (feather headdress), and *manidoowi* (the spirit of a *manidoo*). (*Summer in the Spring* 12)

As both poet and novelist Vizenor has used the language throughout his books to convey sounds, images, and ideas that could not be so precisely stated in English. As an Anishinaabe author, Vizenor uses Anishinaabemowin to achieve his own artistic goals and to help keep it, and the culture it represents, alive.

Vizenor's views about the importance of the Anishinaabe language can be found throughout his work. His earlier books, which center on cultural heritage, frequently stress the importance of maintaining the language. In *The People Named the Chippewa* (1984), he wrote about the history and importance of the original language. He noted the confusion that ensued when missionaries, ethnographers, and government representatives tried to document a culture without knowing the language. People were named to suit the needs of French- and English-speaking immigrants, and the tribal group itself was rarely referred to as "Anishinaabe" in early documents. The Anishinaabe are still officially given names no Native speaker would consider correct. Vizenor describes the dissonance caused by these linguistic difficulties:

> Not only have certain tribal names been invented and ascribed in written form, the personal names of tribal people have been changed and translated without cultural significance. When a tribal person is expected to understand several thousand years of tribal history in the language of dominant societies, his identities are a dangerous burden. Two generations ago the Anishinaabeg, and other tribal cultures, were forbidden to speak their language and practice their religion. . . . The cultural and political histories of the Anishinaabeg were written in a colonial language by those who invented the Indian, renamed the tribes, allotted the land, divided ancestries by geometric degrees of blood, and categorized identities on federal reservations. (*People Named the Chippewa* 19)

It is this renaming, division, and categorization that Vizenor writes against. By weaving the language throughout his works he keeps Anishinaabe words and concepts alive and in a modern context.

Vizenor's use of Anishinaabemowin ranges from didactic passages that provide a translation for each word to instances where no direct translation is provided at all. Despite the range in the amount of information Vizenor provides readers, it should be noted that at no time does his use of Anishinaabemowin render any passage meaningless to nonspeakers. Speakers of the language will sometimes understand a broader implication or make a more specific cultural connection, but he writes in a way that can be read, on the surface at least, by those who speak only English. This could be because English is the first language of the majority of the members of the Anishinaabe community today, including Vizenor himself. This could also be a way for him to "tease" readers into learning the language or at least understanding how it can influence a text.

One of the powers he ascribes to the language is the way that an Anishinaabe name can convey something of personal importance about a person. For example, in *Hotline Healers*, characters stop at the Ozaawaa Casino Station, which is perfect for stories of the risk-taking Brownes, since *ozawaa* can mean any color from gold to brown. In *The Heirs of Columbus*, he invokes traditional stories of migration and Native presence in North America by naming a young girl, Miigis, after the sacred cowrie shell that led the Anishinaabe to settle where they currently live around the Great Lakes. In *Dead Voices*, Bagese, the bear-woman, is named for the Anishinaabe game in which wooden figures are tossed in a dish to see which figures will remain standing. Other uses of Anishinaabe proper nouns include the names of some of the mythic characters already discussed. These characters, Nanabozho and the *wiindigoo*, are specifically Anishinaabe and in some books are mentioned so often that even a reader who does not speak the language will begin to recognize them.

Ikidowinan Akiing / Words in the World

Like other Anishinaabe authors, Vizenor draws on Anishinaabe linguistic and literary traditions while writing in English. He often speaks of the way a simple description of image or action can become a narrative. In *Bearheart*, "Proude spread his graceful fingers out on the table, moving them like shaman animals through the tender fern. His fingers became turtles and touched his spoken words. Words came before him on the wind" (61). Through short lines of poetic prose Vizenor takes readers to a specific place in the woods where ferns grow and words are spoken on the wind. In *Chancers* words are found in song as "Cloud Burst beat the character on the drum harder, thunder in every fierce thrust, and the pitch of his wail cut conversations, scared the sparrows, and mocked the insects" (32). There is a synergy between the word and the sound, placing an image and idea in song.

Vizenor sees in traditional Anishinaabe dream songs "the kind of touch with nature, the twist on natural experience that's almost a transformation, human consciousness derived from other living things" (Blaeser, *Gerald Vizenor* 116). Haiku are short lyrical poems usually made up of 17 syllables in three lines following a five-seven-five pattern. Like Anishinaabe dream songs, haiku stem from a moment of intense personal awareness, sometimes inspired by a dream or vision. The songs and haiku are frequently intended to capture and convey the meaning of a fleeting image. In "Envoy to Haiku" Vizenor tells how he went back to the work of musicologist and ethnologist Frances Densmore, who transcribed the songs of the Anishinaabe in the 1800s, and found in her raw recordings "woodland dream songs and trickster stories that would bear the humor and tragic wisdom of tribal experiences . . . in song, the dreamers listen to the natural turnout of the seasons, and the everlasting sky hears their voices on the wind" (*Shadow Distance* 26). In his 1917 review of Densmore's collection of Ojibwe songs, Carl Sandburg jokingly noted the similarities between the songs and the poems of the imagist, saying, "suspicion arises that the red man and his children committed direct plagiarism on our modern imagists and vorticists" (Sandburg 245). In 1946, Margot Astrov again took up the subject and wrote that tribal songs were "remindful of the best of Japanese haiku that turn the listener into a poet himself, for it is his part to fill in the sketch" (16). At about the same time, A. Grove Day wrote that the imagists "found in the short verses like the Chippewa songs collected by Densmore the sort of compressed word-pictures they sought in other foreign forms like the Chinese poems and Japanese haiku" (32). Numerous contemporary writers, including James Ruppert, Michael Castro, Kenneth Rexroth, Larry Evers, and Karl Kroeber, have taken up the debate over the similarity of these forms. Vizenor has said, "The first American imagist poets were the American Indians" ("The Ojibway" 18). Undoubtedly, the links among Japanese, imagist, and Anishinaabe verse will continue to be debated as opinions change over time.

Vizenor finds poetry in the dream songs, and through them he speaks of alternate realities, histories of personal and collective subconscious. Dreaming is an important part of Anishinaabe stories and spirituality. In Anishinaabe tradition, dreams are a way to understand the waking world and to communicate with other worlds. Francis Densmore notes in *Chippewa Customs* that the abilities to dream and remember the stories of one's dreams were "cultivated from birth" among the Anishinaabe (78). Another important sentiment she recalled from her many interviews is the power and permanence of dreams. "A picture can be destroyed, but stone endures, so it is good that a man have the subject of his dream carved in a stone pipe that can be buried with him. The sign of his dream should not be taken from him" (*Chippewa Customs* 80). Dreams represent an incredible source of personal power and understanding for Vizenor's characters. Griever de Hocus connects with this theory when he warns that "lonesome white people with no shadows hound the tribes and capture our dreams" (*Griever* 56). The theft or forgetting of dreams is the greatest of tragedies.

Dreams and visions are also a means of giving readers collateral information. Often what happens in dreams does not happen in real life, but dreams can voice the unthinkable, the undoable. For example, in *Dead Voices* the narrator is haunted by memories of a past event and, through the description of a dream, allows a dead man to speak and give form to a vision of death (139). The dream allows a reader to experience a character's emotions without the limits of realism. Just as Nanabozho and his brothers were led on their adventures by their visions, Vizenor shows how modern Anishinaabe can find their own path on the trail of "word wars" imposed by the dominant society.

Arnold Krupat, in his studies of Native autobiography as a distinct genre, has also commented on the general importance of dreams and visions to all tribes. In response to Krupat's ethnographies, however, Vizenor proposes that dreams can also support a theory of incredible individuality. Rather than try to identify all the universal connections in dreams, Vizenor advises readers to celebrate each strange and unique imagining. In the novel *Bearheart* Proude Cedarfair emphasizes the power of dreams when he speaks to the federal agents.

> I will not listen to you speaking as an institution. Fools listen to the voices of the government . . . and the fools are lost and starving in the cities. When you speak as individuals in the language of your dreams I will listen, but I will not listen to that foolish green paper talking to me. (26)

Proude holds individual dreams in higher esteem than money. In Vizenor's novels, and in the records of various ethnographers, including Densmore, dreams and visions are highly personal. To the extent that one's environment and experiences are included in the dream or vision, they reflect the dreamer's individual culture or distinct community, but beneath that layer of consciousness they can show how the individual members come together as a community.

> Native visions are an originary sense of presence, and the stories of such unique individual experiences are a contradiction of the communal notions of synecdoche

. . . the sources of visions and identity, and the creation of the self, are more individualistic than communal. These visions and stories are more than communal, and must tease traditions. (*Postindian Conversations* 62)

Teasing tradition is one of Vizenor's specialties. Like a hunter quietly following a trapline, he plots a course for the readers that weaves between the real and imagined, facts and fiction, and may include diverse dimensions of reality.

Vizenor uses the techniques of dream songs and haiku to place the images and the imagination of the Anishinaabe world in his work. He uses "haiku moments" in both poetry and fiction. His spare, descriptive verse implies a connection with certain tribal ideas or experiences in nature. In her study of his work Kim Blaeser wrote that Vizenor is able to "expose an innate connection between the natural and the religious" (135).

Many Anishinaabe dream songs are about the presence of animals in visions. My haiku are the same, and yet, and yet, the contradiction is that imagistic scenes are my impermanence and survivance. Haiku poems were my very first creations, and since then imagistic scenes of nature are always present in my writing. The presence of nature in my novels, even in my essays, is an imagistic survivance as an author. My survivance is in nature and the book. (*Postindian Conversations* 67)

Vizenor constantly makes connections between the rich heritage of Anishinaabe dream songs and a mythic sense of natural presence.

In one of his earlier books, *Summer in the Spring*, Vizenor "reexpresses" traditional songs to show how "the Anishinaabe are a people of visions and dreams and tribal families who celebrate humor, compassionate balances in the world, and mythic imagination" (14). As an example he translates a song:

Across the earth
Everywhere
Making my voice heard. (14)

The shape of the verse may be haiku, but this is the dream song of a hybrid mixed-blood crane.

In his book *Shadow Distance* Vizenor demonstrates the connection he sees between his poetry and prose, by writing poetic envoys before short prose pieces to combine his "experience in haiku with natural reason in tribal literature—a new haiku hermeneutics" (*Shadow Distance* 31). He offers the following as an example:

> redwing blackbirds
> ride the reeds in a slough
> curtain calls

> The crack of bird songs and the flash of color on the wing is a comic romance in sloughs. We pose at lampposts as the blackbirds might, cocked on the side of reeds with the wind close to our ears. Listen, audiences are better in the sloughs; the curtain calls never end. (*Shadow Distance* 31)

The relationship of the poem and envoy is one of further detail, but not necessarily more defined interpretation. The "comic romance," and posing in windy sloughs where "curtain calls never end," recall the scenery and images of his novels. He carries the haiku into his novels. His novels carry him back to haiku. There is less difference between his short haiku and long novels than readers might imagine.

What Vizenor does with his haiku is to create a new "haiku hermeneutics." In his case, this is achieved by combining Anishinaabe content with Japanese versification. He turns to the work of haiku masters, such as his favorite, Bashō, and finds an echo of sentiment, presence, and imagery that is accessible and similar to Anishinaabe oral verse despite the separation of an ocean. By comparing, contrasting, and weaving two compatible threads of tradition together—Japanese and Anishinaabe—he places Anishinaabe literature in an international context and helps to define each form as distinct. Modern binary interpretations do not often allow unity across oceans. In contrast, Vizenor's collected poetic works demonstrate how a detailed knowledge of another culture can enhance the understanding of one's own culture.

Vizenor explains how he has come to understand haiku in the context of the oral Anishinaabe tradition:

> Haiku hermeneutics, that sense of haiku, is a natural habitude in tribal literature; the interpretations of the heard and written must consider the shadow words and sensations of haiku. The turn of the seasons, the course of spiders, the heat of stone, and the shadows of remembrance rush to the words laced in stories and poems. Stories must have their listeners and readers to overcome a natural impermanence.

Oral stories must be heard to endure; haiku are shadow words and sensations of the heard. Words wait for no one on the page. The envoys to haiku are the silent interpretations of a "haiku spirit." (*Shadow Distance* 32)

The spirit of haiku that Vizenor recognizes is not one of the tamed, romantic Native American Indian "spirits of the woods" imagined by the likes of Longfellow. The envoys Vizenor calls "silent interpretations" are signposts inscribed by the author, leading readers to a privileged interpretation of his world.

Just as Vizenor connects dream songs to his haiku, he also carefully and consciously connects his storytelling to Anishinaabe traditions and beliefs. His narrators are often highly conscious of their roles as storytellers, and frequently they provide information about Anishinaabe culture that will enhance the reader's understanding of the story. For example, *Bearheart* opens with a "Letter to the Reader," wherein the narrator explains the "language of bears" and the four worlds of Anishinaabe cosmology. *The Heirs of Columbus* features Stone Columbus, descendant of the explorer, and Point Assinika, home of a new Native nation. *Assinika* means "stones" in Ojibwe and also refers to the story of Nanabozho's brother, who was born a stone and became envious of his brother's wily ways. In the story, Nanabozho always returns to his brother to tell of his adventures and tease the stone-brother about his permanence and inability to ever be anywhere but in one place. But Nanabozho's brother is clever. He says to Nanabozho, "I know what you can do to get rid of me" and suggests that Nanabozho toss him into a fire and then pour cold water on him. Of course, when Nanabozho does this, the brother shatters into billions of pieces and is scattered across the entire earth. Vizenor has said, "I am a stone, and stones are native stories and stones are everywhere" (*Postindian Conversations* 131). He is, then, the cunning brother of Nanabozho. He is cultural memory shattered and sent to be forever permanent in every imaginable corner. He is the sculptor of facets, the shaper of stories, who will not be erased, only transformed.

Vizenor retells many of the Anishinaabe stories of stone. The title of his novel *Earthdivers* is a reference to Nanabozho and the animals diving after a great flood to find a bit of stone, or soil, beneath the waters. To provide an Anishinaabe literary context, Vizenor begins with an informative critical essay about Anishinaabe narrative and how the secular seriousness of most anthropologists and translators erased the humor and complexity of original narratives. He quotes Victor Barnouw's studies of anal themes in Nanabozho stories and A. Irving Hallowell's attempts to determine whether the Anishinaabe think all objects have a spirit. To revise the myths of Indian literature, Vizenor turns to the lives and works of such early Anishinaabe authors as William Whipple Warren, Kahgegagahbowh (George Copway), and Kahkewaquonaby (Peter Jones). He also acknowledges the oral storytellers he has encountered in his lifetime, among them Harold Goodsky, a dancer and humorist from Nett Lake; Bonnie Wallace from Fond du Lac; his uncle John Clement Beaulieu; and Henry Smith of White Earth. The list could go on. By focusing on the specific literature and history of the Anishinaabe, he makes clear the power and sacredness of remembering the exact words, not just the general ideas of the original stories. "We are touched into tribal being with words, made whole in the world with words and oratorical gestures. Tribal families created the earth, birds and animals, shadows and smoke, time and dreams, with their words as sacred memories" (*Wordarrows* vii).

Vizenor has made many "oratorical gestures" drawing on the gift of traditional tales told to him by his grandmother and uncle; the stories published by his great uncles in the newspaper, *The Progress*; the work of such ethnographers as Frances Densmore and William Jones; the publications of other Anishinaabe writers and historians, including William Warren; and his own urban revisions of these stories. He has studied both the past and the present of the Anishinaabe carefully. As a scholar, he has researched and compared many sources. As a novelist, he has incorporated numerous mythic Anishinaabe characters into his stories. His books are filled with references to traditional Anishinaabe stories, many of them revisions of early ethnography. For example, in 1928 Paul Radin recorded a story of "a man who lived all alone and the people were afraid of him because he would call people over to play a game with him and these people never returned" (Helbig 217). There is no doubt that this is *Bearheart*'s Evil Gambler, who asks: "Who will be the first to challenge me at the dish game? Who will throw the four directions with me? Who will be the first to soothe his dark soul with the lust of chance?" (110).

In *Hotline Healers* the character Almost Browne begins the book by saying, "We live forever in stories, not manners . . . so, tease the chance of conception, tease your mother, tease the privy councils of the great spirit, and always tease your own history" (1). Vizenor follows this counsel and "teases" history and reality in many of his novels. His work emphasizes the fact that all of history is simply one culture's shared interpretation of events. In *The Heirs of Columbus*, Vizenor mixes actual quotes from Columbus, the navigator, with the imagined conversation of tribal heirs from White Earth.

Vizenor often places Anishinaabe literature in an international context. Certainly his work is read as inter-national within Native America, but Vizenor has been able to insert his voice in postmodern literary conversations showing how deconstruction and semiotics have long been a part of Native culture. He often begins with a thought or quote from a broader critical context and then connects it to Anishinaabe tradition, challenging the old ideas to move into the future and the contemporary culture of criticism to make space for what was known in the past. The novel *Chancers* begins with a quotation from Elias Canetti that speaks of the redemption of language and the weight of images. "Slowly he lifts the heavy stones, a little higher with every sentence, and there is nothing that can redeem him except his words." Anishinaabe readers will recognize in this image the *gekinoamaade asiin* (teaching rocks) of the elders (Johnston *Bear-Walker*). Or they may recall that Nanabozho's brother, wives, and daughters have all been depicted as stone at one time or another (Erdrich, *Jacklight*; Helbig; Johnston *Bear-Walker*). Or they may be reminded of the pebbles Nanabozho tossed that became butterflies in his hands (Johnston, *Tales the Elders Told*).

At times Vizenor uses fiction to place Anishinaabe narrative parallel to other famous epic narratives. For instance in *Hotline Healers* Almost Brown tells "an ancestral Anishinaabe story about an adventurous hunter" that is proposed as "the true source of the masterpiece Sir Gawaain and the Green Knight" (62). Sir Gawaain is a "mighty negative" since *gaawiin* in Ojibwe means "no." In Almost's tale, Sir Gawaain is a Native hunter who, although he is warned by his *nokomis* not to seek evil demons, sets out from the *Michiziibi* (Mississippi River) to find and tease the evil gambler. When he nears *Maazhi Mashkiki* (Bad Medicine Lake) he becomes nauseated and falls asleep. In his dreams, an *ozhaawashko inini*, a green man, appears carrying a stone axe. Always one to make a deal, the gambler agrees to bear four blows if Sir Gawaain agrees to accept an equal number of blows four seasons later. Sir Gawaain agrees and then proceeds to cut off the *ozhaawasko inini's niinag* and head. With his head and penis severed, the creature is defeated, and he disappears into the lake. He is rumored to have eventually walked out of the water with his head and *niinag* in hand. What begins as a play on words becomes a clever insertion of Ojibwe into Middle English mythology. Vizenor makes the point that Anishinaabe stories are as complex and worthy of serious study as any other mythic narratives. He also highlights some of the differences between cultures by allowing dreams and chance to be acknowledged in his version. These signature references to Anishinaabe cosmology underscore ways in which the two cultures can coalesce. His story is bawdy and connected to the subconscious and spectral world.

Reading his work in an Anishinaabe context, one sees how a distinctly Anishinaabe worldview can find relevancy and contribute to contemporary conversations. From the headwaters of the Mississippi in Anishinaabe country to the terrain of the Monkey King in Matsumisha, Japan, his stories are like stones lifted higher with every sentence. If we listen to him across the years, Vizenor has done what Kahgegagahbowh asked in 1851 when he wrote to his readers: "Go where I never shall be, and you will still be speaking, long, long after my tears will have ceased to flow, and I be numbered with the past" (Copway x).

Aadizookanan / Histories

In Anishinaabe communities, *aadizookaanag* were part of the cold winter months "when the tellers were certain that Naanabozho was not about, listening in the face of an animal or flower, as he does in the summer when stories should not be told" (*Summer in the Spring* 15). One aspect of the stories Vizenor captures (or perhaps releases) is the importance of narrative tradition in Anishinaabe culture.

> The Anishinaabeg did not have written histories; their worldviews were not linear narratives that started and stopped in manifest binaries. The tribal past lived as an event in visual memories and oratorical gestures; woodland identities turned on dreams and visions. . . . Tribal leaders were dreamers and orators, speaking in visual metaphors as if the past were a state of being in the telling. (*People Named the Chippewa* 24)

According to Vizenor, narrative tradition is history with dimension. He considers traditional Anishinaabe literature a form of interactive art that belonged to individual dreamers or to the community audience, or both. As such, it was fluid and somewhat open to interpretation.

Some of the themes mentioned often in his work were certainly known in oral tradition and have also been documented in writing. As a modern Anishinaabe author, Vizenor's relationship to ethnography is complex, as he participates in the preservation of cultural information by weaving oral history and life experience with written documents from a wide range of sources. At times what he does could be considered repatriation of information as he places action back into stories with Anishinaabe characters.

Vizenor writes fiction and nonfiction to elaborate and illuminate the history of the Anishinaabe. His postmodern fictional accounts of history reflect an interest, and participation, in the critical exploration of the recent century.

> My approach is native survivance in stories, that is, to hear more than mere documents, which are already selected, already the common law, already praised to serve cultural dominance. Native stories of survivance are the creation of presence, of tricky time and place, over the absence of natives in the causal histories of civilization. Native histories are natural reason, the memories and seasons of survivance. Listen, the best stories are shamanic, and more visionary than victimry. (*Postindian Conversations* 134)

Vizenor considers his stories a laughing tease of culture in the past and present. Many of his stories are funny in an unnerving way that dares a reader to confront aspects of living not often included in serious literature. For example, his stories "The Edible Menu and Slow Food Tricksters," "The Psychotaxidermist," and "Four Skin Documents" exhibit a playfulness with language and a desire to tease members of the dominant culture along with members of the Anishinaabe community. His characters shout, "you old birch liar" to Robert Frost at poetry readings. He imagines rocking world coffee economics with *coffee anishinaabica,* a bean raised and roasted on the reservation and sold to romantic liberals trying to buy a taste of Native culture. His humor is delightfully and dangerously close to reality, often referencing Vizenor's own background and the Anishinaabe community on White Earth Reservation in Minnesota.

Through his writing, Vizenor demonstrates how the voice of Anishinaabe storytellers is related to their place of origin, to their history of place. He has said, "The tribal singer had the eyes of the animals, the legs of the birds, the wings of the spirits, the heart of the bear, and the breath of the wind. He was the breath and touch of the woodland and prairie and desert" (Blaeser, *Gerald Vizenor* 199). Imagine a singer with animal eyes, bird legs, ethereal wings, and a bear heart, brought to life by the wind. The creature and song born of that image are woven of the woods, the prairies, the world above, and the world below. In addition to making the connection between Anishinaabe culture and literature, Vizenor offers one of many reasons the Anishinaabe continue to write from their distinct perspective. "Today we sing what we believe others have believed and trust the past for the future. Our songs of peace and timeless myths may bring all men together with a good energy to live," he explains ("Tribal People and the Poetic Image"). He suggests that the "tribal singer" and the Anishinaabe author write to unite their particular past with the present and to create a future that can be shared with other cultures. In many of his texts, Vizenor follows this model, drawing on the Anishinaabe worldview to illuminate broader issues.

Vizenor's earliest "native histories" began with the poetry of dream songs. The short introduction to *Summer in the Spring* begins with a factual, yet poetic, summary of Anishinaabe history. Beginning with the term *Anishinaabe*, which means "original people," he recounts their 500-year migration along the shores of Lake Superior, or *Gitchigaming*, "the great sea of the Anishinaabe" (8). He notes the arrival in the seventeenth century of voyageurs and missionaries, and the establishment of a Christian fur-trading post on *Mooninkwanekaning*, now known as Madeline Island. One of the Jesuits who came during this period noted of the Anishinaabe that "they nearly all show more intelligence in their business, speeches, courtesies, intercourse, tricks, and subtleties than do the shrewdest citizens of merchant France" (Thwaites, vol. 15, 157). But after the War of 1812, territorial governor Lewis Cass sent Indian agents such as Henry Schoolcraft to "prepare the Indians of Northern Michigan for a peaceful cession of their land" (Schoolcraft, *Literary Voyager or Muzzeniegun* xix). Schoolcraft believed "the just and humane dealings, which characterize the whole policy of the American government," were "proof of its superior treatment of the race [Anishinaabe]" (Schoolcraft, *Literary Voyager or Muzzeniegun* 114). Vizenor's version of history differs.

> Weakened by several epidemics, tribal families were bound to remember the hymns of a new civilization, while the hymns were peddled like military secrets to the nervy voyageurs who learned the languages and humor of the woodland and enmeshed the people in the predatory economics of peltry. . . . Thousands of white settlers with terminal creeds procured the land with new laws and liens and enslaved the Anishinaabe in the furies of discovery. . . . The rhythms of the land were broken by the marching cadence of Christian patriotism. (*Summer in the Spring* 9)

Vizenor's characteristically tricky phrasing and quick capture of complicated sentiments are precursors to the style of writing he later used in his fiction, where he continues to offer alternate readings of events. Consider the difference between what Kahgegagahbowh (George Copway) says of himself in 1851 and the words Vizenor wrote for his Anishinaabe character Lusterbow in 1988. Copway tells his readers, "I come and at the feet of noble Britons drop the tears of pleasure, and pay homage, not to man, but to the greatness of the Palefaces" (Copway 1). Lusterbow, by comparison, "renounced the strict summons to mature in a base and possessive civilization, and he would never wait on a mission porch to have his mind mended by the government, even when his mind needed mending" (*Trickster of Liberty* 4). While Vizenor was seeking to revisit the subject of Anishinaabe history, he was also using his poetic instinct to convey more than one dimension of events. More than listener, voyeur, or even witness, Vizenor attempts to make the reader a participant in his production of texts.

One of the characters Vizenor returns to repeatedly is the model of mixed identity, Nanabozho. The Nanabozho stories Vizenor selected for one of his earliest books, *Summer in the Spring*, were first printed a century earlier in *The Progress*, the first newspaper published on White Earth Reservation in Minnesota. In these articles, two elder members of the *Midewiwin* religious community described the spiritual history of the people. Day Dodge and Saycosegay were reported to have seen over 90 winters at the time they dictated these stories for translation; consequently they were probably born in the late 1700s. The tales dictated by these two elders from White Earth Reservation in Minnesota echo the stories of Basil Johnston and Joe McLellan, from Ontario and Manitoba, with the exception of only a few minute details. In both versions, the earth is created in the same manner, and it is Nanabozho who, with the help of animals, re-creates it after a great flood. Nokomis, his grandmother, figures prominently, and Nanabozho has the same prowess and playfulness. In Johnston's tales, the *manidoo* of the west is Nanabozho's father, while in Vizenor's versions, his father is the *manidoo* of the north. In both cases, the father abandons Nanabozho and his mother and is eventually sought by his son somewhere near the edges of the known world.

Versions of Nanabozho, Nokomis, and the Evil Gambler are the Anishinaabe characters who appear in Vizenor's books most often. Nanabozho, the half-man, half-*manidoo* champion of the Anishinaabe culture, and the Evil Gambler, who balances the equation by continually confronting Nanabozho and the Anishinaabe, receive mention in Vizenor's early works strictly as they are represented in traditional tales, but in his later novels these figures take on many faces. He uses these characters to confront the difficult postcolonial issues of identity, sovereignty, anthropology, politics, and narrative structure in an imaginative way.

Nanabozho appears frequently in Vizenor's books. In *Bearheart*, Vizenor creates modern versions of the characters from his early short story "Nanabozho and the Gambler." Sir Cecil Staples, the "monarch of gasoline," is an evil gambler who wagers a few gallons against people's lives. Proude Cedarfair, a grandfatherly counterpart of Nokomis, or an heir to Nanabozho, is a human figure who seeks to save the community. Like Nanabozho, he can win against the gambler. These characters, along with Vizenor's reference to the Anishinaabe dish game, make his story recognizably Anishinaabe. In *Griever*, Vizenor creates a version of Nanabozho that could be the cousin of a similar character in Chinese tradition. Griever de Hocus travels with a rooster and interrogates everything he encounters. Simultaneously, like the Chinese Monkey King and Nanabozho, he is a liberating radical leader, a master of cultural and political reconstruction. The evil gamblers Griever encounters are communist and capitalist rulers who emphasize their dangerousness and difference while overlooking all they have in common. Wenabozho also appears as the inspiration for a monastic document, and the name of a railroad, in *Hotline Healers*. The document is the *Manabozho Curiosa*—a bestiary in the most literal and sexual sense possible. While there is no evidence at all that the document existed, Vizenor's careful research about the attitudes, behavior, and possible conversion of the early missionaries certainly leads readers to the conclusion that there is no reason to assume with certainty that it did not. *Dead Voices* contains both Nanabozho and some evil anthropologists who were born in a sewer. These various appearances of Nanabozho and the Evil Gambler accomplish two goals. First, they demonstrate the flexibility of traditional mythic figures to become a relevant part of contemporary Anishinaabe history. Vizenor uses them to create stories about everything from economics to religious conversion. Second, these figures teach readers the wide range of emotions and situations that suit these Anishinaabe characters. They are not saints; nor are they wholly sinners. They demonstrate how crazy or compassionate the *manidoog* can be. These are figures of mythic power and importance, but because they do not manifest infinite omniscience, they can speak more directly to the human condition.

Nanabozho stories are notorious for confronting bawdy, raunchy reality. They show that in Anishinaabe literature, as in life, everything is not always as it seems and that humor and imagination are essential. There are Nanabozho tales to explain everything from why a man's *niinag* is rounded at the end to why the wind of a *boogit* smells. From Minnesota to Michigan the stories are much the same. The fact that printed versions are usually sanitized is a theme for another discussion altogether. Vizenor, Erdrich, and other Anishinaabe authors put the bawdy humor back into Anishinaabe literature. As Vizenor has said: "The trickster is a liberator and healer in a narrative, a comic sign, communal signification and a discourse with imagination" (*Narrative Chance* 187). Larry Gross has further explained the role of Nanabozho:

> The trickster does not die; he comes back to life in new guises, new narratives. The trickster can face the onslaught of the European invasion, and rather than "vanish" as seems to have been the hope of earlier Euro-Americans, the trickster mutates into something even greater. Maintaining the role of culture hero in new stories and new roles, the trickster liberates the Anishinaabe from the oppression of colonialism and opens healing vistas of the imagination. ("*Bimaadiziwin*" 28)

Beneath the shock value is a serious lesson about repression, authenticity, and a willingness to confront chaos with chaos. As Vizenor's character Bagese the bear-woman says, "what seems to be a game is not a game, the opposites are never the other, the plurals, even the pronouns we write, are not in the natural world" (*Dead Voices* 111).

Vizenor shakes the stories of Nanabozho loose amid the chaos of modern life. He and others have called Nanabozho a trickster (Johnston, *Manitous*; Helbig; Jahner; Murray and Rice). Vizenor has called himself a trickster (*Postindian Conversations* 20). He has written the story of an Anishinaabe character titled *The Trickster of Liberty*. But in the context of Anishinaabe literature the word requires some explanation. Frederic Baraga's *Dictionary of the Ojibway Language*, first published in 1878, has no equivalent for the English word "trick," nor does Richard Rhodes's *Eastern Ojibwa-Chippewa-Ottawa Dictionary*, published in 1993. Only the *Concise Dictionary of Minnesota Ojibwe* by John Nichols and Earl Nyholm, published in 1995, has an entry for "trickster," and the definition is "name of the *aadizookaan* character viewed as culture hero and trickster, Wenabozho, also Nenabozho." The tricky image of the talking coyote, or deer, bear, or man transformed into a god among a pantheon of human and animal spirits is an invention of literary critics. It is a useful term when trying to understand Native American literature across various tribes, but so much more can be gained by diving down into the actual facts and fantasies of the tribe to see how the stories of Nanabozho have gifted the people over centuries. There is more to the character than the riddles and magic he uses in some stories. A close reading from an Anishinaabe perspective allows a reader to see "wild stories break from the stones," to borrow the phrasing Vizenor uses in his poem "Shaman Breaks." Vizenor himself speaks of the role of the "trickster" in *Manifest Manners*:

> The trickster is reason and mediation in stories, the original translator of tribal encounters; the name is an intimation of transformation, men to women, animals to birds, and more. . . . Tricksters are the translation of creation; the trickster creates the tribe in stories, and pronounces the moment of remembrance as the trace of liberation. The animals laughed, birds cried, and there were worried hearts over the everlasting humor that would liberate the human mind in trickster stories. Trickster stories are the translation of liberation, and the shimmer of imagination is the liberation of the last trickster stories. (15)

Insert the name "Nanabozho" in place of the word "trickster" and the stories make more sense in an Anishinaabe context. What is denied in the pantribal interpretation of the trickster is the raw power of transformation and possibility. The word "trickster" implies mere deception and cunning, but Nanabozho and his family, the *wiindigoo*, the *missepishu* and *memegwesiiwag*, are characters capable of understanding passion, pain, and longing while at the same time transcending human limits. They are as likely to turn into rabbits as they are to make love to the wind. Their power lies in their ability to fall flat on their faces or command nature to reshape the lakes. They are real enough to be present on earth and yet are able to walk with the dead (Johnston, *Manitous* 151). When Vizenor moves from euphemistic literary figures to specific characters known to the Anishinaabe, magic becomes miracle, and the spirit, rather than the mind, is affected. "Trickster" is a useful word, but Nanabozho has a face (or maybe two). In *Hotline Healers*, Vizenor explains how the character relates to his fiction:

> Nanabozho is the trickster of creation, the natural traces of men, women, bear, and birch, a wild tease heard on the wind and in the tricky stories of the seasons. Tricksters are stories, the traces and hum of the seasons, and the cover of winter. Tricksters are the chancy ruins of silence. The crows and animals are the tricksters of human pleasure. . . . Trickster stories are survivance, not salvation, pleasure not abstinence, imagination not devotion, humor not termination. The trickster is on

the rise, not the end of stories. Trickster is the wind, not the other, not mortal, not immortal, the natural tease of the obvious. Trickster is an erotic trace with no presence or salvation. Naanabozho is our carnal creation in tricky stories that never end in silence. (161–62)

Nanabozho is a character who created the world while dog-paddling in waters where his own feces were floating. This is a character who wears fire to steal it, can become a tree stump, and goes off as a young man on a journey to find and punish his father (McLellan). Knowing Nanabozho stories does not make Vizenor's wild scenes of lust and violence more comfortable, but certainly more understandable. The details of Nanabozho's life add to a reader's understanding of Anishinaabe literature. Literature by Anishinaabe authors can be read, and even created, with absolutely no knowledge of Nanabozho. Literature identified as Anishinaabe, however, cannot exclude this heritage of "carnal creation." Vizenor is one of many Native American Indian authors drawn to the trickster figure indigenous to his area. With Nanabozho he can write within the Anishinaabe landscape. Nanabozho is part of the seasons. He can defeat the winter *wiindigoog* and become a part of the winter stories. Vizenor also uses the Anishinaabe trickster to specifically confront the ironies imposed by French and English missionaries and explorers living among the Ojibwe. He relies on the trickster to "tease the obvious" and bring stories of pleasure, imagination, and humor to bear on modern life. His tricksters denounce ideas of dependent salvation, abstinence, devotion, and termination. For the Anishinaabe, the trickster figure can be a formidable resource.

> Tricky stories are the cure. Listen, is there a wiser antidote to fear, fate, and dominance than wit, natural reason, and irony? The Anishinaabe even tried to outwit the coldest, mundane count of winter with tricky stories. The mind, a good story, can even change the weather, and that's the start of a new season. Stories are the cure, not the pose of traditions or victimry. So Wenabozho, that Anishinaabe trickster and curative weather conniver, creates wild scenes, lusty situations, and outwits wicked posers, native reactionaries, and even the manners of oral traditions. The trickster assumes the natural presence of wind, stones, trees, birds, animals, and is always in motion. (*Postindian Conversations* 38)

Vizenor also claims that "tricksters are better than the real, much better than flesh and blood, because Wenabozho and other tricksters are stories of liberation, not mere representations. The trickster is a very sophisticated literary practice in Anishinaabe stories" (*Postindian Conversations* 59).

Vizenor's tricksters take other forms at times. In *Dead Voices*, Bagese the bear-woman is a trickster who survives through interpretation. Vizenor recalls thinking of Bagese as "in his life" before she was firmly on the page.

> *Dead Voices* comes out of that tricky tease of silence more than twenty years ago during my second winter quarter at the University of California, Berkeley. I could barely focus on anything that winter because there were demons in the water, in the mirrors, at every corner. I could hear the demons on the wind. . . . I have always turned to nature when the page is cold and conversations cut to the soul. Bagese was there, and she teased me right back into the chance of my own story. . . . She created me as one of the figures in the game. . . . Bagese struck that dish on the stone four times to get me on my feet. . . . Bagese, my grandmother, and a shadow of Nokomis were there to tease me and so we created the *wanaki* game. (*Postindian Conversations* 144)

Teasing him back into his own story is a woman named after an Anishinaabe game of chance and Nokomis, the grandmother of Nanabozho and the grandmother who cared for Vizenor after his mother's departure. He relies on these characters of myth and memory to stress the power of chance to influence the outcome of anyone's story. He uses these characters to show how survival is dependent in many ways on chance circumstances. In his life Vizenor was given the chance to hear the Anishinaabe stories of his ancestors. In his book, Bagese the trickster represents a way to use stories as a means of survival, in the midst of the great chaos and stress now inherent in modern life.

In *The Trickster of Liberty* it is Almost Browne, almost born on White Earth Reservation, who is the trickster. Almost carries Nanabozho's voice into the present. He questions and defines Anishinaabe culture in the context of modern society. In *Griever*, it is Griever de Hocus, born on the reservation and visiting Tianjin University, who is the trickster counterpart to the Chinese Monkey King. This particular story is made possible by the premise that many cultures have tricksters; they may be related but remain distinctly different from one another. In both of these books, Vizenor uses an imaginative, inquisitive trickster to interrogate modern society. These trickster figures are an essential part of the narrative because when they appear, the reader comes to expect unnatural events and new perspectives. With their unusual ways of seeing and acting in the world, these characters have become a part of Vizenor's style. Their actions and dialogue shape the way the story unfolds; their visions and journeys provide structure to the narrative.

Vizenor is aware of the theories of Paul Radin and Carl Jung, who see the trickster as a problem-solving figure constructed by humanity to preserve cultural myths and interpret the present. But Vizenor also objects to narrow, linear interpretations that relegate tricksters to the past, causing them to become what Vizenor calls "terminal creeds" (Blaeser, *Gerald Vizenor* 141). Like other Anishinaabe authors, he argues for the survival of the culture by giving the trickster back to the people, putting him back into the stories. Vizenor, Johnston, and Erdrich all invite Nanabozho, Nokomis, Pukawiss, and others to liberate modern fiction and restore erotic satire to the art of storytelling, to the art of survival. Noting that Lyotard defined "postmodern" as "the condition of knowledge in the most highly developed societies," Vizenor defines knowledge in Anishinaabe society and shows it is as highly developed as any (*Narrative Chance* 2). His chapter "Trickster Discourse" turns the tables on various interpretations of Nanabozho. Framing his argument in modern theoretical terms, Vizenor quotes Fredric Jameson.

> The great modernisms were predicated on the invention of a personal, private style, as unmistakable as your fingerprint, as incomparable as your own body . . . linked to the conception of a unique self and private identity, a unique personality and individuality, which can be expected to generate its own unique vision of the world. (*Narrative Chance* 193)

Vizenor then explains that for the Anishinaabe this "unique vision of the world" includes Nanabozho not as a literary artifact, but as a semiotic tool, as a "woodland trickster, a social antagonist in a comic holotrope." "In trickster narratives," says Vizenor, "the listener and readers imagine their liberation; the trickster is a sign and the world is 'deconstructed' in a discourse (194).

Vizenor's narratives are connected to Anishinaabe tradition by time and chance. Stories begin in a place and a season. Time is cyclical and events are remembered in no particular order. Most people are introduced by relation rather than profession. Chance shapes lives. Dreams are afforded great significance. These conventions can be found in the fiction of many cultures, but in Vizenor's books they appear as part of distinctly Anishinaabe narratives. For example, in

Dead Voices, Bagese plays *wanaki*, an Anishinaabe game of chance. The word *wanaki* also means "to be in a place of peace." As Vizenor explains, "the game of peace is to take a chance on the real wherever you live and bring the real, the creatures, stones, leaves, insects, right into your life, rather than the pose of simulations, or the separations of dead voices" (*Postindian Conversations* 138). Bagese, with her Ojibwe name, her traditional game of chance, and her desire to find peace, represents a blend of specifically Anishinaabe heritage in the context of the challenges of the modern world.

Vizenor's style is complex and influenced by many cultures. His use of haiku techniques and trickster narratives is a small part of the sum that is his literature. Yet these aspects of his style are most closely related to Anishinaabe culture. As he uses them, he is aware of the way they relate differently to Anishinaabe culture. Dream songs filled with woodland images, and trickster stories loosely based on the life of Wenabozho, connect his fiction to Anishinaabe history and to the current Anishinaabe community. These elements of his style, echoed in the work of other Anishinaabe authors, demonstrate shared stylistic values in Anishinaabe literature.

Vizenor rewrites the colonial language that has been used to describe the Anishinaabe. He confronts what he considers to be cultural atrocities by setting the record straight on numerous issues. He does not pretend to speak of what he does not know, but he has clearly taken time to learn some of what is necessary for continuance. He writes for the heirs of Anishinaabe *aadizookaanag* and the heirs to the errors of colonial racism and assumptions. He is as interested in correcting Americans' perceptions of the "Indian" as he is in correcting the Anishinaabe's perception of themselves. At most, he tries to teach Americans to see the Anishinaabe as one of many Native American Indian cultures that can possibly provide alternative ways of viewing life and literature. Robert F. Berkhofer, Jr., wrote in *The White Man's Indian*, "the idea and the image of the Indian must be white concoctions . . . the first residents of the Americas were divided, by modern estimates, into at least two thousand cultures and more societies . . . [and] by classifying all these many people as Indians, whites categorized the variety of cultures as a single entity, thereby neglecting their cultural diversity" (20). It is this diversity that Vizenor's work helps to preserve.

Vizenor has written that "language is, in a sense, an attempt to interpret, to narrate dreams older than itself" (*Landfill Meditation* 182). His works are his dreams, the dreams he has inherited, and the dreams he leaves for readers to explore. Not all of the images in Vizenor's visions are pleasant or easily understood. However, as one of the major contributors to Anishinaabe literature, he offers a spectrum of subjects and styles that serve as a reminder of what can be found in the study of a single tribe.

CHAPTER SEVEN

Ziiginibiige: Poured Writing

Many words have been poured into these pages: *bimaadizi* (to live), *bwaajige* (to dream), *jichakaan* (one soul), *jibwaam* (the other soul), *waabaamaa* (to see someone), *waamdaan* (to see something), *Anishinaabeakiing* (the place of the Anishinaabe), *Anishinaabebiigeyaanh* (I write in Anishinaabe) . . . I have tried to be sure that the sound of the stories can be found on the page. This introduction to Anishinaabe language, literature, and storytellers is an invitation to think differently, to bend straight lines into circles and to set familiar circles spinning on the edge of the universe. As Hartley White has said:

> *Endaso-giizhig akina gegoo bakaan gigii-kikendaan, mii i'iw endaso-giizhig apane gikendaasowin. Mii i'iw akeyaa bimaadiziyan. Mii gomaa ji-naazikaman ji-noon-daman ji-wabandaman. Miinawaa maada'ookii a'aw manidoo. Mii i'iw akeyaa nandawaabandaman wenizhishing.* (Every day you learn something different, every day a new piece of knowledge. That's the way you live your life. Then you approach those things a little more to hear them, to see them. And the Spirit shares. That's how you search for the good things.) (219)

Most days I am a teacher; every day I am a student. I teach Anishinaabemowin and Anishinaabe literature at a large university, where we seriously study the work of Louise Erdrich, Jim Northrup, Basil Johnston, and Gerald Vizenor as part of American literature. By getting closer to the details, the subjects, the style, and the language of the Anishinaabe we can hear them better, read them more clearly, and perhaps share the Anishinaabe spirit elder Hartley White describes.

All of the authors surveyed here refer to the power and influence of the region, the *Anishinaabeakiing*. All of them retell one or more of the *aadizookaanag*, the traditional tales of Nanabozho and other mythic figures. All of them grapple with the legacy of cultural genocide that occurred as land was taken and children were sent to boarding school. And all of them *bangii Anishinaabemowag* (speak a little Anishinaabemowin). If we look at them from an Anishinaabe perspective, they appear more alike than different, but reading them as twenty-first-century authors, they range from postmodern to regional. These authors have their own voices and write about many things not related in any way to Anishinaabe culture, but all of them also have taken some time as writers to connect the Anishinaabe culture to their work, and it is those instances I have tried to highlight.

All of them speak of identity and how it can change, how it should be seen as impacted by many factors but also how it is a constant source of centering. They speak too of survival, which could be interpreted as finding and not losing that center while being able to observe action in every direction. They talk of trickster verbs and women who fall out of the sky, some who fly back up into it and men who become trees. All of them say it is important for the Anishinaabe to maintain the features of the culture that define it as separate from all others. Knowledge of the Anishinaabe language, the ability to tell traditional stories of the Great Lakes, and an Anishinaabe view of life in the universe are all essential for the future of the Anishinaabe. The near loss of and attempt to reclaim a language within only four generations stresses the importance of the work of these authors.

Louise Erdrich may be the Anishinaabe author most likely to be read by Americans. Basil Johnston is known throughout eastern and central Canada as an honored storyteller. Gerald Vizenor is the Anishinaabe author most frequently drawn into cultural and critical debates. Jim Northrup is one of the most outspoken and steady Anishinaabe journalists. But surrounding them, connected to them by threads of language and culture, are many more Anishinaabe authors. The circle of Anishinaabe storytellers has always been wide, and although this book has a beginning and an end, there is really no *wayeshkad* or *wayekwaase*, no place to start or stop in reading Anishinaabe literature. One story always leads to another. One speaker picks up where another leaves off. These authors, and the grandfathers, grandmothers, mothers, and fathers who gave them their first stories all have a desire to share some portion of the past and to carry it into the future. Looking at language and literature through their eyes, we find ways not only to see their work anew, but to think differently about all the stories we encounter in any worlds we visit. Louise Erdrich says, "what is the whole of our existence, but the sound of an appalling love"—a love that is unconditional, unexplained and as unending as the human need to discover its source (*Last Report* 229). Long ago I began a poem. I use it now to teach the language, to explain why we teach the language, to tell the story of the language in the language of stories. It is written in a way that allows the Anishinaabemowin to come first, with a literal translation in the middle that gestures toward the third line, an English version. Sometimes these three lines seem too much, sometimes they make all the difference. Often it is the least polished one in the middle, the one that can either be seen as fitting in both worlds or neither, that tells us the most about the way to build bridges between cultures and sustain Anishinaabe language and identity.

> *Bindigeig,*
>> All of you, enter
>> Come in
>
> *Enji-Anishinaabemong*
>> A place of Anishinaabe language
>> Where Anishinaabemowin is spoken
>
> *Enji-manjimendimying*
>> Where we remember
>> Where there is remembering
>
> *Enji-gikendaasoying*
>> Where we know/read/count
>> A place of knowing

Enji-zaagi'iding
>Where there is love
>A place of love

Bizandamig,
>Listen all of you
>Listen

enendamowinan zhaabwidoonan odeong
>ideas saved in the heart
>to what we know by heart

bwajigeying waasa kina nikeyaa
>we dream far in all directions
>as we dream in all directions

aadisokeying, nagamoying, nimiiying ezhi-Anishinaabebimaadiziying
>we tell teaching stories, we sing, we dance in the traditional way
>with traditions of stories, song and dance

kina bimaadizijig miinwa wesii'ig owaabandaanaawaa bidaasigemigog
>all the people and animals see it, the light coming
>and we recognize the lighting of a new fire

Bimaadizig
>Live
>Live

Nisawayi'iing misko-biidaabang idash ni misko-pangishimag
>Between the red dawn and the red place where it falls
>Between the red dawn and the red sunset

Nisawayi'iing giizis idash ni dibiki'giizis
>Between the sun (or the month) and the night sun
>Between sun and the moon

Nisawayi'iing manidoog idash wiindigoog
>Between the small spirits and the cannibals
>Between the spirits we love and the ones who devour

Nisawayi'iing awang idash ankwadong mii ji-mikaman gdo'ojichaakam
>Between the fog and the clouds you can find your soul
>Between the fog and the clouds you can find your soul

Bindigeig, wewnii bizindamig, minobimaadizig
>Come in, carefully listen, live well
>Come in, carefully listen, live well

Maziniaganan Gii Gindanaanan: Works Cited

Adamson, Joni. *American Indian Literature, Environmental Justice and Ecocriticism*. Tucson: University of Arizona Press, 2001.

Akan, Linda. "Pimosatamowin Sikaw Kakeequaywin: Walking and Talking—a Salteaux Elder's View of Native Education." *Canadian Journal of Native Education* 19.2 (1992): 191–214.

Allen, Paula Gunn, ed. *Studies in American Indian Literature: Critical Essays and Course Designs*. New York: Modern Language Association Press, 1983.

Allen, Paula Gunn, and Patricia Clark Smith, eds. *Spider Woman's Granddaughters: Traditional Tales and Contemporary Writing by Native American Women*. New York: Fawcett Columbine, 1989.

Baraga, Frederic. *A Dictionary of the Otchipwe Language Explained in English*. Cincinnati: Jos. A. Hemann, 1853.

Barnouw, Victor. *Wisconsin Chippewa Myths and Tales and Their Relation to Chippewa Life*. Madison: University of Wisconsin Press, 1977.

Beaulieu, David L. "Curly Hair and Big Feet: Physical Anthropology and the Implementation of Land Allotment on the White Earth Chippewa Reservation." *American Indian Quarterly* 8.4 (1984): 282–314.

Beidler, Peter G., and Gay Barton. *A Reader's Guide to the Novels of Louise Erdrich.* Columbia: University of Missouri Press, 2006.

Benton-Banai, Edward. *The Mishomis Book: The Voice of the Ojibway.* St Paul, Minn.: Red Schoolhouse, 1988.

Berkhofer, Robert F., Jr. *The White Man's Indian: Images of the American Indian from Columbus to the Present.* New York: Vintage, 1979.

Black, Mary. "Ojibwa Power Belief System." In *The Anthropology of Power,* ed. Raymond Fogelson ad Richard Adams. New York: Academic Press, 1977.

Blaeser, Kimberly. *Absentee Indians & Other Poems.* East Lansing: Michigan State University Press, 2002.

———. *Gerald Vizenor: Writing in the Oral Tradition.* Norman: University of Oklahoma Press, 1996.

———. "Native Literature: Seeking a Critical Center." In *Looking at the Words of Our People: First Nations Analysis of Literature,* ed. Jeanette Armstrong. Penticton, B.C.: Theytus Books, 1993.

———. *Stories Migrating Home.* Bemidji, Minn.: Loonfeather Press, 1999.

———. *Traces in Blood, Bone and Stone.* Bemidji, Minn.: Loonfeather Press, 2006.

———. *Trailing You.* New York: Talman Company, 1994.

Boatman, John. *My Elders Taught Me: Aspects of Great Lakes American Indian Philosophy.* Lanham: University Press of America, 1992.

Booth, Annie L., and Harvey M. Jacobs. "Ties that Bind: Native American Beliefs as a Foundation for Environmental Consciousness." *Environmental Ethics* 12.1 (1990): 27–38.

Bourgeois, Arthur P. *Ojibwa Narratives of Charles and Charlotte Kawbawgam and Jacques LePique, 1893–1895.* Detroit: Wayne State University Press, 1994.

Bowden, Henry Warner. *American Indians and Christian Missions: Studies in Cultural Conflict.* Chicago: University of Chicago Press, 1981.

Boyden, Joseph. *Three Day Road.* New York: Penguin, 2005.

Brehm, Victoria. "The Metamorphoses of an Ojibwa Manido." *American Literature* 68.4 (1996): 677–706.

Brizinski, Peggy. *Knots in a String.* Saskatoon: University of Saskatchewan Press, 1993.

Broker, Ignatia. *Night Flying Woman.* St. Paul: Minnesota Historical Society Press, 1983.

Brown, Paula. "Changes in Otjibwa Social Control." *American Anthropologist* (1952) 1: 1–57.

Bruhac, Joseph. *Survival This Way: Interviews with American Indian Poets.* Tuscon: University of Arizona Press, 1987.

Burnaby, Barbara, and Jon Reyhner, eds. *Indigenous Languages Across the Community.* Flagstaff: Northern Arizona University, 2002.

Carson, William. "Ojibwa Tales." *Journal of American Folklore* (1917) 7: 491–533.

Castillo, Susan Perez. "Postmodernism, Native American Literature and the Real: The Silko-Erdrich Controversy." *Massachusetts Review* 32.1 (1991): 285–94.

Chaillier, Grace, and Rebecca Tavernini, eds. *Voice on the Water: Great Lakes Native America Now.* Marquette: Northern Michigan University Press, 2011.

Chamberlain, A. F. "Nanibozhu Amongst the Otchipwe, Mississagas, and Other Algonkian Tribes." *Journal of American Folklore* (1891) 7: 193–252.

Champagne, Duane. "UNDRIP (United Nations Declaration on the Rights of Indigenous Peoples): Human, Civil, and Indigenous Rights." *Wicazo Sa Review* 28.1 (Spring 2013): 9–22.

Chavkin, Allan, ed. *The Chippewa Landscape of Louise Erdrich.* Tuscaloosa: University of Alabama Press, 1999.

Child, Brenda J. *Boarding School Seasons: American Indian Families, 1900–1940.* Lincoln: University of Nebraska Press, 2000.

Christensen, Rosemary Ackley. "Ojibwe Language: A Competence Exchange Model for Administrative Curriculum Makers and First Language Speakers." *Native American Values: Survival and Renewal,* Thomas E. Schirer and Susan M. Branstner, eds., 30–46. Sault Ste. Marie: Lake Superior State University Press, 1993.

Chute, Janet E. *The Legacy of Shingwaukonse: A Century of Native Leadership.* Toronto: University of Toronto Press, 1998.

Clements, William C. "The Jesuit Foundations of Native North American Literary Sources." *American Indian Quarterly* 18.1 (1994): 43–59.

Coleman, Sister Bernard, Ellen Frogner, and Estelle Eich. *Ojibwa Myths and Legends.* Minneapolis: Ross and Haines, 1962.

Colombo, John Robert. *Windigo: An Anthology of Fact and Fantastic Fiction.* Saskatoon: Western Producer Prairie Books, 1982.

Conway, Thor, and Julie Conway. *Spirits on Stone: The Agawa Pictographs.* San Luis Obispo, Calif.: Heritage Discoveries Publications, 1990.

Copway, G. "Kahgegagahbowh." *Recollections of a Forest Life, or The Life and Travels of Kah-Ge-Ga-Gah-Bowh.* London: C. Gilpin, 1851.

——— . *The Traditional History and Characteristic Sketches of the Ojibway Nation.* 1850; Toronto: Coles, 1972.

Corbiere, Mary Ann. "Teaching Native Languages So They Will Survive." In *Celebration of Indigenous Thought and Expression*, ed. Thomas Shirer and Susan Branstner. Sault Ste. Marie, Mich.: Lake Superior State University Press, 1997.

Danziger, Edward Jefferson, Jr. *The Chippewas of Lake Superior*. Norman: University of Oklahoma, 1977.

Deloria, Vine, Jr. *Red Earth, White Lies: Native Americans and the Myth of Scientific Fact*. New York: Scribner, 1995.

——. *Spirit and Reason: The Vine Deloria, Jr., Reader*. Ed. Barbara Deloria, Kristen Foehner, and Sam Scinta. Golden, Colo.: Fulcrum Publishing, 1999.

Deloria, Vine, Jr., and Clifford M. Lytle. *God Is Red*. New York: Dell Publishing, 1973.

——. *The Nations Within: The Past and Future of American Indian Sovereignty*. New York: Pantheon, 1984.

Dennis, Helen May. *Native American Literature: Towards a Spatialized Reading*. New York: Routledge, 2007.

Dennis, Jerry. *The Living Great Lakes: Searching for the Heart of the Inland Seas*. New York: St. Martin's, 2004.

Densmore, Frances. *Chippewa Customs*. Washington, D.C.: Smithsonian Bureau of Ethnology, Bulletin 86, 1929.

——. *Chippewa Music*. Washington, D.C.: Government Printing Office, 1910.

Devens, Carol. *Countering Colonization: Native American Women and Great Lakes Missions 1630–1900*. Berkeley: University of California Press, 1992.

Dewdney, Selwyn. *Indian Rock Paintings of the Great Lakes*. Toronto: University of Toronto Press, 1967.

——. *The Sacred Scrolls of the Southern Ojibway*. Toronto: University of Toronto Press, 1967.

Dippie, Brian W. *The Vanishing American: White Attitudes and U. S. Indian Policy*. Lawrence: University Press of Kansas, 1982.

Dundes, Alan, ed. *Sacred Narrative: Readings in the Theory of Myth*. Berkeley: University of California Press, 1984.

Dunn, Anne M. *Grandmother's Gift: Stories from the Anishinabeg*. Duluth, Minn.: Holy Cow Press, 1997.

——. *When Beaver Was Very Great: Stories to Live By*. Mount Horeb: Midwest Traditions, 1995.

——. *Winter Thunder: Retold Tales*. Duluth, Minn.: Holy Cow Press, 2001.

Erdrich, Heid. *Cell Traffic: New and Selected Poems*. Tucson: University of Arizona Press, 2012.

Erdrich, Louise. *The Antelope Wife*. New York: HarperCollins, 1998.

——— . *Baptism of Desire*. New York: HarperCollins, 1989.

——— . *The Beet Queen*. New York: Bantam Books, 1986.

——— . *The Bingo Palace*. New York: HarperCollins, 1994.

——— . *The Birchbark House*. New York: Hyperion Books for Children, 1999.

——— . *The Blue Jay's Dance*. New York: HarperCollins, 1995.

——— . *Books and Islands in Ojibwe Country*. Washington, D.C.: National Geographic Society, 2003.

——— . *Four Souls*. New York: HarperCollins, 2004.

——— . *The Game of Silence*. New York: HarperCollins, 2005.

——— . *Grandmother's Pigeon*. New York: Hyperion Books, 1996.

——— . Interview with author. March 2001.

——— . *Jacklight*. New York: Henry Holt, 1984.

——— . *The Last Report on the Miracles at Little No Horse*. New York: HarperCollins, 2001.

——— . *Love Medicine*. New York: HarperCollins, 1993.

——— . *The Master Butchers Singing Club*. New York: HarperCollins, 2003.

——— . *Original Fire*. New York: HarperCollins, 2003.

——— . *The Painted Drum*. New York: HarperCollins, 2005.

——— . *The Plague of Doves*. New York: HarperCollins, 2008.

——— . *The Porcupine Year*. New York: HarperCollins, 2008.

——— . *The Range Eternal*. New York: Hyperion Books, 2002.

——— . *The Red Convertible*. New York: HarperCollins, 2009.

——— . *Shadow Tag*. New York: HarperCollins, 2010.

——— . *Tales of Burning Love*. New York: HarperCollins, 1996.

——— . *Tracks*. New York: Henry Holt, 1988.

——— . "Two Languages in Mind, but Just One in the Heart." *New York Times*, May 22, 2000.

——— . "The Years of My Birth." *New Yorker*, January 10, 2011.

Esbensen, Barbara Juster. *The Night Rainbow*. New York: Orchard Books, 2000.

Ezzo, David. "Female Status in the Northeast." In *Papers of the Nineteenth Algonquian Conference*, ed. William Cowan. Ottawa: Carleton University Press, 1988. 49–62.

Fairbanks, Brendan. "Ojibwe Discourse Markers." Ph.D. diss., University of Minnesota, 2009.

Fiddler, Chief Thomas. *Legends from the Forest*. Moonbeam, Ont.: Penumbra Press, 1985.

Fixico, Donald L. *Termination and Relocation: Federal Indian Policy, 1945–1960*. Albuquerque: University of New Mexico Press, 1986.

Fortunate Eagle, Adam. *Alcatraz! Alcatraz! The Indian Occupation of 1969–1971.* Berkeley: Heydey Books, 1992.

Fox, Mary Lou. "Manitou—Minnissing (Island of the Spirits)." In *Contemporary Native Art of Canada—Manitoulin Island.* Toronto: Royal Ontario Museum Ethnology Department, 1978.

Fuhst, Caroline Helen. *Introduction to the Sound Based Method of Understanding Anishinaabemowin: Nisosataagaadeg Akina Initaagawaziwinan E-Noondaagaadegin E-Akidoong Akidoowining.* Canton, Mich.: Niish Ishkoden Productions, 2010.

Gaikesheyongai, Sally. *The Seven Fires: An Ojibway Prophecy.* Toronto: Sister Vision, Black Women and Women of Colour Press, 1994.

Giese, Paula. "Roots." Posted at http://www.hanksville.net/stories/words.html.

Gilman, Chandler Robbins. *Life on the Lakes: Being Tales and Sketches Collected During a Trip to the Pictured Rocks of Lake Superior.* 2 vols. New York: George Dearborn Publisher, 1836.

Golden, Renny, Michael McConnell, Peggy Mueller, Cinny Poppen, and Marilyn Turkovich. *Dangerous Memories: Invasion and Resistance since 1492.* Chicago: Chicago Religious Task Force, 1991.

Gordon, Hanford L. *Legends of the Northwest.* St. Paul, Minn.: St. Paul Stationery Co., 1881.

Grady, Wayne. *The Great Lakes: The Natural History of a Changing Region.* Vancouver: Greystone Books, 2007.

Graham, Loren. *A Face in the Rock.* Berkeley: University of California Press, 1995.

Greene, Merritt. *Forgotten Yesterdays: A Tale of Early Michigan.* Hillsdale, Mich.: Hillsdale School Supply, 1964.

Gross, Lawrence W. "*Bimaadiziwin*, or 'The Good Life' as a Unifying Concept of Anishinaabe Religion." *American Indian Culture and Research Journal* 26.1 (2002): 15–32.

——. "Cultural Sovereignty and Native American Hermeneutics in the Interpretation of the Sacred Stories of the Anishinaabe." *Wicazo Sa Review* 18.2 (2003).

Hallowell, A. Irving. "Bear Ceremonialism in the Northern Hemisphere." *American Anthropologist* 28 (1926): 1–175.

——. *Culture and Experience.* Philadelphia: University of Pennsylvania Press, 1955.

——. "Ojibwa Ontology, Behavior, and World View." In *Culture in History: Essays in Honor of Paul Radin*, ed. Stanley Diamond. New York: Columbia University Press, 1960.

Hanzeli, Victor Egon. *Missionary Linguistics in New France: A Study of Seventeenth- and*

Eighteenth-Century Descriptions of American Indian Languages. The Hague: Mouton, 1969.

Harrison, K. David. *The Last Speakers: The Quest to Save the World's Most Endangered Languages.* Washington, D.C.: National Geographic, 2010.

——. *When Languages Die: The Extinction of the World's Languages and the Erosion of Human Knowledge.* New York: Oxford University Press, 2007.

Hedrick, Ulysses P. *The Land of the Crooked Tree.* New York: Oxford University Press, 1948.

Helbig, Aletha K. *Nanabozhoo Giver of Life.* Brighton, Mich.: Green Oak Press, 1987.

Helstern, Linda Lizut. "Gerald Vizenor: An Annotated Bibliography of Criticism." *Studies in American Indian Literatures* 11.1 (1999): 30–80.

Henry, Gordon. *The Failure of Certain Charms.* London: Earthworks, 2008.

——. *The Light People: A Novel.* East Lansing: Michigan State University Press, 2003.

Hernandez-Avila, Ines, ed. *Reading Native American Women: Critical/Creative Representations.* New York: Altamira Press, 2005.

Highway, Tomson. *Ernestine Shuswap Gets Her Trout.* Vancouver: Talon Books, 2005.

——. *The Rez Sisters.* Saskatoon: Fifth House, 1988.

Hilger, Inez. *Chippewa Child Life and Its Cultural Background.* St. Paul: Minnesota Historical Society, 1992.

Hinton, Leanne. *Flutes of Fire: Essays on California Indian Languages.* Berkeley, Calif.: Heyday Books, 1996.

——. *How to Keep Your Language Alive: A Commonsense Approach to One-on-One Language Learning.* Berkeley, Calif.: Heyday Books, 2002.

Hinton, Leanne, Johanne Nichols, and John J. Ohala, eds. *Sound Symbolism.* Cambridge: Cambridge University Press, 1994.

Hinton, Leanne, and Lucille J. Watahomigie, eds. *Spirit Mountain: An Anthology of Yuman Story and Song.* Tucson: Sun Tracks and University of Arizona Press, 1984.

Hoffman, W. J. "The Midewiwin or Grand Medicine Society of the Ojibway." *Bureau of American Ethnology Seventh Annual Report.* Washington, D.C.: Bureau of American Ethnology, 1891.

Hoxie, Frederick E., ed. *Indians in American History: An Introduction.* Arlington Heights, Ill.: Harlan Davidson, 1988.

Isernhagen, Hartwig. *Momaday, Vizenor, Armstrong: Conversations on American Indian Writing.* Norman: University of Oklahoma, 1999.

Jahner, Elaine. "Allies in the Word Wars: Vizenor's Uses of Contemporary Critical Theory." *Studies in American Indian Literatures* 9.2 (1985): 64–69.

Jaimes, M. Annette, ed. *The State of Native America: Genocide, Colonization and Resistance.* Boston: South End Press, 1992.

Johnston, Basil. *Anishinaubaemoowin: First Year High School.* Cape Croker First Nation, Ont.: Winter Spirit Creations, 2001.

——. *The Art of Norval Morrisseau and the Writings of Basil H. Johnston.* Calgary: Glenbow Museum, 1999.

——. *The Bear-Walker and Other Stories.* Toronto: Royal Ontario Museum, 1995.

——. *By Canoe & Moccasin: Some Native Place Names of the Great Lakes.* Lakefield, Ontario: Waapoone Publishing & Promotion, 1986.

——. *Crazy Dave.* Toronto: Key Porter Books, 1999.

——. *Dibaudjimootaudiwin.* Cape Croker First Nation, Ont.: Winter Spirit Creations, 2001.

——. *Honour Earth Mother.* Lincoln: University of Nebraska Press, 2003.

——. "How Do We Learn Language?" In *Talking on the Page: Editing Aboriginal Oral Texts,* ed. Laura J. Murray and Keren Rice. Toronto: University of Toronto Press, 1999.

——. *How the Birds Got Their Colours: Gah w'indinimowaut binaesheehnyuk w'idinauziwin-wauh.* Toronto: Kids Can Press, 1978.

——. *Hudson Bay Watershed: A Photographic Memoir of the Ojibway, Cree, and Oji-Cree* with John Macfie. Toronto: Dundurn, 1991.

——. *Indian School Days.* Norman: University of Oklahoma Press, 1989.

——. *K'd'Inawaewininaun: Our Language.* Cape Croker First Nation, Ont.: Winter Spirit Creations, 2001.

——. Letter to the author. June 5, 2001.

——. *The Manitous: The Spiritual World of the Ojibway.* New York: HarperCollins, 1995.

——. *Moose Meat and Wild Rice.* Toronto: McClelland and Stewart, 1978.

——. *Ojibway Ceremonies.* Lincoln: University of Nebraska Press, 1990.

——. *Ojibway Heritage.* Lincoln: University of Nebraska Press, 1976.

——. *Ojibway Tales.* Lincoln: University of Nebraska Press, 1978.

——. *The Star-Man and Other Tales.* Toronto: Royal Ontario Museum, 1997.

——. *Stories.* Unpublished manuscript, 2008.

——. *Tales of the Anishinaubaek.* Toronto: Royal Ontario Museum, 1993.

——. *Tales the Elders Told: Ojibway Legends.* Toronto: Royal Ontario Museum, 1981.

——. *Think Indian: Languages Are beyond Price.* Owen Sound, Ont.: Kegedonce Press, 2011.

———. *Verbs: Ae-idumoowinuguk Doodumoo-kittoowinun.* Cape Croker First Nation, Ont.: Winter Spirit Creations, 2001.

Jones, Peter. *History of the Ojebway Indians.* Freeport, N.Y.: Books for Libraries Press, 1970.

Jones, William. "The Algonkin Manitou." *Journal of American Folklore* (1905) 7: 183–210.

———. *Ojibwa Texts Part 1.* New York: G. E. Stechert Publications of the American Ethnographic Society, 1917.

———. *Ojibwa Texts Part 2.* New York: G. E. Stechert Publications of the American Ethnographic Society, 1919.

Judson, Katharine B., ed. *Myths and Legends of the Mississippi Valley and the Great Lakes.* Chicago: McClurg, 1914.

———. *Native American Legends of the Great Lakes and the Mississippi Valley.* DeKalb: Northern Illinois University Press, 2000.

Kane, Grace Franks. *Myths and Legends of the Mackinacs and the Lake Region.* Cincinnati: Editor Publishing Co., 1897.

Keady, Maureen. "Walking Backwards into the Fourth World: Survival of the Fittest in *Bearheart*." *American Indian Quarterly* 9.1 (1985): 61–65.

Keeshig-Tobias, Lenore. *Bineshiinh Dibaajmowin: Bird Talk.* Toronto: Sister Vision, Black Women and Women of Colour Press, 1991.

Kegg, Maude. *Portage Lake: Memories of an Ojibwe Childhood.* Edmonton: University of Alberta Press, 1991.

Kellogg, Louise P., ed. *Early Narratives of the Northwest 1634–1699.* New York: Scribner's Sons, 1917.

Kidder, Homer H. *Ojibwa Narratives of Charles and Charlotte Kawbawgam and Jacques LePique, 1893–1895*, ed. Arthur P. Bourgeois. Detroit: Wayne State University Press, 1994.

Kimewon, Howard, and Margaret Noori. *Anishinaabemowin Maajaamigad.* Sarnia, Ont.: Ningwakwe Learning Press, 2009.

King, Alanis. *The Manitoulin Incident.* Wikwemikong, Ont.: Debajemujig, 1994.

King, Thomas, ed. *All My Relations: An Anthology of Contemporary Canadian Native Fiction.* Norman: University of Oklahoma Press, 1992.

Kohl, Johann G. *Kitchi-Gami: Wanderings Round Lake Superior.* Minneapolis: Ross and Haines, 1860.

Kovach, Margaret. *Indigenous Methodologies: Characteristics, Conversations and Contexts.* Toronto: University of Toronto Press.

Kroeber, Alfred L. *Configurations of Culture Growth.* Berkeley: University of California Press, 1944.

Kroeber, Karl. "Deconstructionist Criticism and American Indian Literature." *Boundary 2* 7 (1979): 72–87.

———. "1492–1992: American Indian Persistence and Resurgence." *Boundary 2* 19.3 (1992): 231.

———, ed. *Traditional Literatures of the American Indian: Texts and Interpretations.* Lincoln: University of Nebraska Press, 1981.

Krupat, Arnold. *Ethnocriticism: Ethnography, History, Literature.* Berkeley: University of California Press, 1992.

———, ed. *For Those Who Come After: A Study of Native American Autobiography.* Berkeley: University of California Press, 1985.

———. *New Voices in Native American Literary Criticism.* Washington, D.C.: Smithsonian Institution Press, 1993.

———. *Voice in the Margin: Native American Literature and the Canon.* Berkeley: University of California Press, 1989.

LaDuke, Winona. *All Our Relations: Native Struggles for Land and Life.* Cambridge, Mass.: South End Press, 1999.

———. "Like Tributaries to a River." *Sierra* 81 (November/December 1996): 38–45.

———. "Wild Rice: Maps, Genes and Patents." Institute for Agriculture and Trade Policy, 2001.

———. *The Winona LaDuke Reader: A Collection of Essential Writings.* Stillwater, Minn.: Voyageur Press, 2002.

LaFavor, Carole. *Along the Journey River.* New York: Firebrand Books, 1996.

———. *Evil Dead Center.* New York: Firebrand Books, 1997.

Landes, Ruth. *Ojibwa Religion and the Midéwiwin.* Madison: University of Wisconsin Press, 1968.

———. *Ojibwa Sociology.* New York: Columbia University Press, 1937.

———. *The Ojibwa Woman.* New York: Columbia University Press, 1938.

Larry, Charles. *Peboan and Seegwun.* New York: Farrar, Straus and Giroux, 1993.

Larson, Sidner. *Captured in the Middle: Tradition and Experience in Contemporary Native American Writing.* Seattle: University of Washington Press, 2000.

Lee, Robert, ed. *Loosening the Seams: Interpretations of Gerald Vizenor.* Bowling Green, Ohio: Bowling Green State University Popular Press, 2000.

Leekley, Thomas B. *The World of Manabozho: Tales of the Chippewa Indians.* New York: Vanguard Press, 1965.

Leuthold, Steven. *Indigenous Aesthetics: Native Art Media and Identity*. Austin: University of Texas Press, 1998.

Levi, Sr. M. Carolissa. *Chippewa Indians of Yesterday and Today*. New York: Pageant, 1956.

Longfellow, Henry Wadsworth. *The Song of Hiawatha*. Avenel, N.J.: Gramercy Books, 1968.

Lyotard, Jean-François. *The Postmodern Condition: A Report on Knowledge*. Minneapolis: University of Minnesota Press, 1989.

Madsen, Deborah. *Understanding Gerald Vizenor*. Columbia: University of South Carolina Press, 2009.

Maristuen-Rodakowski, Julie. "The Turtle Mountain Reservation in North Dakota: Its History as Depicted in Louise Erdrich's *Love Medicine* and *Beet Queen*." *American Indian Culture and Research Journal* 12.3 (1988): 33–48.

McClurken, James. *Gah-Baeh-Jhagwah-Buk: The Way it Happened, A Visual Culture History of the Little Traverse Bay Bands of Odawa*. East Lansing: Michigan State University Museum, 1991.

McKenney, Thomas. *Sketches of a Tour of the Lakes*. New York: Fielding Lucas, 1827.

McLellan, Joe. *The Birth of Nanabosho*. Winnipeg: Pemmican Publications, 1989.

———. *Nanabosho Dances*. Winnipeg: Pemmican Publications, 1991.

———. *Nanabosho Steals Fire*. Winnipeg: Pemmican Publications, 1990.

McLellan, Joe, and Matrine McLellan. *Nanabosho and the Cranberries*. Winnipeg: Pemmican Publications, 1998.

———. *Nanabosho and Kitchie Odjig*. Winnipeg: Pemmican Publications, 1997.

McNally, Michael. *Ojibwe Singers: Hymns, Grief and a Native Culture in Motion*. New York: Oxford University Press, 2000.

McNickle, D'Arcy. *Native American Tribalism: Indian Survivals and Renewals*. London: Oxford University Press, 1973.

Medicine, Beatrice. "'Warrior Women'—Sex Role Alternatives for Plains Indian Women." In *The Hidden Half: Studies of Plains Indian Women*, eds. Patricia Albers and Beatrice Medicine. Lanham: University Press of America, 1983. 213–228.

Michelson, Truman. "Ojibwa Tales." *Journal of American Folklore* (1911) 4: 249–62.

Miller, Carol. Review of *Ojibway Ceremonies* by Basil Johnston. *Studies in American Indian Literatures* 3.2 (1991): 60–62.

Miller, Cary. *Ogimaag: Anishinaabeg Leadership: 1760–1845*. Lincoln: University of Nebraska Press, 2010.

Minnesota Chippewa Tribe, The. *A History of Kitchi Onigaming: Grand Portage and Its People*. Cass Lake, Minn.: Grand Portage Local Curriculum Committee, 1983.

Moore, James T. *Indian and Jesuit: A Seventeenth-Century Encounter*. Chicago: Loyola
   University Press, 1982.

Moses, Daniel David, and Terry Goldie. *An Anthology of Canadian Native Literature in
   English*. Toronto: Oxford University Press, 1997.

Murray, Laura J., and Keren Rice. *Talking on the Page: Editing Aboriginal Oral Texts*.
   Toronto: University of Toronto Press, 1996.

Muswagon, George. *First Nations Family Justice: Mee-noo-stah-tan Mi-ni-si-win*.
   Thompson, Manitoba, Awasis Agency, 1997.

National Congress of American Indians. Tribal Directory. http://www.ncai.org/.

Nichols, John D., and Earl Nyholm. *A Concise Dictionary of Minnesota Ojibwe*.
   Minneapolis: University of Minnesota Press, 1995.

Northrup, Jim. *Anishinaabe Syndicated: A View from the Rez*. St. Paul: Minnesota
   Historical Society Press, 2011.

——— . "Dash Iskigamiziganing." In *Sing: Poetry from the Indigenous Americas*, ed.
   Allison Adelle Hedge Coke. Tucson: University of Arizona Press, 2011.

——— . Interview with the author. April 2001.

——— . *The Rez Road Follies*. Stillwater, Minn.: Voyageur Press, 1997.

——— . "The Rez Road Follies Stage Version." In *Stories Migrating Home*, ed. Kimberly
   Blaeser. Bemidji, Minn.: Loonfeather Press; Stillwater, Minn.: Voyageur Press,
   1999.

——— . *Rez Salute: The Real Healer Dealer*. Golden, Colo.: Fulcrum, 2012.

——— . "Ricing Again." In *North Writers: A Strong Woods Collection*, ed. John
   Henricksson. Minneapolis: University of Minnesota Press, 1991.

——— . "Shinnob Jep." In *Nitaawichige: Selected Poetry and Prose by Four Anishinaabe
   Writers*. Duluth, Minn.: Poetry Harbor Publications, 2002.

——— . "2,000 Seasons." In *Do You Know Me Now: An Anthology of Minnesota
   Multicultural Writing*, ed. Elisabeth Rosenberg. Bloomington: Normandale
   Community College, 1992.

——— . "Veteran's Dance." In *Returning the Gift: Poetry and Prose from the First North
   American Native Writers Festival*, ed. Joseph Bruchac. Tucson: University of
   Arizona Press, 1994.

——— . *Walking the Rez Road*. Stillwater, Minn.: Voyageur Press, 1993.

Otto, Simon. *Walk in Peace: Legends and Stories of the Michigan Indians*. Grand Rapids:
   Michigan Indian Press, 1990.

Overholt, Thomas. *Clothed In Fur: An Introduction to an Ojibway World View*.
   Washington, D.C.: University Press of America, 1982.

Owens, Louis. *Other Destinies: Understanding the American Indian Novel*. Norman: University of Oklahoma Press, 1992.

Parrish, Randall. *The Sword of the Old Frontier, a Tale of Fort Chartres and Detroit: Being a Plain Account of Sundry Adventures Befalling Chevalier Raoul de Coubert During the Year 1763*. New York: Burt Co., 1905.

Peacock, Margaret. *Southern Feather's Story*. St. Ignace, Mich.: Museum of Ojibwa Culture, 1988.

———. *The Story of Wafted Across*. St. Ignace, Mich.: Museum of Ojibwa Culture, 1988.

Peacock, Thomas D. *A Forever Story: The People and Community of the Fond du Lac Reservation*. Cloquet, Minn.: Fond du Lac Band of Lake Superior Chippewa, 1998.

Peschel, Keewaydinoquay. Review of *Ojibway Heritage* by Basil Johnston. *Studies in American Indian Literatures* 3.3 (1979): 43–44.

Peyton, John L. *The Stone Canoe and Other Stories*. Blacksburg, Va.: McDonald and Woodward Publishing Co., 1989.

Pflug, Melissa A. *Ritual and Myth in Odawa Revitalization*. Norman: University of Oklahoma Press, 1998.

Plain, Aylmer Nicholas. *Ojibway and English Hymns*. Sarnia, Ont.: Plain, 1972.

Plain, Ferguson. *Amikoonse: Little Beaver*. Winnipeg: Pemmican Publications, 1993.

———. *Eagle Feather: An Honor*. Winnipeg: Pemmican Publications, 1989.

Pokagon, Simon. *Ogimawkwe Mitigwaki: Queen of the Woods*. East Lansing: Michigan State University Press, 2011.

Radin, Paul. *The Trickster: A Study in American Indian Mythology*. New York: Schocken Books, 1972.

Radin, Paul, and A. B. Reagan. "Ojibwa Myths and Tales." *Journal of American Folklore* (1928) 1: 61–115.

Rainwater, Catherine. *Dreams of Fiery Stars: The Transformations of Native American Fiction*. Philadelphia: University of Pennsylvania Press, 1999.

Redsky, James. *Great Leader of the Ojibway: Misquonaqueb*. Toronto: McClelland and Stewart, 1972.

Rexroth, Kenneth. "American Indian Songs: The United States Bureau of Ethnology Collection." In *Literature of the American Indians: Views and Interpretations. A Gathering of Indian Memories, Symbolic Contexts, and Literary Criticism*, ed. Abraham Chapman. New York: New American Library, 1961.

Reyhner, Jon. *Education and Language Restoration*. Philadelphia: Chelsea House, 2006.

———. "Rationale and Needs for Stabilizing Indigenous Languages." Educational Resources Information Center, 1996.

———. "Some Basics of Indigenous Language Revitalization." Educational Resources Information Center, 1999.

———. "Strategies for Keeping Indigenous Languages Alive." Educational Resources Information Center, 1998.

Reyhner, Jon, and Louise Lockard. *Indigenous Language Revitalization: Encouragement, Guidance and Lessons Learned*. Flagstaff: Northern Arizona University, 2009.

Rhodes, Richard A. *Eastern Ojibwa-Chippewa-Ottawa Dictionary*. New York: Mouton de Gruyter, 1993.

Richter, Daniel K., and James H. Merrell, eds. *Beyond the Covenant Chain: The Iroquois and Their Neighbors in Indian North America, 1600–1800*. Syracuse: Syracuse University Press, 1987.

Ross, Rupert. *Dancing with a Ghost: Exploring Indian Reality*. Markham, Ont.: Octopus Publishing Group, 1992.

Roulette, Roger. Interview with author. April 2010.

Ruoff, LaVonne Brown. *American Indian Literatures: An Introduction, Bibliographic Review, and Selected Bibliography*. New York: Modern Language Association of America, 1990.

———. "Gerald Vizenor: Compassionate Trickster." *American Indian Quarterly* 9.1 (1985): 67–73.

———. "Woodland Word Warrior: An Introduction to the Works of Gerald Vizenor." *Melus* 13.1–2 (1986): 13–43.

Ruppert, James. "Mediation and Multiple Narrative in Contemporary Native American Fiction." *Texas Studies in Literature and Language* 28.1 (1986): 209–25.

———. *Mediation in Contemporary Native American Fiction*. Norman: University of Oklahoma Press, 1995.

Sagard, Gabriel. *Le grand voyage du pays des hurons*. [1632]. Project Gutenberg, 2007. www.gutenberg.org.

Sale, Kirkpatrick. *The Conquest of Paradise: Christopher Columbus and the Columbian Legacy*. New York: Knopf, 1990.

Sandburg, Carl. Review of *Chippewa Music* by Frances Densmore. *Poetry: A Magazine of Verse* 9 (February 1917): 245–55.

Sapir, Edward. *American Indian Languages*. New York: Mouton de Gruyter, 1990.

———. *Culture*. New York: Mouton de Gruyter, 1999.

———. *Ethnology*. New York: Mouton de Gruyter, 1994.

Sauer, Carl O. *Sixteenth Century North America*. Berkeley: University of California Press, 1971.

Schenck, Theresa M. *The Voice of the Crane Echoes Afar: The Sociopolitical Organization of the Lake Superior Ojibwa, 1640–1855.* New York: Garland Publishing, 1997.

Schoolcraft, Henry R. *Algic Researches.* New York: Harper, 1839.

———. *The Fire Plume: Legends of the American Indians.* New York: Dial Press, 1969.

———. *The Literary Voyager or Muzzeniegun.* East Lansing: Michigan State University Press, 1962.

———. *Personal Memories of a Residence of Thirty Years with the Indian Tribes on the American Frontiers.* Philadelphia, 1851.

———. *Schoolcraft's Ojibwa Lodge Stories: Life on the Lake Superior Frontier.* East Lansing: Michigan State University Press, 1997.

Schwarz, Herbert T. *Windigo and Other Tales of the Ojibway.* Toronto: McClelland and Stewart, 1969.

Scott, Steven D. *The Gamefulness of American Postmodernism: John Barth & Louise Erdrich.* New York: Peter Lang, 2000.

Sibley, David Allen. *The Sibley Guide to Birds.* New York: Chanticleer Press, 2000.

Silberman, Robert. "Gerald Vizenor and *Harold of Orange*: From Word Cinemas to Real Cinema." *American Indian Quarterly* 9.1 (1985): 4–21.

Silko, Leslie Marmon. *Ceremony.* New York: Penguin, 1977.

———. "Here's an Odd Artifact for the Fairy Tale Shelf." *Studies in American Indian Literature* 10.4 (1986): 177–84.

Skinner, Alanson. "Plains Ojibwa Tales." *Journal of American Folklore* (1919) 4: 280–327.

Smith, Jeanne. "Transpersonal Selfhood: The Boundaries of Identity in Louise Erdrich's *Love Medicine.*" *Studies in American Indian Literature* 3.4 (1991): 13–26.

Smith, Theresa S. *The Island of the Anishnaabeg: Thunderers and Water Monsters in the Traditional Ojibwe Life-World.* Moscow: University of Idaho Press, 1995.

Snelling, William Joseph. *Tales of the Northwest.* Minneapolis: Ross & Haines, 1971.

Spielmann, Roger. *You're So Fat! Exploring Ojibwe Discourse.* Toronto: University of Toronto Press, 1998.

Squier, E. G. "Manabozho and the Great Serpent." *American Review* (1848) 10: 395–422.

St. Germain, Pat. Review of *Crazy Dave. Winnipeg Sun*, September 25, 1999.

Stannard, David E. *American Holocaust: Columbus and the Conquest of the New World.* New York: Oxford University Press, 1992.

Stookey, Lorena L. *Louise Erdrich: A Critical Companion.* Westport, Conn.: Greenwood Press, 1999.

Stripes, James D. "The Problem(s) of (Anishinaabe) History in the Fiction of Louise Erdrich: Voices and Contexts." *Wicazo Sa Review* 7.2 (1991): 26–33.

Swann, Brian, ed. *On the Translation of Native American Literature*. Washington, D.C.: Smithsonian Institution Press, 1992.

——. *Smoothing the Ground: Essays on Native American Oral Literature*. Berkeley: University of California Press, 1983.

——. *Song of the Sky: Versions of Native American Song-Poems*. Amherst: University of Massachusetts Press, 1993.

Swann, Brian, and Arnold Krupat, eds. *I Tell You Now: Autobiographical Essays by Native American Writers*. Lincoln: University of Nebraska Press, 1987.

——, eds. *Recovering the Word: Essays on Native American Literature*. Berkeley: University of California Press, 1987.

Tanner, Helen Hornbeck. *The Chippewa of Eastern Lower Michigan*. New York: Garland, 1974.

Tedlock, Dennis. *The Spoken Word and the Work of Interpretation*. Philadelphia: University of Pennsylvania Press, 1983.

Thwaites, Reuben Gold, ed. *The Jesuit Relations and Allied Documents: Travels and Explorations of the Jesuit Missionaries in New France 1610–1791*. New York: Pageant, 1959.

Tinker, George. *Missionary Conquest: The Gospel and Native American Cultural Genocide*. Minneapolis: Fortress Press, 1993.

Treuer, Anton. *Living Our Language: Ojibwe Tales and Oral Histories*. St. Paul: Minnesota Historical Society Press, 2001.

Treuer, David. *The Hiawatha*. New York: Picador, 2000.

——. *Little*. St. Paul, Minn.: Graywolf, 1995.

——. *Native American Fiction*. St. Paul, Minn.: Graywolf, 2006.

——. *The Translation of Dr. Apelles: A Love Story*. St. Paul, Minn.: Graywolf, 2006.

Troop, Edna Willa. *Blackbird: A Story of Mackinac Island*. Detroit: Citator, 1907.

Turill, David A. *Michilimackinac: A Tale of the Straits*. Fowlerville, Mich.: Wilderness Adventure Books, 1989.

Valentine, Lisa Philips. *Making It Their Own: Severn Ojibwe Communicative Practices*. Toronto: University of Toronto Press, 1995.

Valentine, Rand. "Amik Anicinaa bewigoban: Rhetorical Structures in Albert Mowatt's Telling of an Algonquin Tale." In *Nikotwasik Iskwahtem Paskihtepayih!* ed. John Nichols and Arden C. Ogg. Memoir 13, Algonquian and Iroquoin Linguistics, 1996.

Vecsey, Christopher. "The Ojibwa Creation Myth." In *Imagine Ourselves Richly: Mythic Narratives of North American Indians*. New York: Crossroad, 1988.

———. *On the Padres' Trail*. South Bend, Ind.: University of Notre Dame Press, 1996.

———. *The Paths of Kateri's Kin*. South Bend, Ind.: University of Notre Dame Press, 1997.

———. *Traditional Ojibwa Religion and Its Historical Changes*. Philadelphia: American Philosophical Society, 1983.

———. *Where the Two Roads Meet*. Notre Dame, Ind.: University of Notre Dame Press, 1999.

Velie, Alan. *Four American Indian Literary Masters: N. Scott Momaday, James Welch, Leslie Marmon Silko, and Gerald Vizenor*. Norman: University of Oklahoma Press, 1982.

———. "The Trickster Novel." In *Narrative Chance: Postmodern Discourse on Native American Indian Literatures*, ed. Gerald Vizenor. Norman: University of Oklahoma Press, 1993.

Vennum, Thomas. "A History of Ojibwa Song Form." In *Selected Reports in Ethnomusicology* 3.2, ed. Charlotte Heth. Los Angeles: Department of Ethnomusicology, University of California, Los Angeles, 1980.

———. *The Ojibwa Dance Drum*. Washington, D.C.: Smithsonian Institution Press, 1982.

———. *Wild Rice and the Ojibwa People*. St. Paul: Minnesota Historical Society Press, 1988.

Vizenor, Gerald. *Almost Ashore*. Cambridge: Salt Publishing, 2006.

———. *Anishinabe Adisokan: Tales of the People*. Minneapolis: Nodin Press, 1970.

———. *Bear Island: The War at Sugar Point*. Minneapolis: University of Minnesota Press, 2006.

———. *Bearheart: The Heirship Chronicles*. Minneapolis: University of Minnesota Press, 1990.

———. *Chair of Tears: A Novel*. Lincoln: University of Nebraska Press, 2012.

———. *Chancers*. Norman: University of Oklahoma Press, 2000.

———. *Crossbloods: Bone Courts, Bingo, and Other Reports*. Minneapolis: University of Minnesota Press, 1990.

———. *Dead Voices: Natural Agonies in the World*. Norman: University of Oklahoma Press, 1992.

———. "Dennis Banks: What Sort of Hero?" *Minneapolis Tribune*, July 22, 1978, A4.

———. *Earthdivers: Tribal Narratives on Mixed Descent*. Minneapolis: University of Minnesota Press, 1981.

———. *Empty Swings*. Minneapolis: Nodin Press, 1967.

———. *Escorts to White Earth, 1868–1968: 100 Years on a Reservation*. Minneapolis: Four Winds, 1968.

———, ed. *The Everlasting Sky: Voices of the Anishinaabe People.* St. Paul: Minnesota Historical Society Press, 2000.

———. *Father Meme.* Albuquerque: University of New Mexico Press, 2008.

———. *Fugitive Poses. Fugitive Poses: Native American Indian Scenes of Absence and Presence.* Lincoln: University of Nebraska Press, 1998.

———. *Griever: An American Monkey King in China.* Normal: Illinois State University Fiction Collective, 1987.

———. *Harold of Orange.* Film directed by Richard Weise. Minnesota-Film-in-the-Cities, 1983. Screenplay in *Shadow Distance*, 297–333.

———. *The Heirs of Columbus.* Hanover, N.H.: Wesleyan University Press / University Press of New England, 1991.

———. *Hiroshima Bugi: Atomu 57.* Lincoln: University of Nebraska Press, 2003.

———. *Hotline Healers: An Almost Browne Novel.* Hanover, N.H.: University Press of New England, 1997.

———. *Interior Landscapes: Autobiographical Myths and Metaphors.* Minneapolis: University of Minnesota Press, 1990.

———. *Landfill Meditation: Crossblood Stories.* Hanover, N.H.: University Press of New England, 1991.

———. Letter to M. Noori. May 2001. Copy in possession of the author.

———. *Matsushima.* Minneapolis: Nodin Press, 1984.

———. *Manifest Manners: Postindian Warriors of Survivance.* Hanover, N.H.: University Press of New England, 1994.

———, ed. *Narrative Chance: Postmodern Discourse on Native American Indian Literatures.* Norman: University of Oklahoma Press, 1993.

———, ed. *Native American Literature: A Brief Introduction and Anthology.* New York: HarperCollins, 1995.

———. *Native Liberty: Natural Reason and Cultural Survivance.* Lincoln: University of Nebraska Press, 2009.

———. "The Ojibway." *Twin Citian* 8.10 (May 1966): 18–19.

———. *The People Named the Chippewa: Narrative Histories.* Minneapolis: University of Minnesota Press, 1984.

———. *Raising the Moon Vines.* Minneapolis: Nodin Press, 1968.

———. *Seventeen Chirps.* Minneapolis: Nodin Press, 1967.

———. *Shadow Distance: A Gerald Vizenor Reader.* Hanover, N.H.: University Press of New England, 1994.

———. *Shrouds of White Earth*. Albany: State University of New York Press, 2010.

———. *Summer in the Spring: Ojibwe Lyric Poems and Tribal Stories*. Minneapolis: Nodin Press, 1981.

———, ed. *Touchwood: A Collection of Ojibway Prose*. Minneapolis: New Rivers Press, 1987.

———. "Tribal People and the Poetic Image: Visions of Eyes and Hands." In *American Indian Art: Form and Tradition*. Minneapolis: Walker Art Center, 1972.

———. *Tribal Scenes and Ceremonies*. Minneapolis: University of Minnesota Press, 1990.

———. *The Trickster of Liberty: Tribal Heirs to a Wild Baronage*. Minneapolis: University of Minnesota Press, 1988.

———. *Wordarrows: Indians and Whites in the New Fur Trade*. Minneapolis: University of Minnesota Press, 1978.

Vizenor, Gerald, and A. Robert Lee. *Postindian Conversations*. Lincoln: University of Nebraska Press, 1999.

Vollum, Judith, and Thomas Vollum. *Ojibwemowin: The Ojibwe Language*. Vermilion, Minn.: Ojibwe Language Publishing, 1994.

Warren, William W. *History of the Ojibway People*. St. Paul: Minnesota Historical Society Press, 1984.

Warrior, Robert Allen. *Tribal Secrets: Recovering American Indian Intellectual Traditions*. Minneapolis: University of Minnesota Press, 1995.

Weaver, Jace. *Other Words: American Indian Literature, Law and Culture*. Norman: University of Oklahoma Press, 2001.

White, Hartley. "Onizhishin o'ow Bimaadiziwin: This Is a Good Way of Life." In *Living Our Language: Ojibwe Tales and Oral Histories*, ed. Anton Treuer. St. Paul: Minnesota Historical Society Press, 2001.

White, Richard. *The Middle Ground: Indians, Empires, and Republics in the Great Lakes Region 1650–1815*. Cambridge: Cambridge University Press, 1991.

Witgen, Michael. *An Infinity of Nations: How the Native New World Shaped Early North America*. Philadelphia: University of Pennsylvania Press, 2012.

Wiget, Andrew. "His Life in His Tail: The Native American Trickster and the Literature of Possibility." In *Redefining American Literary History*, ed. A. La Vonne Brown Ruoff and Jerry W. Ward Jr. New York: Modern Languages Association, 1990.

Williams, Angeline. *The Dog's Children*. Ed. Leonard Bloomfield and John Nichols. Winnipeg: University of Manitoba Press, 1991.

Winchell, N. H. *The Aborigines of Minnesota*. St. Paul: Minnesota Historical Society

Press, 1911.

Wong, Hertha D. Sweet. *Louise Erdrich's "Love Medicine": A Casebook*. New York: Oxford University Press, 2000.

———. *Sending My Heart Back across the Years: Tradition and Innovation in Native American Autobiography*. New York: Oxford University Press, 1992.

Young, Mary Isabelle. *Pimatisiwin: Walking in a Good Way. A Narrative Inquiry into Language as Identity*. Winnipeg: Pemmican Publications, 2005.

Youngbear-Tibbets, Holly. "Without Due Process: The Alienation of Individual Trust Allotments of the White Earth Anishinaabeg." *American Indian Culture and Research Journal* 15.2 (1991): 93–138.

Zanger, Martin. "Straight Tongue's Heathen Wards: Bishop Whipple and the Episcopal Mission to the Chippewas." In *Churchmen and the Western Indians: 1820–1920*, ed. Clyde Milner and Floyd O'Neil. Norman: University of Oklahoma Press, 1985.

Nanaandawaabanjigan: Index

Stookey, Lorena, 42

T

Termination Act, 29
Three Fires Confederacy, 5–6, 69
thunder beings, 46
thunderbirds, 35, 117, 136
translation: from Anishinaabemowin to
    English, 2, 3, 13, 14, 16, 19, 21, 25, 31,
    69, 79, 115, 121, 126, 132, 133, 163, 171;
    inability to offer complete, 51, 54–55,
    62, 86, 93, 97, 135; as mediation tool,
    22, 23, 26, 33, 38, 40, 51, 112, 125, 130,
    165, 174, 183; of proper nouns, 159;
    unwillingness toward, 84, 107, 134
Treaty of Greenville (1795), 4
trees (*mitigoog*): apple, 133; birch, 46,
    133, 134; lost to logging industry,
    45; as markers, xxi, 7; pine, 23;
    sound of, 7–8; sugar maple, 94–95;
    transformation of humans into, 28,
    175, 182
Treuer, Anton, 30
Treuer, David, 33, 35
Turtle Mountain Band of Chippewa
    Indians, 40

U

unceded: identities, xx; nations, 73
underwater culture, 45, 64, 66, 67, 70, 129
United Nations, 29
United States of America: Alaska, 14;
    census data, 4, 14; Civil War and,
    28; colonial process in, 8, 22, 29,
    38, 44–47, 54, 69, 88, 91, 94, 103,
    154–59, 173, 178; culture in, 98–99,

104–6; history, 38, 73, 80–82, 103,
    170; identity as citizen of, 14–15, 28,
    89, 93, 100; Michigan, 5, 16, 28, 149,
    170, 173; Minnesota, 5, 16, 29, 40, 42,
    45, 46, 47, 58, 59, 68, 81, 88, 108, 113,
    153, 173; Montana, 60; New Mexico,
    45; North Dakota, 5, 41, 44; view of
    nature, 108; Wisconsin, 5, 16, 68

V

Valentine, Rand, 9
"Veteran's Dance," 91–93
Vietnam War, 81–81, 87, 90–93, 99, 106
voyageurs, 71, 76, 170

W

War of 1812, 23, 178
Warren, William Whipple, 4, 5, 26–27,
    166
water: biological significance of, xviii,
    32, 51, 95; cultural significance for
    Anishinaabeg, 1, 26, 28, 39, 55,
    58–59; -drum, 76; as geological
    marker, 21, 36, 58, 108; as measure of
    time, 61; as medicine, 11; as metaphor,
    vii, 34, 56, 75, 96–97; as narrative
    device, 165–67; 175–76; as seasonal
    marker, 43. See also *michibizhew*
Wayne, John, 91
White, Hartley, 138, 181
White, Richard, 71
White Earth Nation (Gaa-
    waabaabiganikaag), 150, 155, 169, 171,
    176
White Hawk, James, 151
wiindigoo, xix, 26, 32–33, 45–46, 62, 66,